Buying a Home
in
NEW
ZEALAND

Graeme Chesters

SURVIVAL BOOKS • LONDON • ENGLAND

First published 2006 (as *Buying a Home in Australia & New Zealand*)
Second Edition 2008

Survival Books Limited
26 York Street, London W1U 6PZ, United Kingdom
☎ +44 (0)20-7788 7644, 🖷 +44 (0)870-762 3212
✉ info@survivalbooks.net
🖳 www.survivalbooks.net

British Library Cataloguing in Publication Data.
A CIP record for this book is available
from the British Library.
ISBN: 978-1-905303-18-2

Printed and bound in India by Ajanta Offset

ACKNOWLEDGEMENTS

My sincere thanks to all those who contributed to the successful publication of the second edition of this book, particularly Joe Laredo (editing and proof-reading), Peter Read (additional editing and proof-reading), Di Tolland (desktop publishing), Grania Rogers (photo editing), and everyone else who has contributed in any way who I have omitted to mention. Finally, a special thank-you to Jim Watson for the superb illustrations, cartoons, maps and cover design, and all the photographers who provided the superb photos (see page 286), without which this book would be dull indeed.

THE AUTHOR

Graeme (g.chesters@virgin.net) lives in London (England) and is an experienced non-fiction and travel writer. He has travelled and written extensively on regions as diverse as Europe, Africa, the Middle and Far East, and Australasia. He is the editor of *Living and Working in New Zealand* and the co-author of *Culture Wise New Zealand*, both published by Survival Books. Graeme is also an enthusiastic wine drinker and writer, and is the author of two wine books, including *Shopping for Wine in Spain* (Santana).

WHAT READERS & REVIEWERS

'If you need to find out how France works then this book is indispensable. Native French people probably have a less thorough understanding of how their country functions.'

Living France

'It's everything you always wanted to ask but didn't for fear of the contemptuous put down. The best English-language guide. Its pages are stuffed with practical information on everyday subjects and are designed to compliment the traditional guidebook.'

Swiss News

'Rarely has a 'survival guide' contained such useful advice – This book dispels doubts for first-time travellers, yet is also useful for seasoned globetrotters – In a word, if you're planning to move to the US or go there for a long-term stay, then buy this book both for general reading and as a ready-reference.'

American Citizens Abroad

'Let's say it at once. David Hampshire's Living and Working in France is the best handbook ever produced for visitors and foreign residents in this country; indeed, my discussion with locals showed that it has much to teach even those born and bred in l'Hexagone – It is Hampshire's meticulous detail which lifts his work way beyond the range of other books with similar titles. Often you think of a supplementary question and search for the answer in vain. With Hampshire this is rarely the case. – He writes with great clarity (and gives French equivalents of all key terms), a touch of humour and a ready eye for the odd (and often illuminating) fact. – This book is absolutely indispensable.'

The Riviera Reporter

'A must for all future expats. I invested in several books but this is the only one you need. Every issue and concern is covered, every daft question you have but are frightened to ask is answered honestly without pulling any punches. Highly recommended.'

Reader

'In answer to the desert island question about the one how-to book on France, this book would be it.'

The Recorder

'The ultimate reference book. Every subject imaginable is exhaustively explained in simple terms. An excellent introduction to fully enjoy all that this fine country has to offer and save time and money in the process.'

American Club of Zurich

HAVE SAID ABOUT SURVIVAL BOOKS

'The amount of information covered is not short of incredible. I thought I knew enough about my birth country. This book has proved me wrong. Don't go to France without it. Big mistake if you do. Absolutely priceless!'

Reader

'When you buy a model plane for your child, a video recorder, or some new computer gizmo, you get with it a leaflet or booklet pleading 'Read Me First', or bearing large friendly letters or bold type saying 'IMPORTANT - follow the instructions carefully'. This book should be similarly supplied to all those entering France with anything more durable than a 5-day return ticket. – It is worth reading even if you are just visiting briefly, or if you have lived here for years and feel totally knowledgeable and secure. But if you need to find out how France works then it is indispensable. Native French people probably have a less thorough understanding of how their country functions. – Where it is most essential, the book is most up to the minute.

Living France

A comprehensive guide to all things French, written in a highly readable and amusing style, for anyone planning to live, work or retire in France.

The Times

Covers every conceivable question that might be asked concerning everyday life – I know of no other book that could take the place of this one.

France in Print

A concise, thorough account of the Do's and DONT's for a foreigner in Switzerland – Crammed with useful information and lightened with humorous quips which make the facts more readable.

American Citizens Abroad

'I found this a wonderful book crammed with facts and figures, with a straightforward approach to the problems and pitfalls you are likely to encounter. The whole laced with humour and a thorough understanding of what's involved. Gets my vote!'

Reader

'A vital tool in the war against real estate sharks; don't even think of buying without reading this book first!'

Everything Spain

'We would like to congratulate you on this work: it is really super! We hand it out to our expatriates and they read it with great interest and pleasure.'

ICI (Switzerland) AG

CONTENTS

IMPORTANT NOTE

Readers should note that the laws and regulations for buying property in New Zealand aren't the same as in other countries, and are also liable to change periodically. I cannot recommend too strongly that you check with an official and reliable source (not always the same), and take expert legal advice before paying any money or signing any legal documents. Don't, however, believe everything you're told or read, even – dare I say it – herein!

To help you obtain further information and verify data with official sources, useful addresses and references to other sources of information have been included in most chapters, and in Appendices A to C. Important points have been emphasised throughout the book in **bold** print, some of which it would be expensive or foolish to disregard. Ignore them at your peril or cost! Unless specifically stated, the reference to any company, organisation, product or publication in this book does not constitute an endorsement or recommendation.

Author's Notes

- All prices are shown in New Zealand dollars (NZ$) unless otherwise stated and should be taken as estimates only, although they were mostly correct when going to print and fortunately don't usually change overnight. Although prices are sometimes quoted exclusive of goods and services tax (GST) in New Zealand, most prices are inclusive of tax, which is the method used when quoting prices in this book, unless otherwise stated.

- Times are shown using am (Latin ante meridiem) for before noon and pm (post meridiem) for after noon. Most New Zealanders don't use the 24-hour clock. All times are local, and you should check the time difference when making international calls.

- His/he/him also means her/she/her (please forgive me ladies). This is done to make life easier for both the reader and (in particular) the author, and isn't intended to be sexist.

- British English is used throughout, but American English equivalents are given where appropriate.

- Warning and important points are shown in **bold** type.

- The following symbols are used in this book: ☎ (telephone), 🖹 (fax), 🖥 (Internet) and ✉ (email).

- Lists of **Useful Addresses**, **Further Reading** and **Useful Websites** are contained in **Appendices A, B and C** respectively.

- For those unfamiliar with the metric system of weights and measures, conversion tables are included in **Appendix D**.

- A map of New Zealand is on page 6 and a communications map showing the major airports, railways and roads is in **Appendix E**.

- A glossary of property terms is included in **Appendix F**.

INTRODUCTION

First published in 2006 (as *Buying a Home in Australia & New Zealand*), **Buying a Home in New Zealand** is the best-selling and most comprehensive book published for foreign property buyers in New Zealand. The second edition has been enlarged and updated – and printed in colour! The aim of this book is to provide you with the information necessary to help you choose the most favourable location and most appropriate home to satisfy your personal requirements. Most importantly, it will help you avoid the pitfalls and risks associated with buying a home in New Zealand (which, fortunately, are few).

You may already own a home in another country; however, buying a home in New Zealand (or in any 'foreign' country) is a different matter altogether. One of the most common mistakes many people make when buying a home abroad is to assume that the laws and purchase procedures are the same as in their home country. **This is rarely, if ever, the case!** Buying property in New Zealand is generally very safe, particularly when compared with some other countries. However, if you don't do your homework and follow the rules provided for your protection, a purchase can result in a serious mistake or financial loss.

For many people, buying a home in New Zealand has previously been a case of pot luck. However, with a copy of **Buying a Home in New Zealand** to hand you'll have a wealth of priceless information at your fingertips – information derived from a variety of sources, both official and unofficial, not least the hard won personal experiences of the author, his friends, colleagues and acquaintances. This book doesn't contain all the answers, but what it will do is reduce the risk of making an expensive mistake that you may regret later, and help you make informed decisions and calculated judgements, instead of costly mistakes and uneducated guesses – forewarned is forearmed! Most important of all, it will help you save money and will repay your investment many times over.

Buying a home in New Zealand is a wonderful way to make new friends, broaden your horizons and revitalise your life – and it provides a welcome bolt-hole to recuperate from the stresses and strains of modern life. I trust this book will help you avoid the pitfalls and smooth your way to many happy years in your new home, secure in the knowledge that you've made the right decision.

Good luck!

Graeme Chesters
December 2007

Mitre Peak, Fiordland National Park, South Island

1.

MAJOR CONSIDERATIONS

Buying a home abroad isn't just a major financial commitment, it's also a decision that can have a huge influence on other aspects of your life, including your health, security and safety, your family relationships and friendships, your lifestyle, your opinions and your outlook. You also need to take into consideration any restrictions that might influence your choice of location and type of property, such as whether you'll need (or be able) to learn another language, whether you'll be able (or permitted) to find work, whether you can adapt to and enjoy the climate, whether you'll be able to take your pets with you, and not least, whether you'll be able to afford the kind of home (and lifestyle) that you want. In order to ensure that you're making the right move, it's wise to face these and other major considerations before making any irrevocable decisions.

WHY NEW ZEALAND?

There are many excellent reasons for buying a home in New Zealand. It's one of the most beautiful countries in the world, with varied landscapes offering something for everyone, including magnificent beaches for sun-worshippers (although sunbathers must be aware of the dangers of excessive sun exposure); spectacular countryside for nature lovers; and mountains and seas for fans of adventure activities. It also has vibrant, Mediterranean-style cities for the young at heart, great wines for connoisseurs, innovative cuisine for gourmets, an abundance

of culture for art lovers (which will come as a surprise to some people), a sophisticated sporting infrastructure and competitive sports leagues, and tranquillity for the stressed.

No longer is New Zealand regarded as an isolated, rural backwater located somewhere to the north of Antarctica, where men are men and sheep are worried. As for this sheep-related slur, the country no longer has such a massive ratio of sheep to humans as in the past. In the '70s, New Zealand was known as the country of 60m sheep and 3m people, but by mid-2004, the country's human population had risen to over 4m, while the sheep population had dropped to 39m (compared with a peak of over 70m in 1982 and the first time the number had fallen below 40m for 60 years), the result of the elimination of farm production subsidies to maintain flock numbers and aid exports.

New Zealand men are, of course, still men, but modern ones with (fairly) sophisticated interests and tastes and a (reasonably) egalitarian attitude towards the opposite sex. New Zealanders (of both sexes) have a zest for life and many love sport, the great outdoors and eating and drinking with friends *al fresco*. The pursuit of the good life is a serious business and many people put their family and social lives before their career and the pursuit of success and wealth. Contrary to a clichéd view of New Zealand, the country has more to offer than watching or playing rugby, although the sport is welded into the fabric of New Zealand life and often makes front-page news.

New Zealand enjoys an exhilarating mixture of natural beauty and cultural diversity, its burgeoning sophistication and style combining the best of the Anglo-Saxon tradition with Mediterranean flair and Asian and Pacific spice. In the past, it was said to be a pale imitation of the UK and the US (especially the former), but in the 21st century New Zealand is regarded as combining the best of the UK and the US without many of their drawbacks.

Dart river, Queenstown

It's often said that when buying property in New Zealand you aren't buying a home but a lifestyle.

As a location for a holiday, retirement or permanent home, the country has few rivals and in addition to the incomparable choice of properties and excellent value, it offers a generally fine climate for most of the year, particularly in the North Island.

Nevertheless, it's important to ask yourself exactly why you want to buy a home in New Zealand. For example, are you primarily looking for a sound investment or do you plan to work or start a business in New Zealand? Are you seeking a holiday or retirement home? If you're seeking a second home, will it be mainly used for two- or three-week holidays or for lengthier stays? Do you plan to let it to offset the mortgage and running costs (and the cost of the flights to and from your home country)? If so, how important is the property income? You need to answer these and many other questions before deciding on the best (and most appropriate) place to buy a home in New Zealand.

Often buyers have a variety of reasons for buying a home in New Zealand; for example, some people buy a holiday home with a view to living there permanently or semi-permanently when they retire. If this is the case, there are many more factors to take into account than if you're 'simply' buying a holiday home that you'll occupy for just a few weeks or months a year (when it might be wiser not to buy at all). If, on the other hand, you plan to work or start a business in New Zealand, you'll be faced with a completely different set of criteria.

Can you really afford to buy a home in New Zealand? What about the future? Is your income secure and protected against inflation and currency fluctuations? In the past, some foreigners purchased holiday homes by taking out second mortgages on their family homes and stretching their financial resources to the limits. Not surprisingly, when a recession struck (as it did in the early '90s) many people had their homes repossessed or were forced to sell at a huge loss when they were no longer able to meet mortgage payments.

You shouldn't expect to make a quick profit when buying property in New Zealand and should look upon it as an investment in your family's future happiness, rather than merely in financial terms. This is particularly true in the current uncertain property market. Property values in New Zealand increased (sometimes dramatically) in the early years of the 21st century, but the market slowed considerably in 2005, with falls in some regions. Despite reports forecasting a 'correction' or even a crash, however, prices have continued to increase in the last few years. In mid-2007, the property market remained strong with a steady demand, despite a slow-down in price rises.

☑ **SURVIVAL TIP**

Before making an irrevocable decision regarding buying a home in New Zealand, you should do extensive research, study the possible pitfalls and be prepared to rent for a period before buying.

Advantages & Disadvantages

There are advantages and disadvantages to buying a home in New Zealand, although for most people the benefits far outweigh any drawbacks. The country has many attractions: large areas enjoy a sunny and warm or mild climate for much of the year, although there are more climatic variations than many people imagine (see **Climate** on page 20) and parts of the South Island have decidedly chilly winters and cool summers (similar to the British climate); access to New Zealand has never been easier or cheaper, especially from the UK, thanks mainly to the large volume of flights and the fierce competition between airlines; travel within the Antipodes (i.e. between New Zealand and Australia) is easy and relatively inexpensive, mainly thanks to increased competition on domestic air routes; and New Zealand has a stable political environment and is perceived as being removed from the terrorist threat that stalks much of the rest of the world.

Until recently, New Zealand was often regarded as its neighbour Australia's poor relation (particularly by Australians!), but the early 21st century has seen the country forge a new identity and grow in confidence. Part of the credit for this must go to the huge amount of positive (and free) publicity generated by the multi-Oscar-winning *Lord of the Rings* film trilogy, much of which was filmed in New Zealand, using the country's spectacular scenery as a memorable backdrop (post-production took place in Wellington). The success of the *Lord of the Rings* series propelled its Kiwi director Peter Jackson to fame and fortune. The world's most famous New Zealander, he was noted as much for his scruffy appearance and corpulent frame as for his success as a director.

New Zealand is a greener, milder, more peaceful (some think duller) version of Australia, an enticing destination for those in search of deserted beaches (nowhere in New Zealand is more than 150km/95m from the sea), geysers, crystal-clear lakes, majestic mountains and whitewater rivers, and an outdoor lifestyle (whatever the weather). New Zealand has two marine, three maritime, 14 national and 20 forest parks, plus two World Heritage Areas: Te Waihipounamu in the South Island and the Tongariro National Park in the North Island.

But the country has more to offer than natural beauty. Since the '90s, the easing of licensing regulations and loosening of lifestyles have led to an increase in the number of bars, clubs and restaurants, giving New Zealand a more sophisticated nightlife than previously. It's no longer just a destination for bearded types in bobble hats, hiking boots and waterproofs who spend their time bungee jumping over gorges, scrambling up mountains in driving rain and whiling away their evenings singing songs around the campfire.

New Zealand's people are another of the country's assets, their culture combining European and Maori traditions, and many are forward-thinking, friendly, helpful and independent. As well as an increasingly lively bar, club and restaurant scene, the country offers challenging theatre (particularly in Wellington) and some fascinating art, much of it a blend of Maori, Melanesian and Pakeha (European) influences. Specialities include bone, shell, stone and wood carvings, as well as *tukutuku* (wood panelling) and jewellery made from pebbles and stones, much of it inspired by the local terrain. New Zealand also has a vibrant music scene, but the only pop and rock artists to reach international prominence are the (now-defunct) Split Enz and (the much more

successful, recently reformed) Crowded House.

Among the many other advantages of buying a home in New Zealand are (usually) good rental possibilities, reliable local tradesmen and services (particularly in cities and resort areas), fresh, innovative food and fine wines at reasonable prices, a relaxed pace of life in rural areas (and in some of the towns and cities), good healthcare, plenty of open space and some of the most beautiful scenery in the world.

Last, but by no means least, New Zealand has the great advantage for

native English speakers that most of their citizens speak English (or at least a form of English!) as a first language. Some Britons buying homes in sunnier, warmer countries (i.e. just about anywhere) have struggled to come to terms with the local language, particularly the many who have bought in France, Greece, Italy, Portugal and Spain. Buying in a country that speaks your language has many obvious practical and social advantages, and New Zealand scores over the English-speaking alternatives of Canada, California, Florida and South Africa. It lacks the severe winters of Canada; the high crime, racial tension and proximity to the San Andreas Fault of California (although New Zealand is seismically active); the crime and hurricanes of Florida; and the violence and instability of South Africa.

Naturally, there are also a few disadvantages, including 'leaky building syndrome' in some areas (see pages 92), earthquakes (around 14,000 are recorded annually, but only around 20 have a magnitude greater than 5 on the Richter scale and the last fatal earthquake was in 1968, which killed three people on the South Island's west coast), unexpected renovation and restoration costs (if you don't do your homework), a high rate of burglary in some areas, overcrowding in popular tourist areas during the peak season(s), and traffic congestion and pollution in some towns and cities. For many people, however, particularly those who live anywhere except South-east Asia, the major drawback of owning a holiday home in New Zealand is the length of time and expense of getting to and from it; weekend visits are out of the question and even a week's holiday is too short for comfort. And for those emigrating Down Under, an emergency back in the mother country (for example, in Europe or North America) might entail a very expensive flight, particularly if booked last minute at a busy time of year.

CLIMATE

Being an island nation, New Zealand has a climate dominated by its ocean setting, although it experiences a variety of climatic patterns due to its mountainous terrain. Climatic conditions vary considerably and include sub-tropical, sub-Antarctic, semi-arid (mainly in the Northland region), super-humid, frost-free, and sub-Alpine with permanent snow and ice in the mountainous areas. The eastern regions experience a drier climate than the west, on account of the prevailing westerly winds, the wettest area being the south-west (west of the Southern Alps). Being in the southern hemisphere, New Zealand has the 'opposite' seasons to those in the northern latitudes, i.e. summer is from December to February, autumn March to May, winter June to August and spring September to November. Unseasonal weather is rare.

The most important characteristic of New Zealand weather is its changeability.

The North Island tends to be warmer and drier than the South Island, although the highest mountain peaks often have snow year round. The average rainfall in the North Island is around 1,300mm. Daytime temperatures in Auckland average 23C (73F) in summer and 14C (57F) in winter, while in Wellington they range from 26C (79F) in summer to as low as 2C (35F) in winter. Wellington is renowned for its extremely windy weather, which can make the sea crossing between the two islands rough. Variations in weather and temperature in the South Island are more pronounced, and the Southern Alps have 'wet' (west) and 'dry' (east) sides. On the east side of the Southern Alps rainfall can be as low as 300mm (droughts are fairly common) and temperatures a lot warmer than on the west side. Snow is a permanent feature on the highest peaks. Christchurch averages temperatures of around 22C (72F) in summer and 12C (54F) in winter, while Dunedin averages 19C (66F) in summer and 10C (50F) in winter. Average temperatures, rainfall levels and sunshine hours for the main towns and cities are shown below.

Town/City	Average Temp (C)		Annual Rainfall (mm)	Annual Hours Sunshine
	Summer	Winter		
Bay of Islands	25	15	1,648	2,020
Auckland	23	14	1,268	2,140
Rotorua	23	12	1,511	1,940
Napier	24	13	780	2,270
Wellington	20	11	1,271	2,020
SOUTH ISLAND				
Nelson	22	12	999	2,410
Christchurch	22	12	658	1,990
Queenstown	22	8	849	1,940
Dunedin	19	10	772	1,700
Invercargill	18	9	1,042	1,630

Bear in mind that the temperatures are averages and it can be much warmer or colder on individual days.

PURCHASE RESTRICTIONS

If you're a permanent resident of New Zealand, there are no restrictions on the home you can buy there. If you aren't a permanent resident, you're sometimes limited by the Overseas Investment Act 1973 (OIC Act) to buying a home on less than 5 hectares (12.5 acres) of land. If the land is on, or next to, a 'sensitive' area (e.g. an island or nature reserve), overseas buyers are sometimes limited to buying less than 0.4 hectares (1 acre) of land. Buying apartments, houses and land in urban areas isn't generally affected by OIC Act restrictions.

Your solicitor will advise whether you need to seek agreement from the Overseas Investment Commission (OIC, i.e. the government body that oversees foreign investment policies) for a particular purchase. If you do, your solicitor will insert a condition in the contract making the purchase conditional on obtaining OIC consent.

COST OF PROPERTY

In general, property prices in New Zealand are slightly lower than in Europe because of its small population (i.e. relatively low demand), low cost of land and generally low construction costs. There is, however, a huge gulf between Auckland and the rest of the country. Property is much more expensive in Auckland, mainly because most of the best-paid jobs are to be found there. Auckland also has one of the better climates in New Zealand, and prices are further increased because a majority of immigrants make Auckland their first choice. Wellington is the country's second most expensive area for property purchase. Price variations are less marked in the rest of the country.

After some years of large annual increases in house prices, 2007 saw a slowdown in the property market, and the New Zealand Institute of Economic Research expects the

City/Area	Average Price August 2007	Increase since August 2006
Auckland	$450,000	+13.9%
Canterbury/Westland	$310,000	+13.4%
Hawkes Bay	$275,000	+7.8%
Manawatu/Wanganui	$215,000	+7.1%
Nelson/Marlborough	$334,000	+14%
Northland	$317,500	+19.8%
Otago	$238,000	+8.2%
Central Otago Lakes	$474,500	+2%
Southland	$176,000	+17.7%
Taranaki	$257,500	+7.3%
Waikato/BoP/Gisborne	$325,000	+14%
Wellington	$381,050	+13.4%

housing market to contract over the next few years. The national average house price in New Zealand in August 2007 was around $350,000, up from $310,000 a year earlier (a rise of 12.9 per cent). However, average prices were influenced by the high prices in New Zealand's major cities, particularly Auckland and Wellington.

The table above shows average house prices per region in August 2007 and the percentage increase since August 2006 (from figures published by the Real Estate Institution of New Zealand).

Apartments are often as expensive as houses and townhouses (or even more so), as they're invariably located in city centres, whereas most houses are in suburbs or in the country. Advertised prices are usually around 3 to 8 per cent above a property's market value (i.e. an offer this much below the advertised price is usually accepted) and substantially above its rateable value (see **Property Tax** on page 174).

When calculating your budget, you should also allow for lawyer's fees (see **Conveyance** on page 149) and bear in mind that banks charge a mortgage processing fee equal to 1 per cent of the mortgage amount and require a deposit (usually $500 minimum) on application.

BUYING FOR INVESTMENT

There are various kinds of property investment. Your family home is an investment, in that it provides you with rent-free accommodation. It may also yield a return in terms of increased value (a capital gain), although that gain may be difficult to realise unless you trade down or move to another region or country where property is cheaper. Of course, if you buy property other than for your own regular use, e.g. a holiday home, you'll be in a position to benefit from a more tangible return on your investment. There are four main categories of investment property:

- a holiday home, which can provide your family and friends with rent-free holiday accommodation while (hopefully) maintaining or increasing its value; you may also be able to let it to generate an income;

- a home for your children or relatives, which may increase in value and could also be let when not in use to provide an income;

- a business property, which could be anything from a private home with bed and breakfast or guest accommodation to a shop or office;

- a property purchased purely for investment, which could be a capital investment or provide a regular income, or both. In recent years, many people have invested in property instead of a pension to provide an income on their retirement.

With prices now generally rising in New Zealand more slowly than in previous years, property is an interesting investment proposition: some 'experts' are advising people to buy now before the market picks up again, while others advocate waiting in case prices stagnate further.

> ☑ **SURVIVAL TIP**
>
> A property investment should be considered over the medium to long term, i.e. a minimum of five and preferably 10 to 15 years, as you need to recoup the purchase costs (see **Fees** on page 109) when you sell.

You need to take into account income tax if a property is let and property tax (see page 174) when you sell a second home. Bear in mind that property isn't always 'as safe as houses' and property investments can be risky over the short to medium term.

When buying to let, you must ensure that the rent will cover the mortgage (if applicable), running costs and periods when the property isn't let. Bear in mind that rental rates and 'letability' vary according to the region and town, and that an area with high rents and occupancy rates one year may not be so fruitful the next. Gross rental yields (the annual rent as a percentage of a property's value) are from around 5 to 10 per cent a year in most areas (although gross yields of 15 per cent or more are possible); net yields (after expenses have been deducted) are 2 to 3 per cent lower.

Before deciding to invest in a property, you should ask yourself the following questions:

- Can I afford to tie up the capital for at least five years?

- How likely is it that the value of the property will rise during this period, and will the rise outstrip inflation?

- Can I rely on a regular income from my investment? If so, how easy will it be to generate that income, e.g. to find tenants? Will I be able to pay the mortgage if the property is empty and, if so, for how long?

- Am I aware of all the risks involved and how comfortable am I with taking those risks?

- Do I have enough information to make an objective decision?

See also **Location** on page 57, **Mortgages** on page 142 and **Chapter 9 (Letting)**.

ECONOMY

Although lagging behind Australia, most European Union countries and the US in terms of gross domestic product (GDP), New Zealand is one of the world's wealthiest countries, with a per-capita GDP of US$27,320 in 2007. A period of recession followed the Asian economic crisis in the late '90s and two successive droughts, which caused the country's export market to fall dramatically, but the economy is on an upward trend, and GDP growth was 2.2 per cent for the period July 2006 to June 2007, with an inflation rate of 2 per cent (inflation was an average of 2.6 per cent between 2001 and 2006).

Approximately 70 per cent of GDP derives from services, 25 per cent from industry and 5 per cent from agriculture. The national economy is, however, highly reliant on agriculture, particularly the export of dairy products, meat and wool, and a slump in world prices of these commodities badly affects the country.

The economy is also highly dependent on Far Eastern markets, and the economic crisis that befell that

region in 1997-98 caused a recession in New Zealand. Since then, however, the economy has recovered, and the country is rated by the World Bank as one of the best places in the world to do business.

Agriculture

Modern methods and machinery are used extensively on New Zealand farms, where productivity is amongst the highest in the world. The land is ideally suited to dairy farming, and grass grows almost all year in the north of the country. The main cereal crops include wheat (around 350,000 tonnes per year), barley (over 200,000 tonnes), maize (175,000 tonnes) and oats (70,000 tonnes). Other important crops are kiwi fruit (inevitably!), apples, pears, peas, potatoes and tobacco. The

livestock population of New Zealand includes 40m sheep (ten times as many as the human population), 5m cattle, 350,000 pigs and over 150,000 goats. New Zealand is the world's fifth-largest exporter of wool.

Forestry

Timber production is an important industry in New Zealand, which produces some 20m cubic metres annually, earning around $4bn. Much of it is used for pulp. Most native forests were cut down by the early European settlers in the late 1800s, and an extensive reforestation programme in recent decades has seen the planting of imported varieties of fast-growing trees such as Douglas fir instead of native New Zealand trees such as rimu and miro, most of which are slow-growing. A plantation of a North American species of pine in the Kaingaroa State Forest, said to be the largest planted forest in the world, is commercially exploited by a consortium of government and private industry. Timber production is expected to grow to 35m cubic metres per year by 2015.

Fishing is a small but important industry in New Zealand, where the annual catch is around 600,000 tonnes, much of which is exported. The most common freshwater and marine species are barracuda, blue grenadier, blue whiting, crayfish, lobster, mackerel, orange roughy and squid. New Zealand is also a large producer of shellfish, particularly green-lipped mussels and oysters.

Mining

In the '70s, New Zealand's mineral output increased substantially as new deposits of oil and natural gas were exploited. Annual output is around 5m tonnes of coal, 15m barrels of oil and 6.5bn cubic metres of natural gas. Other minerals produced in large quantities are bentonite, gold, iron ore, limestone, pumice, silica sand and silver. Clay, dolomite, gravel, limestone, magnesite, pearlite and sand are also found in New Zealand, where deposits of thorium and uranium are believed to be present.

Manufacturing

Around 300,000 New Zealanders are employed in manufacturing. The principal products are chemicals, clothing, electrical machinery, metal goods, paper and paper products, printed materials, refined petroleum and timber. All car manufacturing and assembly plants have been closed over the last few years. Manufacturing is modern and automated, although there are insufficient workers and raw materials to support much heavy industry.

Energy

In keeping with the country's environmentally-friendly image, some 60 per cent of New Zealand's electricity is produced by hydroelectric power, most of the rest from coal- and oil-fired plants. In addition, underground steam is used to produce a substantial amount of electricity in the North Island. Major hydroelectric facilities are located on the Waikato river in the North Island and on the Clutha and Waitaki rivers in the South Island. New Zealand has an annual electricity output of around 38bn kilowatt-hours.

Foreign Trade

The value of exports from New Zealand totals nearly $36bn annually.

New Zealand is the largest exporter of dairy products in the world (dairy products are exported chilled to many regions, including the Middle East and the Caribbean) and the fifth-largest exporter of wool. Other important exports include fish, meat and wood. In total, agricultural products account for over half of all exports.

Imports have risen significantly in recent years – in 2005 they exceeded exports in value for the first time – and primarily include chemicals, heavy machinery, iron, manufactured goods, petroleum, plastic materials, steel and textiles. New Zealand import tariffs are generally low (many having been reduced or abolished in recent years) and around half of all imports of manufactured goods are free of duty. Further information

Australia, the US, Japan, China and the UK are the country's major trading partners.

is available from the Ministry of Foreign Affairs and Trade, Private Bag 18-901, Wellington (☎ 04-439 8000, 🖥 www.mft. govt.nz).

STANDARD & COST OF LIVING

The inflation rate in New Zealand is low (around 2 per cent in mid-2007) and the government is committed to maintaining it at around this rate or lower. Prices of many imported goods have fallen in real terms in recent years, particularly cars and electrical appliances. In general, New Zealanders enjoy a high standard of living, although salaries are lower than in Australia, North America and many European countries.

In the Mercer Cost of Living survey (🖥 www.mercer.com/costofliving) of the world's 143 most expensive cities, Wellington was the least costly in Australasia in 111th place, while Auckland was ranked 99th. By comparison, London was 2nd, Paris 13th, New York 15th, Sydney 21st, Los Angeles 42nd and Melbourne 60th. New Zealand cities rate highly in international quality of life surveys, particularly Auckland and Wellington; in the Mercer Human Resources 2007 Quality of Life survey of the top 50 cities in the world, Auckland was placed 5th and Wellington 12th (Sydney was 9th and Melbourne 17th).

It's difficult to estimate an average cost of living in New Zealand, as it depends on where you live as well as your lifestyle. If you live in Auckland, drive a BMW and dine in expensive restaurants, your cost of living will be much higher than if you live in a rural part of the South Island, drive a small Japanese car, and live on home-cooked lamb and kiwi fruit. You can live most economically by buying New Zealand produce when possible and avoiding imported goods, which are more expensive not only because of the distance they must travel but also because they're considered fashionable.

Examples of typical salaries, housing costs and the price of many everyday items can be obtained from Statistics New Zealand (🖥 www.stats.govt.nz), the statistical office of the New Zealand government.

PERMITS & VISAS

Before making any plans to buy a home in New Zealand, you must ensure that you have a valid passport and the appropriate visa to allow you to use the home as you wish. Nationals of Australia and New Zealand can

live and work in either country with no more official documentation than their passport. All other nationalities (with some exceptions) must apply for permission to stay in New Zealand, either temporarily or permanently, **before** their arrival.

⚠ **Caution**

The information in this chapter is intended as a guide only and the rules and regulations concerning permits and visas change frequently, as well as sometimes being ambiguous, confusing and vague. It's important to check the latest regulations with a New Zealand mission or an immigration consultant (such as The Emigration Group – see 🖳 www.emigration. uk.com) before making a visa application.

For more information about permits and visas, see *Living and Working in New Zealand* (Survival Books).

Visitor's Visas & Visitor Permits

If you plan to visit New Zealand for a short period (e.g. for a holiday or business trip or to assess the country before applying for residence), you must apply for a visitor's visa, if applicable. Australian citizens don't need a visa to travel to New Zealand, and nationals of certain countries can use a 'visa waiver scheme', which allows you to travel to New Zealand without a visitor's visa and obtain a visitor permit on arrival. Countries that are party to the visa waiver scheme are Andorra, Argentina, Austria, Bahrain, Belgium, Brazil, Brunei, Canada, Chile, Czech Republic, Denmark, Estonia, Finland, France, Germany, Greece, Hong Kong, Hungary, Iceland, Ireland, Israel, Italy, Japan, Korea (South), Kuwait, Latvia, Liechtenstein, Lithuania, Luxembourg, Malaysia, Malta, Mexico, Monaco, the Netherlands, Norway, Oman, Poland, Portugal, Qatar, Romania, San Marino, Saudi Arabia, Singapore, Slovak Republic, Slovenia, South Africa, Spain, Sweden, Switzerland, the United Arab Emirates (UAE), the UK, Uruguay, the US (except for nationals of American Samoa and Swains Island) and Vatican City. **Everyone else needs a visitor's visa to travel to New Zealand and you won't even be allowed to board a plane to New Zealand without one.**

A visitor's visa is an endorsement in your passport that allows you to travel to New Zealand but not necessarily to remain there. Those who travel to New Zealand with a visa or visa waiver must complete an arrival card on their outward journey, which serves as an application for a visitor permit, which is processed on arrival. A visitor permit allows you to stay for a short period (usually three months, or six months if you're a UK citizen) as a tourist, to see friends or relatives, study, take part in sporting and cultural events, undertake a business trip or undergo medical treatment. It doesn't state on the permit that you may use it to look for a job or visit New Zealand with a view to living there but it doesn't forbid either activity and many people use it for these purposes.

To obtain a visitor's visa or, if you're travelling under the visa waiver scheme, to be granted a visitor permit on arrival, you must have a valid return ticket, sufficient money to support yourself (usually around $1,000 per month or $400 if staying with friends or relatives) and a passport valid for three months beyond the date you intend to leave New Zealand. You must also intend to stay in New Zealand for no longer than the period of the permit. If you comply with these requirements, you may travel to New Zealand and should be granted a visitor permit on arrival.

You can also be refused a visitor permit or visitor's visa if any clause of Section 7 of the Immigration Act 1987 applies to you, i.e. if you:

- have been deported from any country;
- are the subject of a New Zealand 'removal order';
- have committed a criminal offence which resulted in imprisonment of 12 months or more;
- are believed to have criminal associations or are suspected of constituting a danger to New Zealand's security or public order.

The above restrictions also apply to Australians, who don't need a visa or visitor permit to visit New Zealand.

Visitors may stay for a maximum of nine months (which can be made up of a number of shorter periods) in an 18-month period. Once you've reached the maximum, you're required to remain abroad for nine months before returning to New Zealand as a visitor. Visitor permits can be extended by a further three months on application to the New Zealand Immigration Service (NZIS), although this is at their discretion, and you may be required to be able to support yourself financially without working.

Visitor's visas can be applied for at offices of the NZIS (also called Immigration New Zealand, or *Te Ratonga Manene* in Maori, and a service of the Department of Labour) and New Zealand diplomatic missions abroad. Like Australia, New Zealand operates a system whereby applications for visas in major cities such as London and New York can be cleared almost instantly via an electronic link with the NZIS computer in New Zealand. Fees are usually charged for visas and permits and vary according to the country where you apply. They must be paid in local currency by bank draft or money order or in cash (if you're applying in person). Personal cheques and credit cards aren't usually accepted. Fees aren't refundable, even if a visa isn't granted. A list of NZIS offices, branches and agencies in New Zealand and worldwide can be found on its website (🖳 www.immigration. govt.nz). New Zealand embassies, consulates and high commissions (see **Appendix A** for a list) also provide information about immigration.

Note that as a visitor to New Zealand you aren't entitled to use publicly funded health services unless you're a resident or citizen of Australia or a UK national or hold a permit valid for at least two years (e.g. a long-term business visa). Unless you fall into one of these categories, it's strongly recommended that you have comprehensive medical insurance for the duration of your visit (see **Health Insurance** on page 188 and **Holiday & Travel Insurance** on page 193).

Work Visas & Permits

A work visa allows you to travel to New Zealand in order to undertake a period of temporary work. It isn't usually applicable to those intending to take up long-term residence in the country and applies mostly to contract workers and other short-term employees. Work visas are granted to foreigners when no suitable New Zealand citizen or resident is available to do a job. Their issue isn't based on a points system and each case is treated on its merits, taking into account the availability of local labour.

To obtain a work visa you must have a firm offer of a job in writing and apply to the NZIS, which can be done outside or within New Zealand (if, for example, you arrive as a visitor and then wish to work).

The visa fee is between around $200 and $280 (depending on where it's issued) and isn't refundable, even if your application is rejected.

On arrival in New Zealand you'll be issued with a work permit, which applies to a particular job only and for a specified period, usually a maximum of three years (but often for a much shorter period).

RETIREMENT

There's no particular immigration category for those wishing to retire to New Zealand, and those aged over 55 aren't eligible to apply for residence under the Skilled Migrant category. Most retirees seek residence under the Family stream, although those with business experience and capital may qualify under the Skilled/Business stream. See *Living and Working in New Zealand* (Survival Books) for more information about immigration categories.

LANGUAGE

If you want to make the most of the way of life and your time in New Zealand, it's essential to learn English as soon as possible. For people living in the country long term, learning English isn't an option but a necessity and you should take evening classes or a language course before you leave home, as you'll probably be too busy for the first few months after your move, when you most need the language. Your business and social enjoyment and success in New Zealand will be directly related to the degree to which you master English

---

☑ **SURVIVAL TIP**

If you come to New Zealand without being able to speak English, you'll be excluded from everyday life and will feel uncomfortable until you can understand what's going on around you (and you won't be allowed to stay long-term).

However bad your grammar, however poor your vocabulary and however terrible your accent, an attempt to speak English will be much better appreciated than your fluent Arabic, Danish, Serbo-Croat or whatever, which only people from that community will understand anyway. Like most native English speakers, few New Zealanders learn other languages.

HEALTH

One of the most important aspects of living in New Zealand (or anywhere else for that matter) is maintaining good health, and the country is among the world's 'healthiest'. Despite the common stereotype of the Kiwis as beer-swilling sports watchers stuffing themselves with barbecued meats, many have become health freaks in recent years. Fitness and health centres flourish in most towns, and even jogging (*footing*) has become fashionable in recent years. Smoking has declined considerably and is now a minority habit.

The quality of healthcare in New Zealand is high and comparable with other developed countries. Most illnesses and chronic conditions can be treated in New Zealand hospitals, with the exception of a few highly specialist areas (such as certain transplants), when it may be necessary to travel abroad. The standard of public health is generally high, although there are some differences between racial groups, with Maoris in particular suffering ill health more often than people of European origin. New Zealanders tend to suffer more from alcohol-related diseases than Europeans, but less from smoking-related conditions. A disturbing trend in recent years has been that diseases associated with poverty, such as rickets and TB in children, are on the increase after being virtually wiped out. The infant mortality rate is almost 6 deaths per 1,000 live births (around average for OECD countries) and average life expectancy at birth is around 78 years.

New Zealand provides 'free' or subsidised healthcare to its citizens, permanent residents and certain visitors. The system is comparable to those in European countries such as France or Germany, where the state covers the bulk of the cost of medical treatment but expects most patients to make a contribution. 'Free' care isn't as comprehensive as under the British National Health Service, which aims to provide free care to almost everyone, including emergency treatment for visitors. On the other hand it's nothing like that in the US, where every last pill, potion and sticking plaster must be paid for.

The New Zealand Ministry of Health (⌨ www.moh.govt.nz) is responsible for funding state healthcare, the provision of which is delegated to District Health Boards (DHBs), whose job is to meet the government's health objectives and spend their budgets in the most cost-effective way possible. DHBs use their funding to 'buy' healthcare services from various 'suppliers', including family doctors, hospitals, nursing homes and other health organisations. This system has been in existence since 1993 and introduced the commercial market into the public healthcare sector. It has seen most hospitals reformed as Crown Health Enterprises (CHEs or 'cheeses'

in local slang), which are in effect in competition with each other. As each of the 21 DHBs has substantial freedom to adopt its own system and framework, there tends to be a lack of national consistency in the health system.

The state healthcare system has come under huge pressure in recent years due to an increasing demand for services amid severe financial constraints, as politicians have sought to reduce the spiralling health budget to fund tax cuts. A number of hospitals have been closed and the number of people on waiting lists for non-emergency treatment, once unknown in New Zealand, has sometimes soared to almost 100,000. There has also been disruption to healthcare as successive governments have experimented with various measures aimed at providing a better service for less money (a formidable task). The latest healthcare innovation is the Health Information Strategy for New Zealand – launched in August 2005 – which aims to mitigate current challenges, including the ageing population, the rising incidence of chronic diseases such as diabetes and cardiovascular disease, the emergence of new infectious diseases such as SARS, and the high cost of new technology and treatments.

The New Zealand public and media are concerned at a perceived lack of funds behind the country's state healthcare, and medical staff generally feel they're underpaid and obliged to work with over-stretched resources. There have been several high-profile cases of people needing urgent treatment having to wait too long. The New Zealand Medical Association (NZMA, 💻 www.nzma.org.nz) also highlights the shortage of rural GPs and professionals in some specialist areas, such as psychiatry, as well as the 'brain drain' of doctors who have accumulated vast student debts and are attracted by salaries and working conditions abroad.

Although you won't be denied orthodox medical attention in New Zealand (assuming you don't mind waiting), alternative treatments are also popular. A recent survey by *Consumer* magazine claimed that half of New Zealanders have tried alternative therapies, usually for conditions for which they had been seeing a 'traditional' doctor. The most popular alternative therapies are chiropractic, herbal medicine, homeopathy and osteopathy. New Zealand doctors are generally sympathetic to these therapies and occasionally refer patients to alternative practitioners.

PETS

New Zealanders are enthusiastic animal lovers and many people keep dogs and cats. However, cats have received a 'bad press' in recent years, as they're believed to be responsible for the decimation of New Zealand's wildlife. Cats aren't indigenous to New Zealand and flightless birds such as the kiwi had few natural predators until the first European settlers landed their pets on the country's shores.

> ⚠️ **Caution**
>
> **If you plan to take a pet to New Zealand, it's important to check the latest regulations, which are complex. Given the distance (unless you're travelling from Australia) and container regulations, it's best to entrust the transportation of pets to a specialist shipping company.**

New Zealand has strict regulations regarding the import of animals in order to prevent animal diseases entering the country, and pets and other animals cannot be imported without authorisation from customs. You must obtain an import permit, which is available from the Executive Co-ordinator, Biosecurity New Zealand, PO Box 2526, Wellington (☎ 04-470 2754, 🖥 www.biosecurity.govt.nz). Note that if your pet needs to undergo a period of quarantine, the import permit will be approved only when accompanied by a letter from a MAF-approved quarantine establishment (there are only three) confirming that your cat or dog has a reserved place. You require a 'zoo-sanitary certificate' and a health certificate from a veterinary surgeon in your home country, and your pet will need to undergo a period of quarantine after its arrival in New Zealand (except as described below).

All animals must be vaccinated against rabies and must have had a Rabies Neutralising Antibody Tritation test no less than six months before they enter quarantine. A repeat test must be done within 30 days of the start of quarantine. Cats and dogs imported from Australia, Hawaii, Norway, Singapore, Sweden and the UK needn't be quarantined, provided they're microchipped, are older than 16 weeks and have been resident in the exporting country for a minimum of six months before travel. The cost of transporting a cat or small dog from Europe or the US, including all necessary paperwork, is likely to be at least $650, with quarantine accommodation costing from around $40 per day.

For further information contact the Ministry of Agriculture and Forestry, PO Box 2526, Wellington (☎ 04-474 4100, 🖥 www.maf.govt.nz), a New Zealand diplomatic mission or NZ Customs head office (☎ 0800-428 786 freephone from within New Zealand or ☎ 09-300 5399 from abroad) or regional offices: Auckland International Airport, PO Box 73-003 (☎ 09-275 9059), Christchurch, PO Box 14-086 (☎ 03-358 0600) or Wellington, PO Box 2218 (☎ 04-473 6099). Customs also have a comprehensive website (🖥 www.customs.govt.nz).

Lake Wanaka, Southern Alps

2.

THE BEST PLACE TO LIVE

O nce you've decided to buy a home in New Zealand, your next task will be to choose the region and what sort of home. Deciding where to live can be difficult enough, but the choice can be overwhelming if you're seeking a holiday, investment or retirement home.

If you're unsure where and what to buy, the best decision is to rent for a period (see page 95).

The secret of successfully buying a home in New Zealand (or anywhere else for that matter) is research, research and more research, preferably before you even set foot in the country. You may be fortunate and buy the first property you see without doing any homework and live happily ever after. However, a successful purchase is much more likely if you thoroughly investigate the towns and communities in your chosen area, and compare the range and prices of properties and their relative values. It's a lucky person who happens upon the ideal home, and you have a much better chance of finding your dream home if you do your homework thoroughly.

New Zealand is around the same size as the UK and has a variety of landscapes, including mountain ranges, extensive subtropical and temperate forests. Unlike most developed countries, New Zealand has large areas that are still largely uninhabited and there is only a limited amount of grassland.

GEOGRAPHY

New Zealand lies in the South Pacific Ocean south-east of Australia and comprises two main islands, called the North Island and the South Island (they were named in the 19th century by the British, who obviously exercised a great deal of imagination in christening them), plus numerous smaller islands (of which Stewart and Chatham are the most important). Associated with New Zealand are Ross Dependency (in Antarctica) and Niue, Tokelau and the Cook Islands (in the Pacific Ocean). The capital of the country is Wellington, although Auckland is the largest city. Contrary to popular belief (and much to the relief of most New Zealanders – not to mention Australians), New Zealand isn't just off the coast of Australia, but some 2,000km (1,250mi) away across the Tasman Sea. New Zealand covers an area of 270,534km² (104,461mi²), which makes it comparable in size to the UK.

New Zealand is a mountainous country, some 60 per cent of which is between around 200m (655ft) and 1,070m (3,500ft) above sea level, including over 220 mountains above 2,000m (6,550ft). The principal mountain ranges in the North Island extend along the eastern side, where the north central region has three active volcanoes: Mount Ruapehu (2,797m/9,176ft), the highest point

on the island, Mount Ngauruhoe (2,291m/7,516ft) and Tongariro (1,968m/6,456ft). Mount Taranaki (2,518m/8,261ft), a solitary extinct volcanic cone, is near the western extremity of the island.

The North Island has numerous rivers, most of which rise in the eastern and central mountains, including the Waikato River (435km/270mi), the longest river in New Zealand. It flows north out of Lake Taupo (606km²/233mi²), the country's largest lake (where mineral springs are also found), into the Tasman Sea in the west. The North Island has an irregular coastline, particularly on its northern extremity, the Auckland Peninsula, where it's just 10km/6mi wide.

The South Island has a more regular coastline than the North Island and in the south-west is characterised by deep fjords. The chief mountain range of the South Island is the Southern Alps, a massive range extending almost the entire length of the island from the south-west to the north-east (17 peaks in the range are over 3,000m/9,842ft high). Mount Cook (3,754m/12,316ft) is the highest point in New Zealand and rises from the centre of the range, which also contains a number of glaciers. Most of the rivers of the South Island, including the Clutha River (338km/210mi long), the longest river on the island, rise in the Southern Alps. The largest lake is Lake Te Anau (342km²/132mi²) in the

southern part of the Southern Alps. The Canterbury plains in the east and the Southland plains in the extreme south are the only extensive flat areas on the South Island.

The islands of New Zealand emerged in the Tertiary period and comprise a history of marine sedimentary rocks since the early Paleozoic era. Much of the topography of New Zealand has resulted from the warping and splitting of rock layers, although volcanic action has also played a part in its formation, particularly that of the North Island, where it continues to this day. Geysers and hot mineral springs occur in the volcanic area, particularly around Rotorua.

New Zealand is within an earthquake zone and minor (usually unnoticeable) tremors occur almost monthly, although records show that serious earthquakes occur, on average, only once every 210 years.

Much New Zealand plant life is unique, and of the 2,000 indigenous species some 1,500 are found only here, including the golden kowhai and the scarlet pohutukawa. The North Island is home to predominantly subtropical vegetation, including mangrove swamps in the north. The forest, or so-called bush, of the North Island is mainly evergreen with a dense undergrowth of mosses and ferns. Evergreen trees include the kahikatea, kauri (the traditional wood used for house building in New Zealand), rimu and totara, all of which are excellent timber trees. The only extensive area of native grassland in the North Island is the central volcanic plain. The eastern part of the South Island is, for the most part, grassland up to an elevation of around 1,500m, while most of the island's forests are in the west (consisting mainly of native beech and Alpine vegetation at high altitudes).

With the exception of two species of bat, New Zealand has no indigenous mammals. The first white settlers (who arrived early in the 19th century) found a kind of dog and a black rat, both of which had been introduced by the Maoris around 500 years earlier and are now almost extinct. All other wild mammals are descended from the deer, ferrets, goats, opossums, pigs, rabbits and weasels imported by early settlers.

No snakes and few unusual species of insect inhabit New Zealand (unlike Australia, which is infested with them), although it does boast the tuatara, a lizard-like reptile with a third eye, believed to be a distant relative of the dinosaurs.

New Zealand has a large population of wild birds, including 23 native species, which include the songbirds bellbird and tui, and flightless species such as the kakapo, kiwi (from which New Zealanders take their colloquial name), takahe and weka. The survival of flightless birds is attributed to the absence of predatory animals (with the exception of domestic cats). The blackbird, magpie, myna, skylark, sparrow and thrush are among the most prevalent imported species.

New Zealand's rivers and lakes contain a variety of native edible fish, including eel, freshwater crustaceans (particularly crayfish), lamprey and whitebait. Trout and salmon have been introduced and are found throughout the country. The surrounding ocean is the habitat of blue cod, flounder, flying fish, hapuku, shark, snapper, swordfish, tarakihi and various species of whale, in addition to a variety of shellfish including mussels, oysters and toheroas.

CITIES

New Zealand, a country of only just over 4m people, boasts two of the world's top 12 cities, according to a 2007 ranking of the world's top 50 cities according to quality of life by Mercer Consulting (⌨ www.mercer. com). Auckland was fifth (after Zurich, Geneva, Vancouver and Vienna), while Wellington came 12th, just behind Copenhagen and ahead of Amsterdam.

Auckland

Auckland and its neighbouring cities (Manukau, North Shore and Waitakere) make up the Auckland urban area, which occupies the Auckland isthmus (less than 2km/1.25mi wide at its narrowest point). Although it isn't the country's capital, Auckland is most new arrivals' introduction to New Zealand, most flights from Europe and North America landing there. It's also New Zealand's largest and most prominent city and home to almost a third of the country's population (around 1.3m people live in the Auckland area).

Auckland isn't simply New Zealand's largest city, it's also one of the world's largest cities, nearly twice the size of London, but with only a seventh of the population.

The Auckland area is the country's fastest growing region and around 70 per cent of New Zealand's overseas migrants settle there. The population is set to reach 1.6m in the next 30 years. Around 60 per cent of Aucklanders claim European (mainly British) descent, although there are also large Maori and Pacific Island communities (Auckland has the largest Polynesian population of any city in the world).

Auckland is regularly acclaimed as one of the world's best cities in terms of quality of life, with plenty of attractions, including a mild climate, lots of jobs, good educational opportunities, many leisure facilities and a modest cost of living (although property prices vary widely in Auckland, according to the suburb and even the street). It's known as the City of Sails (appropriately, it hosted the America's Cup in 1999 and 2003), with an abundance of beaches and offshore islands, and a lifestyle centred on the sea. It's also the country's economic centre: the Auckland area is home to around a third of New Zealand's workforce and nearly 40 per cent of all business enterprises. Most of the major international corporations operating in New Zealand have their head offices in Auckland, and the city's main industries and employers include business services, communications, distribution (45 per cent of New Zealand's wholesalers are based there), education, manufacturing and property services. Construction, finance, insurance and retailing are growing in importance.

The Pacific almost surrounds the city, and there are lush, subtropical forests on the hills and islands nearby. Auckland has a temperate climate, with warm, humid summers and cool, damp, sometimes quite long winters. The climate varies somewhat across the city due to the local geography, being particularly affected by the neighbouring hills.

The people of Auckland and other New Zealanders have a generally jovial 'love-hate' relationship. The stereotypes dictate that Aucklanders see the rest of the country's inhabitants as unsophisticated bumpkins, while other New Zealanders see Aucklanders as arrogant yuppies.

The 'quarter acre bungalow' (a three- or four-bedroom house or bungalow on around a quarter of an

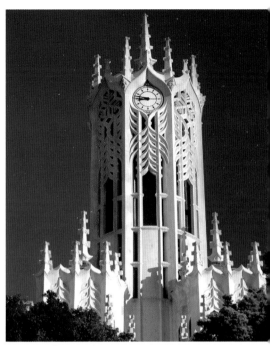

University of Auckland

acre of land) is the most common type of home in Auckland, which is one of the reasons why the city has grown so large and has an over-reliance on the motor car. The regional council is trying to address this issue by building more apartments and townhouses. In view of Auckland's severe traffic congestion, recent investment has been made in local rail services to try to encourage people out of their cars. Some Aucklanders commute by ferry to avoid the increasing traffic congestion, particularly on the Harbour Bridge.

Christchurch

Christchurch lies on the east coast of the South Island and has a population of around 375,000, making it New Zealand's second-largest city, although it feels quite compact. It's the main city of the Canterbury region and is known as the Garden City due to its abundance of public parks and residential gardens. Christchurch derives its name and existence from a colonisation programme operated by members of Christchurch College, Oxford, which not surprisingly has given it a distinctly English feel (it's reputed to be the most English of New Zealand's cities and is sometimes called the 'Oxbridge' of the Antipodes). It has fewer Maori and Pacific Islanders in the population than in much of the rest of New Zealand.

> Christchurch used to have a reputation as a dull place, but in recent years it has been livened up by an influx of Asian students and tourists. The city now has a wide selection of bars, including karaoke bars, and sushi restaurants, is increasingly popular with young people and apparently has the liveliest gay Japanese nightlife outside Tokyo (which is quite a boast).

The city has attractive Victorian Gothic architecture, as well as some ultra-modern buildings, notably the Christchurch Art Gallery.

Christchurch is a very flat city, only a few metres above sea level, with a generally temperate climate and summer temperatures which are often kept in check by a north-easterly breeze. A regular feature of the weather is the 'nor-wester', a hot wind that can reach gale force and cause substantial property damage. Christchurch is subject to smog in winter and this sometimes gives air pollution readings higher than World Health Organization recommendations (perhaps explaining why Christchurch has one of New Zealand's highest numbers of GPs per resident). Winters can be quite cold, with regular frosts and snow a few times a year.

Manufacturing and retailing are the largest employers, and agriculture, new technologies and tourism are also important to Christchurch's economy, the latter boosted by the city's proximity to ski resorts and the Southern Alps. Christchurch has played an important role in the history of Antarctic exploration.

Dunedin

Sitting at the far south end of the South Island, Dunedin (or 'Dunners' as it's called by younger people) is the largest city in Otago and the second-largest in the South Island. It's spread across the hills and valleys around the head of Otago harbour and has a population of around 125,000. Dunedin was settled by Scots in the mid-19th century (it was named after the Gaelic word for 'Edinburgh') and, thanks to the ensuing gold-rush, became New Zealand's largest and wealthiest city; consequently it has some of the most beautiful and best preserved Edwardian and Victorian architecture in the British Commonwealth.

Dunedin was the site of New Zealand's first botanical garden, newspaper and university (the University of Otago) and is surrounded by spectacular scenery. It still has a slightly staid image, but that's changing, driven by a vibrant music scene, a growing boutique fashion industry, an increasing population of artists, a thriving cafe culture and a growing number of students (around 20,000). Dunedin College of Education, Otago Polytechnic and the University of Otago are the major educational institutions and important local employers. Dunedin's climate is moderate, with proper 'seasons', which can come as a shock to Aucklanders and those from the far north. Winter can be frosty and there's significant snowfall every few years. Spring weather can be very changeable, but between November and April the weather is usually mild and settled.

The city offers the advantages of a buzzing university-city lifestyle without the drawbacks of the high cost of living, traffic jams, long commutes (most suburbs are under 15 minutes from the Central Business District) and high crime rate associated with big cities. It also has plenty of natural attractions close by, including miles of white beaches, golf courses, excellent fishing and good trekking country. Dunedin is famous as a centre for ecotourism: the world's only mainland royal albatross colony and several penguin and seal colonies lie within the city boundaries. Employment is provided by Dunedin's vibrant niche industries, including biotechnology, engineering, fashion and software engineering, and its deep-water port.

Dunedin railway station, South Island

Dunedin has three minor claims to fame: it has the world's most southern motorway, a 10km (6mi) section of State Highway One; it's home to Baldwin Street which, according to the *Guinness Book of Records*, is the steepest street in the world, with an alarming 1:2.9 incline; and it's the furthest city from London.

Gisborne

Gisborne is New Zealand's most easterly city, situated on the east coast of central North Island. It's the closest city to the international dateline, making it the first to see the sun each day. Gisborne lies at the confluence of three rivers, the Taruheru, Turanganui and Waitamata – hence its nickname 'City of Bridges'.

The Gisborne district has a population of 45,000 (with around 32,000 in the city itself) and a pleasant climate, with warm summers and mild winters. It's one of the sunniest places in New Zealand, with around 2,200 hours of sunshine per year. Gisborne is surrounded by rich farmland, producing beef, lamb, mutton, pork, citrus and kiwi fruit, wine and wool. It's also a good surfing spot (some 60 per cent of locals surf) and noted for its parks and recreational facilities.

Agriculture, forestry and associated manufacturing businesses are the backbone of Gisborne's economy, which is also one of New Zealand's three major grape growing areas, particularly for Müller-Thurgau and chardonnay. Wood processing is growing in importance, as are food processing, light manufacturing and tourism-related industries.

Hamilton

Hamilton is New Zealand's fifth-largest city (and fourth-largest metropolitan area) and largest inland metropolitan area, with a population of around 125,000, including 25,000 students. It lies by the spectacular Waikato river in the Waikato district of the North Island, an hour and a half's drive (or rail journey) south of Auckland. The region has some of New Zealand's best agricultural land, and Hamilton used to be primarily an agricultural service centre but now has a diverse economy. Education and research are important to the city's economy, notably through the University of Waikato and the agricultural research centre at Ruakura, the sources of much agricultural innovation in New Zealand. Hamilton hosts the annual National Agricultural Fieldays at Mystery Creek, the southern hemisphere's largest agricultural trade exhibition. Mystery Creek is New Zealand's largest event centre, hosting events such as the National Boat Show and the National Car Show. Hamilton isn't a major tourist resort.

Manufacturing and retail are also important to Hamilton's economy, as is the provision of health services, particularly at the Waikato

Base Hospital. Hamilton is home to New Zealand's only aircraft-manufacturing business and also has its largest concentration of trailer-boat manufacturers.

Hamilton city centre is lively but some people find the city's newer suburbs bland and lacking in character. The city has a growing problem with traffic congestion.

Invercargill

Invercargill is the southernmost city in New Zealand and one of the world's most southerly settlements, with a population of around 50,000. It lies on the Southlands Plains on the Oreti (or New) River, bordered by large stretches of conservation land and marine reserves, and is the commercial centre of the Southland region. The city has been regenerated in recent years with the opening of many bars, cafes, restaurants and shops.

Invercargill has a reputation as a friendly city and is a pleasant spot, with wide streets, historic buildings, good shopping and plenty of gardens and parks. It stresses the fact that it offers urban living without most of its associated drawbacks, including unaffordable housing and traffic jams.

Farming, especially dairy and sheep, is key to the local economy. Invercargill is the gateway to New Zealand's southern coastline and Stewart Island, the only place in the world where you can see kiwis in their natural environment. Its climate is temperate oceanic, similar to that of the UK (which might not be an attraction to potential British migrants!). Owing to its southerly latitude, the city enjoys 16 hours of daylight on the summer solstice (21st December).

Napier

Napier is an important port city on Hawke's Bay on the east coast of the North Island, with a population of around 55,000. It lies 332km (210mi) by road north-east of Wellington and is renowned for its '30s architecture and its variety of entertainments. It's a popular year-round holiday destination and a retirement centre, enjoying a Mediterranean-like climate of long,

Invercargill church, South Island

warm summers and short, mild winters. The weather is dry (by New Zealand standards) and Napier has one of the best sunshine records in New Zealand, although it's prone to catching the tail end of tropical cyclones from the central Pacific, which are sometimes still storm strength when they reach Hawke's Bay.

Napier claims to be the Art Deco Capital of the world. A huge earthquake (7.9 on the Richter scale) in 1931, along with the subsequent fires, destroyed much of Napier and the city was rebuilt in the styles of the era. As a result, it has one of the world's best range of '30s architecture, including Spanish Mission, Stripped Classical and, above all, Art Deco. Napier's Art Deco has its own flavour, including Maori motifs and the Frank Lloyd Wright-influenced buildings of Louis Hay.

Napier is the largest city in the Hawke's Bay region, which is the most significant crossbred wool centre in the southern hemisphere and one of New Zealand's largest apple, pear and stone-fruit producing areas. The region is also noted for its vineyards and wines, and Napier has one of New Zealand's busiest ports, shipping fruit, meat, pulp, timber and wool worldwide. Other local industries include electronics and fertiliser manufacturing.

Marine Parade, Napier, North Island

Nelson

Nelson lies on the eastern side of the Tasman Bay at the north end of the South Island. The combined population of Nelson and (adjoining) Richmond is around 55,000, ranking it as New Zealand's tenth most populous city. Nelson has the highest proportion of British expatriates in New Zealand: around 9 per cent of the population was born in the UK or Ireland. Nelson claims to be at the geographical centre of New Zealand, but the true centre is 35km (22mi) to the south-west.

Nelson is a centre of adventure tourism, ecotourism and caving, and is close to lakes, mountains and a national park. It also enjoys good beaches and a sheltered harbour.

Nelson is thought by many to have New Zealand's best (i.e. least changeable) climate and regularly tops the statistics for sunshine hours, averaging over 2,400 per year.

The economy is based on forestry, horticulture, seafood and tourism (Nelson is a holiday resort and retirement city), Port Nelson being the largest fishing port in Australasia. Other local growth industries include arts and crafts (there are over 350 professional artists in Nelson), aviation, engineering and information technology.

New Plymouth

New Plymouth is the port and main city of the Taranaki region on the west coast of the North Island and is the only deep water port on New Zealand's west coast. It has a population of just over 50,000 and is a service centre for the region's main economic activities, which include dairy farming and gas, oil and petrochemical exploration and production (it's the centre for New Zealand's energy exploration).

New Plymouth is a vibrant city and has a variety of attractions, including its excellent botanical gardens, a controversial 45m-high artwork (the Wind Wand) and views of Taranaki mountain (also called Mount Egmont). Locals boast that, because New Plymouth is a coastal city with a mountain close by, you can waterski and ski on the same day. Public transport, however, is limited and you really need a car to get around easily.

Palmerston North

Palmerston North lies at the foot of the spectacular Tararua mountain range, on the banks of the Manawatu river in the centre of the Manawatu plains in the Manawatu-Wanganui region of the North Island. It's around 140km (87mi) north of the capital, Wellington, and is home to around 80,000 people, including a large student population. Palmerston's cost of living is lower than almost any other New Zealand city, although much of its property lacks character.

Palmerston North, known simply as 'Palmy' by the locals, is a major rail and road junction and the service centre for the surrounding region. The climate is noted for being windy, especially in spring, and it has some of the largest electricity-generating wind farms in the southern hemisphere. Nearly 45 per cent of the workforce is employed in education, government and research, a further quarter in the retail and wholesale sectors.

Palmerston North's population has been falling in recent years, possibly because it isn't on the coast, which is where many people want to live. As a result of the population decline, the city has been trying to attract more residents, including a drive to persuade the British Lions rugby supporters who visited the city for a rugby match in summer 2005 to consider emigrating there!

Rotorua

Rotorua lies on the south shore of Lake Rotorua in the Bay of Plenty region of the North Island. It has a population of around 55,000 and a strong Maori heritage, claiming to be the heartland of New Zealand's Maori culture. The city is a spa resort, famous for its geothermal activity, geysers and hot mud pool, and it attracts over 1.3m visitors per year. This geothermal activity means that the city has a smell of sulphur, although most people stop noticing it after a couple of days. As well as tourism, farming and forestry are important to the local economy and manufacturing and retailing are growing in significance, focusing on food, engineering and timber products.

Rotorua is a pretty city, with botanical gardens, some interesting historic architecture and a thriving bar and restaurant scene, and it's one of New Zealand's prime trout fishing spots. There are 16 beautiful lakes in the region and Rotorua has a convenient, central location, within easy driving distance of Auckland, Hamilton and Tauranga.

> Rotorua's climate is temperate, cooled slightly by its altitude (290m/950ft). The weather is often sunny, rain is distributed fairly evenly throughout the year and it's less windy than much of the rest of the country, as it's sheltered by mountains and rock formations.

Tauranga

Tauranga is a city in the Bay of Plenty region of the North Island, 105km (65mi) east of Hamilton and 85km (53mi) north of Rotorua. It lies on a large harbour, protected by Matakana Island, and this sheltered position gives it a warm, dry climate, making it a popular retirement and holiday destination.

Tauranga has a population of 105,000 and is the fastest-growing city in New Zealand, mostly due to the influx of retirees and sun and surf seekers. Mainstays of the local economy include beef and dairy farming, construction, the production of food, drink and tobacco, and manufacturing (especially machinery and metal products).

Wanganui City

Wanganui City is a pretty city, located on the South Taranaki Bight, close to the mouth of the Whanganui River (which is spelt differently, presumably to confuse everybody) in the south-west of the North Island. It has a temperate climate with slightly above the national average sunshine hours (2,100 per year).

Wanganui City is home to 40,000 people and has some well preserved older residential buildings – bungalows, houses and villas. Its economy is based on the fertile land which surrounds the city. There's also some engineering industry and port facilities.

It's home to one of New Zealand's top private schools, Wanganui Collegiate.

Wellington

Wellington is an arty, compact city, centred on an impressive harbour in a dramatic landscape at the southern end of the North Island, roughly in the centre of New Zealand. Although sometimes overshadowed by Auckland (partly because, apart from Air New Zealand and Qantas, few international airlines fly to Wellington), it's a wealthy, sophisticated city, the country's financial and political capital, the seat of the national government and the site of most of New Zealand's public-sector jobs. It has boomed over the last five years, with thriving arts, culture and cafe and restaurant scenes (there are over 300 cafes and restaurants in Wellington). At 185,000, its population is only around a seventh of Auckland's.

In recent years, Wellington has been best known as the production base for the hugely successful and lucrative *Lord of the Rings* film trilogy. Appropriately, the city is the centre of New Zealand's creative and film industries, and over half the country's software developers are based there. Those who work in the fields of biotechnology, information technology and telecommunications will also find plenty of job opportunities.

On the downside, some people find Wellington's weather unpleasant: summers are cool, with an average temperature of around 20C (68F), and the average minimum in winter is 6C (43F). However, the main drawback is the wind; along with Chicago, Wellington is dubbed the Windy City, which can make aircraft take-offs and landings an ordeal for nervous passengers. Gales are prevalent in the summer and when

Parliment Library, Wellington

autumn turns into winter, although winters are often calm.

The wind in Wellington is sometimes so strong that it threatens the ferries that ply the waters between the North and the South Islands. In 1968, 50 people died when the car ferry Wahine sank during a particularly violent storm.

Whangarei

Whangarei is the largest urban area in the Northland region of the North Island, with a population of 50,000. It's the northernmost city in New Zealand, with a damp, subtropical climate, situated between forested hills and a spectacular deep-water harbour, surrounded by fertile farmland, orchards and plenty of beaches.

Whangarei is a lively harbour town and the commercial and service centre for the Northland region, particularly its farming and forestry industries. Other local industries include fishing, oil refining (at Marsden Point), luxury yacht building, tourism and wine production. Whangarei is the site of Parahaki, New Zealand's largest Maori Pa (fortified village).

REGIONS

The North Island

The regions/unitary districts of the North Island described below are arranged geographically, roughly from north to south, rather than alphabetically; see map on page 265.

Northland

Northland is (unsurprisingly) the northernmost of New Zealand's administrative regions, located in what Kiwis sometimes call the 'far north' or the 'winterless north' (because of the kind climate, with warm, humid summers and mild winters.). It occupies the top 80 per cent (285km/178mi) of the North Auckland Peninsula, encompassing just over 5 per cent of New Zealand's total area. To the west is the Tasman Sea and to the east the Pacific Ocean. Much of the terrain is rolling hill country, and farmland and forest (farming and forestry are the region's main industries) occupy over half the land.

> The west coast of Northland is dominated by several long straight beaches, the most famous of which is the inaccurately named Ninety Mile Beach, which is 'only' 80km (50mi) long, and two large inlets, Kaipara Harbour and Hokianga Harbour. The east coast is more rugged, with bays, peninsulas and several large natural harbours.

Northland is home to kauri forests (the kauri is a coniferous tree native to the northern North Island, which grows up to 50m/165ft tall), although many of these were cut down in the 19th century.

Northland is New Zealand's least urbanised region, only around half of its population of 165,000 living in urban areas. Whangarei is the region's largest population centre, home to around 50,000 people, but only seven other centres have populations of over 1,000. Around a third of the population is Maori, most of the rest being of European descent. Pacific Islanders are under-represented, compared with the rest of New Zealand.

Northland's economy is based on agriculture (particularly beef cattle), fishing, forestry and horticulture (particularly citrus fruit). Wood and paper manufacturing are also important and the region is a popular tourist destination, especially the Bay of Islands (with around 150 small islands). Northland has New Zealand's only oil refinery, at Marsden Point near Whangarei.

Auckland

Auckland is the second-smallest region (after Nelson), set on and around the isthmus of Auckland in the north of the North Island. Its coastline is bordered by the Tasman Sea and the Pacific, and the region has many fine beaches. Despite its size, the Auckland region is by far the country's most populous, home to around 1.3m people – roughly a third of New Zealand's population.

The region is dominated by the cities of the Auckland metropolitan area but also encompasses smaller towns, rural areas and the islands of the Hauraki Gulf.

Waikato

Waikato is in the northern central area of the North Island. The coastal area is mainly rough hill country, bounded by the Tasman Sea, with three large natural harbours: Aotea, Kawhia and Raglan. The area around Ragland is noted for its volcanic black sand beaches and fine surfing, and Waikato has some spectacular subterranean caverns.

East of the coastal hills is the Waikato river floodplain, which has a wet, temperate climate and rich farmland and is home to most of the region's population. Waikato's economy is heavily reliant on agriculture, and the land is intensively farmed with crops and livestock, while the upper reaches of the Waikato river are used to generate electricity and the northern region produces good wines. Other industries include business services, communications and tourism, but these

are less highly developed than in many other parts of New Zealand.

Waikato is home to around 385,000 people and the city of Hamilton is the region's main centre (population 125,000), while the towns of Cambridge, Te Awamutu and Tokoroa each have between 10,000 and 15,000 inhabitants.

The people of Waikato sometimes use the nickname Mooloo for themselves or their province, but nobody seems to know why.

Bay of Plenty

The Bay of Plenty is both a body of water (so named by Captain Cook) and the region surrounding it. Its population is around 260,000 and the region is dominated by two cities: Tauranga (population 105,000) and Rotorua (55,000). As a compromise between the two, the town of Whakatane was chosen as the seat of the Regional Council (rather like the choice of Canberra as Australia's capital, which was a compromise between Melbourne and Sydney). Agriculture (notably avocados, citrus fruits and kiwifruit) and tourism are the region's economic mainstays (the coastal region is one of New Zealand's sunniest areas), the geothermal region around Rotorua being one of New Zealand's most popular tourist destinations.

Gisborne

Gisborne, also called the East Cape or East Coast region, is a unitary authority in the north-east corner of the North Island. It's an isolated, sparsely-inhabited part of the country, and other than the city of Gisborne there are no large settlements. Of the region's 45,000 people, two-thirds live in the city, which is home to a higher than average proportion of Maoris. Inland from the coast, the terrain is mainly forested hills and the region's main industries are agriculture, forestry, horticulture, tourism and wine production.

Hawke's Bay

Hawke's Bay is a region on the east coast of the North Island; the 100km (62mi) circular bay from which it takes its name is confusingly called Hawke Bay. To add to the confusion, the region is often referred to as 'The Hawke's Bay' and the use of the apostrophe seems to have become optional (surely a bad example to children!).

The region comprises hilly coastal land around the bay, the Wairoa river floodplains in the north, the Heretunga Plains around Hastings in the south and a mountainous interior. The population is 145,000, of whom 55,000 live in the city of Napier. Hawke's Bay has a significant Maori population (around 20 per cent). The climate is temperate and dry (it's one of New Zealand's most 'Mediterranean' areas), and the region is known for its horticulture, with extensive orchards and vineyards, while in the more hilly areas, cattle and sheep farming and forestry are important.

Taranaki

Taranaki is situated on a peninsula on the west coast of the North Island. Mount Taranaki is the region's dominant feature, the second-highest mountain on the North Island. The region covers a modest area of 7,258km² (2,800mi²) and has a population of 105,000, just under half of whom live in the city of New Plymouth.

Taranaki is very fertile due to its rich volcanic soil and high rainfall (the third-highest in New Zealand). Dairy farming is dominant and the milk factory outside Hawera is the second-largest in the southern hemisphere. Taranaki also has on- and offshore gas and oil deposits; the Maui gas field off the north coast provides most of New Zealand's gas and supports two methane plants. The region has some excellent surfing and windsurfing areas, some of which are world-class.

Manawatu-Wanganui

Manawatu-Wanganui is a region near the bottom of the North Island. As its rather cumbersome name indicates, it's dominated by and named after the rivers Manawatu and Wanganui, the latter being the longest navigable river in New Zealand. Manawatu-Wanganui is the North Island's second-largest region and the sixth-largest in New Zealand, covering 22,215km² (8,575mi² – 8.1 per cent of the country's total land area). Its population of 230,000 makes it New Zealand's fifth-most populous region. The two major urban areas are Palmerston North (population 80,000) and Wanganui (population 40,000). The remainder of the region's population lives outside a large urban area.

The region has a range of low, medium and high terrains, including a series of mountain ranges (notably the Ruahine and Tararua Ranges) which incorporate the three main active volcanoes on the North Island.

The region's soils are productive if fertilised and it's one of New Zealand's most important pastoral

Mt Taranaki, North Island

areas. Manufacturing has also become important to the economy, although most businesses are agriculture-based. The region has areas of great ecological significance and a seventh of its land is part of New Zealand's conservation estate. The rugged interior is an important training area for New Zealand's defence forces, which have three bases in the region.

Manawatu-Wanganui's climate is generally mild, but more extreme inland. Chateau Tongariro 'boasts' New Zealand's lowest recorded temperature (-13.6C, in 1937). Sunshine hours in much of the region are around the national average (1,900 hours per year), but Palmerston North is often cloudy, with an average of 1,725 hours.

Wellington

Wellington is a region in the extreme south of the North Island, bordered to the west, south and east by water. To the west lies the Tasman Sea, to the east the Pacific, and to the south, connecting the two, the Cook Strait, a narrow, unpredictable stretch of water between the North and South Islands, only 28km (17mi) wide at its narrowest.

Over three-quarters of the region's 450,000 people live in the four cities in the south-west corner of the region, 185,000 of them in the capital, Wellington. The region of Wellington has some fine beaches on the narrow coastal strip, while the inland area comprises undulating and rough hills.

The economy is largely dependent on the government sector, along with business services (many of which supply the government).

The South Island

The regions/unitary districts of the South Island described below are arranged geographically, roughly north to south, rather than alphabetically. See map on page 265.

Tasman

Tasman is the region at the northern tip of the South Island. Its northern corner includes the prominent, narrow peninsula, Farewell Spit, and the

Kahurangi National Park. The south and east of the region are dominated by undulating countryside. Tasman has three national parks, which comprise almost 60 per cent of its area. The population is around 45,000, only 1.1 per cent of New Zealand's total, and most of Tasman's urban population (around 11,000) lives in the Richmond area.

> **Tasman has the country's highest percentage of people of European background – nearly 97 per cent.**

Community spirit is important in the region and Tasman has a higher proportion of people involved in voluntary work than any other region.

Tasman's major industries are agriculture (it's New Zealand's main hop growing area and a growing wine producing region), fishing and forestry, and there's a significant population of artists and craftspeople (more than in any other region of New Zealand). It's also a popular place to retire.

Marlborough

The Marlborough region is in the north-east of the South Island. The southern section is mountainous, while the central area comprises extensive plains (where much of the region's population of 44,000 lives), in the middle of which is the town of Blenheim (population 29,000). This area has a temperate climate (it's one of New Zealand's sunniest, driest areas) and fertile soils, and it has become the centre of New Zealand's wine production industry, while inland is sheep country. The north coast of Marlborough, made up of the drowned valleys of the Marlborough Sounds, is very attractive. Agriculture and natural resources are the mainstays of the economy.

Nelson

The region of Nelson mostly comprises, and is dominated by, the city of Nelson. It's New Zealand's smallest region but also the fastest-growing, home to 87,000 people (half of whom live in Nelson). Geographically, the region is split into five areas: the alpine lakes and rivers around Nelson Lakes; the parks around Golden Bay; the coastline of the Abel Tasman National Park; the horticultural land of Mapua, Motueka and Moutere; and the urban centres of Nelson and Richmond. The economy is based on agriculture and natural resources.

West Coast

West Coast is a long, thin region, 600km (375mi) in length, covering much of the west coast of the South Island. It seems a land apart to many New Zealanders, being remote, if beautiful, and the locals have a distinctive identity. The region is often known simply as 'the coast' and its inhabitants are called coasters.

To the west of the West Coast region lies the Tasman Sea, and to the east are the Southern Alps. Much of the land is rugged and most of the population lives on the coastal plains. The region is noted for its beautiful, varied terrain, with wild coast, mountains and native bush, some of which is temperate rain forest.

⚠ **Caution**

West Coast has very high rainfall (hence the rain forest and the fact that it's sometimes called the 'wet coast') due to the prevailing north-west winds and the proximity of the Southern Alps.

West Coast has a small population (around 32,000), and the main towns are Greymouth, Hokitika and Westport. Local industries include farming, fishing, forestry, mining for alluvial gold and coal, tourism and wood processing. The region is home to one of New Zealand's last independent dairy co-operatives, Westland Dairy Company, which remained independent when most farmer-owned dairies merged to form Fonterra, the world's largest farmer-owned dairy co-operative.

Canterbury

Canterbury is New Zealand's largest region, covering 42,200km² (16,290mi²) and the majority of the east coast of the South Island. The Canterbury Plains make up much of the region and the land is suitable for reasonably intensive agriculture, but prone to droughts.

Much of Canterbury's population (of 520,000) lives in a series of large and small settlements spread north-east to south-west along the plains and joined by State Highway 1. Christchurch is the region's main city (population 375,000). The economy is dependent on various manufacturing industries, particularly beverages, food and tobacco, and tourism is also important.

Otago

The Otago region is in the south-east of the South Island. It covers 32,000km² (12,350mi²), making it New Zealand's second-largest region, but has a population of just 195,000. The major centre is Dunedin (population 125,000). Kaitangata is a major coal source, but the economy is heavily reliant on agriculture and farming (particularly dairy, deer and sheep) and their related manufacturing industries, especially food and tobacco. Tourism is also important to the economy, as is Otago University.

Southland

Southland is (unsurprisingly) New Zealand's most southern region and is home to 95,000 people. It's an area of physical contrast, including Fiordland, a rugged area of fiords, lakes and

Queensland, South Island

mountains; rolling hills and plains; and Stewart Island across the Foveaux Strait, which is rich in native bush and wildlife. Southland also has a variety of climates – wet in Fiordland and drier in the north – but generally has New Zealand's lowest summer and winter temperatures and one of the highest rainfalls. By way of slight compensation for the grim weather, the air quality in the region is better than in much of the rest of the country, and it's green, lush and thinly populated.

Southland has long been the centre of New Zealand's sheep farming industry and has recently diversified into beef production, dairy farming,

deer farming, forestry and horticulture. Other major industries are dairy processing, fertiliser production, fishing, manufacturing, meat processing and tourism. Southland also has a vibrant cottage industry producing carvings, pottery and sculptures, and the region is rich in raw materials, including 65 per cent of New Zealand's coal reserves.

Southland has one city, Invercargill (population 50,000), and many of the region's people have Scottish ancestry. Its farming success is mainly the result of Scottish agricultural experience.

LOCATION

The most important consideration when buying a home anywhere is usually its location – or, as the old adage goes, the three most important considerations are location, location and location! If you're looking for a good investment, a property in reasonable condition in a popular area is likely to be greatly preferable to an exceptional property in an out-of-the-way place. Even if you aren't concerned with making money from your property, there's little point in buying a 'dream home' if it's right next to a motorway or a rubbish dump or is so inaccessible that a trip to the baker is a major expedition. New Zealand offers almost everything that anyone could want, but you must choose the right property in the right spot. The wrong decision regarding location is one of the main causes of disenchantment among foreigners who have purchased property in New Zealand.

Many people's choice of location is based on previous holidays, friends' recommendations, accessibility or simply an area's reputation. However, if you're likely to be spending the rest of your life in your new home, and even if you'll be spending only the occasional holiday there, it's worth taking the time and trouble to consider every aspect of its location first hand.

☑ **SURVIVAL TIP**

When choosing a permanent home, don't be too influenced by where you've spent an enjoyable holiday or two. A place that was acceptable for a few weeks' holiday may be far from suitable for year-round living.

The 'best' place to live in New Zealand obviously depends on your preferences and it's impossible to specify a best location for everyone. The important thing is to identify the positive and possible negative aspects of each of your selected locations in order to help you to choose the one that suits you and your family best.

If you have a job in New Zealand, the location of a home will probably be determined by its proximity to your place of employment. Obtain a map of the area and decide the maximum distance you're prepared to travel to work, then draw a circle of the appropriate radius with your workplace in the middle. If you intend to look for employment or start a business, you must live in an area that allows you the maximum scope. Unless you have reason to believe otherwise, you'd be foolish to rely on finding employment in a particular area. If, on the other hand, you're seeking a holiday or retirement home, you'll have a huge choice of areas.

If you have little idea about where you wish to live, read as much as you can about the different cities and regions of New Zealand (see page 50) and spend time investigating your areas of interest. Note that the climate, lifestyle and cost of living can vary considerably from region to region (and even within a particular region). Before looking at properties, it's important to have a good idea of the kind of home you're looking for and the price you wish to pay, and to draw up a shortlist of the areas or towns of interest. If you don't do this, you're likely to be overwhelmed by the number of properties to be viewed. Estate agents usually expect serious buyers to know where they want to buy within a 30 to 40km (20 to 25mi) radius and some even expect clients to narrow their choice down to specific towns and villages.

Don't believe the times and distances stated in adverts and by estate agents.

According to some agents' magical mystery maps, all homes in New Zealand's North Island are convenient for Auckland and a stone's throw from the beach. Check distances and ease of access yourself.

If possible, you should visit an area a number of times over a period of a few weeks, both on weekdays and at weekends, in order to get a feel for the neighbourhood (don't just drive around, but walk!). A property seen on a balmy summer's day after a delicious lunch and a few glasses of chilled wine may not be nearly so attractive on a subsequent visit without sunshine and the warm inner glow.

You should also try to visit an area at different times of the year, e.g. in both summer and winter, as somewhere that's wonderful in summer can be forbidding and inhospitable in winter (or vice versa). If you're planning to buy a winter holiday home, you should also view it in the summer, as snow can hide a multitude of sins! In any case, you should view a property a number of times before deciding to buy it. If you're unfamiliar with an area, most experts recommend that you rent for a period before deciding to buy (see **Renting before Buying** on page 95). This is particularly important if you're planning to buy a permanent or retirement home in an unfamiliar area. Many people change their minds after

a period and it isn't unusual for families to move once or twice before settling down permanently.

When house hunting, obtain large-scale maps of the area where you're looking. These make it easy to mark off the places that you've seen. You could do this using a grading system to denote your impressions. If you use an estate agent, he will usually drive you around and you can return later to those that you like most at your leisure (provided you've marked them on your map!).

You should also check the medium-term infrastructure plans for the area, with both the local and national authorities, particularly with regard to planned road and railway construction. Although a rural plot may seem miles from anywhere today, there could be plans for a motorway passing along the boundaries within the next five or ten years.

Bear in mind that foreign buyers aren't welcome everywhere, particularly when they 'colonise' a town or area (see **Community** below). However, foreigners are generally welcomed by the local populace, not least because they boost the local economy and bring work skills that are in short supply. Permanent residents in rural areas who take the time and trouble to integrate with the local community are invariably warmly welcomed.

The 'best' place to live in New Zealand depends on a range of considerations, including the following.

Accessibility

Is proximity to public transport services, e.g. an international airport, port or railway station, or access to a motorway important? Bear in mind that outside the main cities public transport in New Zealand is often thin on the ground. And don't believe all you're told about the distance or travelling times to the nearest motorway, airport, railway station, port, beach or town, but check it for yourself.

Although it isn't so important if you're buying a permanent home in

New Zealand and planning to stay put, one of the major considerations when buying a holiday home is communications (e.g. air links and links to airports) with your home country.

If you buy a remote country property, the distance to local amenities and services could become a problem, particularly if you plan to retire to New Zealand. If you're buying a home with a view to retiring there later, check the local public transport services, as you may not always be able (or wish) to drive. See also **Getting Around** on page 69.

Although budget and smaller airlines have recently made accessible previously remote parts of New Zealand, such services are

notoriously fickle and it isn't wise to buy in a particular area purely because it's served by cheap flights; airlines create and cancel routes (and are bought and sold) at the drop of a hat and you could be left stranded.

Amenities

What local health and social services are provided? How far is the nearest hospital with an emergency department? What shopping facilities are provided in the neighbourhood? How far is it to the nearest town with good shopping facilities, e.g. a supermarket? How would you get there if your car was out of commission? If you live in a remote rural area, you'll need to be much more self-sufficient than if you live in a town.

Don't forget that New Zealand can seem quite large if you live in a remote area, and those living in rural areas will need to use a car for everything. It has been calculated that it costs some $10,000 a year (including depreciation costs) to run a new small car doing around 15,000km (9,300mi) a year (which is less than average). Note also that many rural villages have few shops or facilities and aren't usually a good choice for a retirement home.

Climate

For most people the climate (see page 20) is one of the most important factors when buying a home in New Zealand, particularly a holiday or retirement home.

Bear in mind both the winter and the summer climate as well as the position of the sun and the direction of the prevailing wind. The orientation or aspect of a building is vital and you must ensure that balconies, terraces and gardens face the right direction.

Community

When choosing the area, decide whether you want to live among your own countrymen and other foreigners in a largely expatriate community, or whether you prefer (and are prepared) to integrate into an exclusively Kiwi environment.

However, unless you speak English fluently or intend to learn it, you should think twice before buying a property in a village. The locals in some villages resent 'outsiders' moving in, particularly foreigners, although those who take the time and trouble to integrate into the local community are usually warmly welcomed.

☑ SURVIVAL TIP

If you're buying a permanent home, particularly if it's an apartment, it's important to check out your prospective neighbours. For example, are they noisy, sociable or absent for long periods? Do you think you'll get on with them? Good neighbours are invaluable, particularly when buying a holiday home in New Zealand.

Crime

What is the local crime rate? In some areas the incidence of burglary is extremely high, which not only affects your security but also increases your insurance premiums. Is crime increasing or decreasing? Note that professional crooks like isolated houses, particularly those full of expensive furniture and other belongings, which they can strip bare at their leisure. You're much less likely to be a victim of theft if you live in a village, where strangers stand out like sore thumbs. See also **Crime** on page 213.

Employment

How secure is your job or business and are you likely to move to another area in the near future? Can you find other work in the same area, if necessary? What about your partner and children? If there's a possibility that you'll need to move in some years' time, you should rent, or buy a property that will be relatively easy to sell.

Garden

If you're planning to buy a country property with a large plot, bear in mind the high cost and amount of work involved in its upkeep. If it's to be a second home, who will look after the house and garden when you're away? Do you want to spend your holidays mowing the lawn and cutting back the undergrowth? Do you want a home

with a lot of outbuildings? What are you going to do with them? Can you afford to convert them into extra rooms or guest accommodation?

Local Council

Is the local council well run? Unfortunately, some are profligate and simply use any extra income to hire a few more of their cronies or spend it on grandiose schemes, and some councillors abuse their positions to further their own ends. What are the views of other residents? If the municipality is efficiently run, you can usually rely on good local social and sports facilities and other services.

Natural Phenomena

Check whether an area is particularly susceptible to natural disasters, such as bush fires, cyclones, droughts, earthquakes, floods or violent storms.

> ⚠ **Caution**
>
> **If a property is near a waterway, it may be expensive to insure against floods, which are a constant threat in some areas**

In fact, many areas of New Zealand, particularly in the North Island, are susceptible to flash floods after torrential rain. It's therefore wise to avoid properties located near rivers and streams (which can quickly become raging torrents after heavy rain) or situated in hollows. See also **Inspections & Surveys** on page 118.

Noise

Noise can be a problem in some cities, resorts and developments. Although you cannot choose your neighbours, you can at least ensure that a property isn't next to a busy road, industrial plant, commercial area, discotheque, night club, bar or restaurant (where revelries may continue into the early hours). Look out for objectionable neighbouring properties which may be too close to the one you're considering and check whether nearby vacant land has been 'zoned' for commercial use. In community developments (e.g. apartment blocks) neighbouring properties may be second homes which are let short term, which means you may need to tolerate boisterous holidaymakers as neighbours throughout the year (or at least during the summer months).

Don't assume that rural life is necessarily tranquil. Other kinds of noise can disturb your peace and quiet, including chiming church bells, barking dogs, crowing cockerels and other farmyard animals, and aircraft if you live near a civil or military airfield. On the other hand, those looking to buy a rural property should note that there may be times when noisy activities such as lawn mowing are prohibited (e.g. at lunchtime on Saturdays and all afternoon on Sundays).

When buying an apartment, note the following:

● Polished floorboards are popular in apartment buildings, but bare floors can be noisy. Check how disturbing it is when someone walks across the floor in the apartment immediately above.

● Interior bathrooms (i.e. those with no windows) often have ventilation systems with extractor fans that are situated on the roof of the apartment block. These extractor fans can generate a lot of noise, which particularly affects the inhabitants of top-floor apartments.

● Air-conditioning units are usually situated on the outside of buildings and often have noisy fans. Check that there are no air-conditioning units near to bedrooms and exterior sitting areas (e.g. balconies) in the apartment you're thinking of buying (although, of course, there's no guarantee that they won't be installed in the future).

Parking

If you're planning to buy in a town or city, is there adequate private or free on-street parking for your family and visitors? Is it safe to park in the street? In some areas it's important to have secure off-street parking if you value your car. Parking is a problem in many towns and most cities, where private garages or parking spaces can be very expensive. Bear in mind that an apartment or townhouse in a town or community development may be some distance from the nearest road or car park. How do you feel about carrying heavy shopping hundreds of metres to your home and possibly up several flights of stairs?

> ⚠ **Caution**
>
> **Traffic congestion is a problem in many towns and tourist resorts, particularly during the high season.**

Position

New Zealanders tend to place a great deal of importance on the position and orientation of their homes. Properties in positions that catch the sun usually sell at a premium over those in shady spots because they tend to be not only brighter but also warmer in winter. In Wellington, for example, any property that's sheltered from the wind and isn't forever in the shadows cast by the surrounding hills is likely to be worth significantly more (though, of course, it will probably cost you more) and will also be more pleasant to live in.

Property Market

Do houses sell quickly in the area? Generally you should avoid neighbourhoods where desirable houses routinely remain on the market for six months or longer (unless the property market is in a slump and nothing is selling).

Schools

Consider your children's present and future schooling needs. What is the quality of local schools? Are there any bi-lingual or international schools nearby? Note that, even if your family has no need or plans to use local schools, the value of a home may be influenced by the quality and location of schools.

Sports & Leisure Facilities

What is the range and quality of local leisure, sports, community and cultural facilities? What is the proximity to sports facilities such as a beach, golf course, ski resort or waterway? Bear in mind that properties in or close to ski and coastal resorts are considerably more expensive, although they also have the best letting potential. If you're interested in a winter holiday home, which area should you choose?

Tourists

Bear in mind that if you live in a popular tourist area, you'll be inundated with tourists in summer – all year in warmer regions or those with skiing. They won't only jam the roads and pack the public transport, but may even occupy your favourite table at your local cafe or restaurant! Although a 'front-line' property on the beach or in a marina development may sound attractive and be ideal for short holidays, it isn't usually the best choice for permanent residence. Many beaches are hopelessly crowded in the high season, streets may be smelly from restaurants and fast food outlets, parking impossible, services stretched to breaking point, and the incessant noise may drive you crazy. You may also have to tolerate water restrictions in some areas.

Town or Country?

Do you wish to be in a town or do you prefer the country? Bear in mind that if you buy a property in the country, you'll probably have to put up with poor public transport (or none at all), long travelling times to a town, solitude and remoteness. You won't be able to pop along to the local shop or drop into the local bar for a glass of your favourite tipple with the locals, or have a choice of restaurants on your doorstep. In a town or large village, the weekly market will be just around the corner, a doctor and chemist close at

Auckland

hand, and if you need help or run into any problems, your neighbours will be close by.

On the other hand, in the country you'll be closer to nature and have more freedom (e.g. to make as much noise as you wish) and possibly complete privacy, e.g. to sunbathe or swim *au naturel*. Living in a remote area in the country will suit nature lovers looking for solitude who don't want to involve themselves in the 'hustle and bustle' of town life (not that there's much of this in New Zealand's rural towns). If you're after peace and quiet, make sure that there isn't a busy road or railway line nearby or a local church within 'donging' distance (see **Noise** above).

Many people who buy a remote country home find that the peace of the countryside palls after a time and they yearn for the more exciting nightlife of a city or tourist resort. If you've never lived in the country, it's wise to rent first before buying. Note also that, while it's cheaper to buy in a remote or unpopular location, it's usually much more difficult to find a buyer when you want to sell.

GETTING THERE

Although it isn't so important if you're planning to live permanently in New Zealand and stay put, one of the major considerations when buying a holiday or part-time retirement home is the cost of getting to and from New Zealand, and you should ask yourself the following questions:

- How long will it take to get to a home in New Zealand, taking into account journeys to and from airports, ports and railway stations?

- How frequent are flights at the time(s) of year when you plan to travel?

- Are direct flights available?

- What is the cost of travel from your home country to the region where you're planning to buy a home in New Zealand?

- Are off-season discounts or inexpensive charter flights available?

You should bear in mind that it may take you up to a week to recover from the journey Down Under (if you've come from Europe, for example), especially if you suffer badly from jet lag. Obviously, the travelling time and cost of travel to a home in New Zealand will be more significant if you're planning to spend frequent holidays there rather than one long visit a year.

☑ SURVIVAL TIP

Allow plenty of time to get to and from airports, ports and railway stations, particularly when travelling during peak hours, when traffic congestion can be horrendous. Also, take into account the time that security checks may take.

Airline Services

New Zealand is served by some 25 international airlines, most of which fly to Auckland or Christchurch. New Zealand's main domestic airline (and also its international airline) is Air New Zealand (☎ freephone 0800-737 000, 💻 www.airnz.co.nz), which is regularly acclaimed as one of the world's best airlines.

Air New Zealand (ANZ) was originally state owned but was then privatised. In 2001 it came near to bankruptcy when it attempted to buy the remaining 50 per cent of Ansett Australia (it already owned 50 per cent), which had gone into liquidation. The New Zealand government, in an attempt to save the airline, announced a $500m rescue package, which made the government the majority shareholder in the company. (Many New Zealanders believe that the airline shouldn't have been privatised in the first place).

ANZ has a comprehensive route network, with over 470 flights per day to 26 domestic destinations, and flights to a wide range of destinations in Asia, Australasia, Europe and North America (and two in Mexico).

ANZ's main domestic competitors are Freedom Air and Qantas (💻 www.qantas.com.au). Freedom Air (💻 www.freedomair.com) serves Auckland, Christchurch, Dunedin, Central North Island, Palmerston North and Wellington (as well as Australian destinations).

Mount Cook also operates domestic services, although it's a partner airline to ANZ (operating services on their behalf), as are Air Nelson and Eagle Air, rather than real competitors. A number of other competitors have started up or been proposed over the years, although most have fallen by the wayside. Many domestic services provide in-flight bar facilities, which is something of an innovation in New Zealand, where the sale of alcohol is subject to strict licensing hours. Smoking isn't permitted on the domestic services of any airline. Surprisingly, however, the health-conscious New Zealanders haven't banned that other risk to the wellbeing of air travellers – airline food!

There are also a number of mini-airlines serving minor destinations, often using aircraft with as few as four seats. For example, Great Barrier Airlines (🖳 www.greatbarrierairlines.co.nz) and Mountain Air (🖳 www.mountainair.co.nz) both operate a service to Great Barrier Island (a paradise-like island, likened to Fiji or Tahiti) in the Hauraki Gulf off Auckland.

Airports

New Zealand's main international airport is Auckland, which is connected by direct flights to most main cities in Asia, several cities in the US and Europe (with frequent flights to and from London), plus several Polynesian destinations. The airports at Wellington and Christchurch also dub themselves 'international' but offer a much smaller number of international flights, mainly to Australia, although Christchurch serves some other countries, including the UK.

Wellington is the country's domestic air hub, as many flights from all points north and south stop at Wellington to allow passengers to change planes. There are also domestic airports at Blenheim, Dunedin, Gisborne, Hamilton, Hastings, Hokitika, Invercargill, Kaitaia, Te Anau, Mount Cook, Napier, Nelson, New Plymouth, Palmerston North, Queenstown, Rotorua, Taupo, Tauranga, Wanganui, Whakatane and

Whangerei. Their facilities range from a modest but modern terminal building to a motley collection of huts.

Auckland International airport is 21km (13mi) south of the city at Mangere and has three, separate terminals. There's an AirBus shuttle connecting the airport with the city centre every 20 or 30 minutes, costing $15 single and $22 return. The privately operated Johnston's Shuttle Link and the SuperShuttle also run to the city centre, taking 35 minutes and costing around $15 one way. Airport information is available on ☎ 09-256 8813 or at 🖳 www.auckland-airport.co.nz.

Wellington International Airport is 7km (5mi) south of the city at Rongotai. It has been designated a 'low noise' airport and may be used only by the quietest planes, which, even so, aren't permitted to arrive or depart at night. Wellington's airport is notoriously windy and renowned among pilots as a difficult place to land and take off. As with Auckland, there are three terminals. Shuttle buses take 20 minutes to reach central Wellington and cost around $11. Airport information is available on ☎ 04-385 5100 or at 🖳 www.wellington-airport.co.nz.

Christchurch International Airport, whose facilities have recently been greatly improved, is 11km (7mi) north of the city centre and is easily reached by bus, for a fare of between $7 and $20. For information, ☎ 03-358 5029 or visit 🖳 www.christchurch-airport.co.nz.

Fares

ANZ's services were notoriously expensive until the now-defunct Ansett arrived on the scene, which prompted more competitive pricing. However, standard fares are still high, and it's necessary to shop around and compare prices to obtain the best deal. The cheapest fares are to be had by booking at least seven days ahead. Sample fares are Auckland to Wellington one way for between $100 and $240, Auckland to Christchurch one way for between $105 and $285, and Wellington to Christchurch one

way for between $80 and $190. International return flights cost around GB£700 from London to Auckland between April and June, rising to between GB£1,100 and GB£1,500 during the high season (December/January).

A departure tax of $25 is levied on passengers on departing international flights, which must be paid before you pass through immigration. At Auckland International Airport it can be paid at the Bank of New Zealand offices on the ground and first floors.

GETTING AROUND

Although the population of New Zealand is dispersed over a wide area, the country has a reasonable internal transport service, which is centred around road, rail and air links, plus the essential umbilical ferry link connecting the North and South Islands. Unless you live in a remote country area, you shouldn't find it too difficult to get around without your own transport. Probably the most impressive feature of New Zealand's public transport is that the different elements are closely integrated and if you start a journey by bus, continue by rail and then take to the air, you usually find that services are timed to connect. If your luggage is lost, stolen or damaged on public transport in New Zealand, you should make a claim to the relevant authority, as you may receive an ex-gratia payment.

Name	Route
The Overlander	Auckland-Wellington
Capital Connection	Palmerston North-Wellington
TranzCoastal	Christchurch-Picton
TranzAlpine	Christchurch-Greymouth

Although car ownership and usage in New Zealand is high, this shouldn't be taken as a sign that public transport is unreliable (although it does have a few shortcomings, such as finishing too early in some cases), but rather that the roads are relatively uncongested and therefore driving still has many advantages over public transport. Even in metropolitan Auckland and Wellington, commuters travelling into the centre often drive (although traffic jams are encouraging more drivers to consider public transport).

All public transport timetables in New Zealand use the am/pm time system rather than the 24-hour clock.

Like many countries, New Zealand has started to take the needs of disabled travellers seriously only within the last decade or so. Domestic airlines and trains cater fully for disabled travellers, but you should tell them that you need special assistance when booking. As most taxis are simply converted saloon cars, you can use them only if you can gain access to a standard car. There are wheelchair-accessible taxis in cities, although you need to book (particularly for the return journey), as their number is limited. There are no special facilities for the disabled on coach and bus services, although discount fares are widely available. Further information can be obtained from the Disability Information Service, 314 Worcester Street, Christchurch (☎ 03-366 6189).

Rail Services

New Zealand's rail network is operated by Tranz Scenic, the country's only passenger rail company (🖳 www.tranzscenic.co.nz). The network is limited, mainly due to the mountainous terrain in many parts of the country and, of course, by the fact that lines cannot cross the Cook Strait. The service itself is modern and comfortable (part of the Auckland-Wellington line has recently been electrified), but neither frequent nor fast, although stops at many small stations on long-distance lines have been eliminated, making journey times shorter. As a result, rail services are widely promoted as a tourist attraction rather than a day-to-day amenity. In this regard the rail service is excellent, as many lines pass through native forests, past volcanic peaks and through alpine passes providing spectacular, panoramic views. There are four main railway routes, each with a colourful name, as above.

There's only one class of travel whichever service you choose. If you're a student or disabled, you qualify for a 50 per cent discount off the standard fare. You must provide proof of identity and must book.

Some services provide free refreshments and/or a free lunch, and there are also buffet cars selling more substantial meals and a bar on some services. Some trains have tourist commentaries (which you must listen to whether you're a tourist or not). If you wish to take a bicycle on a train, check when booking, as they aren't allowed on many services and only limited space is available when they are.

Smokers may have a tough time travelling by train in New Zealand, as smoking isn't permitted on any train, even though some of the journeys are long.

There are no underground services anywhere in New Zealand, but there are fast and reliable commuter rail networks in Auckland and Wellington. Auckland's commuter rail network is operated by Rideline (💻 www.rideline.co.nz), which also runs buses and ferries. There are two lines running from the railway station, one to Waitakere in the west and the other to Papkura in the south. The website has extensive details of routes, fares and offers. Wellington's commuter rail network is run by Tranz Metro, which has four lines – to Johnsonville, Paraparaumu, Melling and Wairarapa. Details can be found on the website (💻 www.tranzmetro.co.nz).

Buying Tickets

The easiest way to book a trip by train is to call Tranz Scenic on ☎ 0800-872 467 and pay by credit card, although you can also book at travel agents' (a booking fee is charged) or free at stations. Tranz Scenic also has numerous agents overseas where you can book tickets and you can also book online (💻 www.tranzscenic.co.nz). If you travel on a train without a ticket (or with an invalid ticket or pass), you must pay the full fare plus a modest surcharge, but you won't be forced to leave the train in the middle of nowhere!

Given the limited rail services in New Zealand, there are no season tickets, although a number of discounted tickets are available on each journey.

Stations

Tranz Scenic stations have few facilities. This is mainly because, in many cases, there's only one arrival or departure a day, and hence no demand for bars and buffets, or the range of other services you usually find at major railway stations. There's an enquiry office open from before the first train leaves (or at least 7.30am) until 5.30pm, for information and bookings. Taxis and buses don't stop at stations throughout the day, but tend to congregate when a train arrives. This means that you may have to wait in a queue, although you're unlikely to be left stranded as there's usually a connecting bus service timed to meet the last train.

Stations aren't always conveniently situated for city centres; for example Auckland's is on Beach Road, a 15-minute walk from the city centre, and isn't on a regular bus route. Wellington's station is on Waterloo Quay, on the edge of the central area near one of the city's bus stations, and is served by the city's commuter railway services, as well as being connected by shuttle bus to the Interislander ferry terminal.

Bus, Tram & Coach Services

Most towns and cities have a good public bus service, and some cities operate double-decker buses, like those in the UK. Bus services have been deregulated and privatised to some extent in recent years, although in many cases the original public bus company is still the largest operator. One of the drawbacks of the public bus service is that it ends early. On Saturdays and Sundays the last services are at around 5pm. Even in Auckland, you won't find a public bus running after 11.30pm during the week (many routes finish much earlier) and some services are discontinued altogether at weekends. On the other hand, one benefit of bus deregulation is that small private firms have been allowed to enter the public transport business, and some operate services late into the evening and at weekends when the main operators

Tram, Christchurch

have suspended their services. Some services, using minibuses and cars, can be ordered by telephone when required.

In Wellington the bus system is run by Stagecoach and has frequent services, including an after-midnight service from the entertainment district to suburbs. Timetables and other information are available from ☎ freephone 0800-8017000.

Christchurch buses are among the best in the country, with cheap and frequent services, and a free Shuttle runs around the city centre at ten-minute intervals. Information is available from Bus Info (☎ 03-366 8855). Auckland bus services include the Link, which runs at ten-minute intervals around the main parts of the city in a loop.

On New Zealand buses you usually buy your ticket from the driver as you enter the bus. Some buses accept the exact fare only.

As several companies now operate in most towns, there's no centralised place where you can obtain timetable information. Check your telephone directory for details of where to obtain information about services and a copy of timetables. In larger cities there's more than one bus station serving the different companies and routes. In Wellington, the main stations are at Waterloo Quay and Courtenay Place. In Auckland, buses use the Downtown and Midtown terminals (although Midtown is only a series of lay-bys rather than a purpose-built terminal).

Bus Fares

Fares for town bus services are calculated on a zone basis and depend on how many zones you travel through. In Auckland, bus journeys within the city cost from 50¢ and a journey on the Link $1.60. In Wellington, it costs $1 for the city zone, $1.50 for one other zone (known as a section) and $2.50 for a journey that includes two zones. Bus fares in Christchurch are $1.90 for a Metrocard single trip and $3.80 for all day travel.

☑ **SURVIVAL TIP**

Most towns and cities offer daily and weekly passes, which work out much cheaper if you plan to do a lot of travelling by bus.

The Auckland Discovery Day Pass costs $14 for unlimited rides on buses, ferries and trains, while in Wellington a Daytripper pass costs $5. In both cases you cannot begin your journey until 9am on weekdays, although there are no restrictions at weekends.

Trams

Trams operate in several cities in New Zealand, including Wellington, where they're called trolley buses and operate on several routes in the city centre and inner suburbs. The cost is the same as for buses (see above), and the Daytripper pass issued for buses can also be used on trams. Wellington also has a cable car operating between Lambton Quay and the Botanic Gardens in Kelburn. This is a popular tourist attraction but is also used daily by commuters, as it's an easy way to travel up one of Wellington's steepest hills. Trams operate on a city-centre loop in Christchurch, stopping at nine points along the way; they mostly attract tourists but are also handy for commuters and shoppers in the city centre. You can buy a one-hour, half-day or full-day ticket from the conductor on board (the service operates between 9am and 6pm).

Coaches

New Zealand has comprehensive and reliable long-distance coach services, which are generally preferable to long-distance trains. Unlike trains, there are several coach services per day on the main routes such as Auckland-Wellington. Services are provided by two major companies: InterCity Group (NZ) Limited (operating as InterCity Coachlines, 🖥 www.intercitycoach. co.nz) serves 600 destinations, while Newmans, its main competitor, also serves an impressive number of destinations (🖥 www.newmanscoach. co.nz). There are also around a dozen smaller companies, such as Northliner Express Coachlines.

Coach services, even of competing companies, are well co-ordinated so that they connect not only with other coach services but also with other modes of transport. So, for example, if you take the train from Auckland to Wellington, the Interislander ferry across the Cook Strait and then a coach to Christchurch, it's possible to plan a route which connects smoothly, allowing just enough time to get from one terminus to another.

Coaches are modern and provide facilities such as toilets, reclining seats and air-conditioning. On routes that are popular with tourists the driver usually provides a commentary on sights and places of interest. On services operating in more remote areas, you may find that half the coach is given over to freight and parcels.

Snacks and drinks aren't available on board coaches but they stop regularly for refreshments, although drivers tend to choose the more expensive places (so it pays to take your own snacks with you). Smoking isn't permitted on coaches.

It's usually possible just to turn up and travel by coach, except at busy times such as during summer and public holiday periods. However, if you know when you want to travel, it makes sense to book, as it costs no extra when booking direct. Bookings can be made by telephone or via the internet; the telephone numbers and website addresses of the three main companies are:

- **InterCity Coachlines** – ☎ Auckland 09-913 6100, Christchurch 03-379 9020, Dunedin 03-474 9600, Wellington 04-472 5111, 💻 www.intercitycoach.co.nz;

- **Newmans** – ☎ 09-913 6200, 💻 www.newmanscoach.co.nz;

- **Northliner** – ☎ 09-307 5873, 💻 www.newzealandnet.com/northliner.

You can also book at InterCity Travel Centres in the main towns or with a travel agent (where you're charged a booking fee).

When booking, take note of exactly where your service operates from, which depends on the coach company and isn't necessarily the same location as the departure point of local city buses.

In Wellington, Newmans services operate from the Interislander ferry terminal, while InterCity services operate from near the railway station. In Auckland, InterCity services depart from Hobson Street, whereas Newmans operate from Quay Street.

Coaches are often the cheapest way of travelling long distances in New Zealand, although discounted fares on the trains can be cheaper. For example, the standard one-way adult fare from Auckland to Wellington (which takes around ten hours) is around $110, from Rotorua to Wellington (eight hours) $100 and

from Picton to Christchurch (6 hours 15 minutes) $50. If you're travelling from the North to the South Island or vice versa, it's worth noting that the Interislander ferry fare (see below) isn't included in the coach price, and you need to pay separately for the North and South Island legs of your trip (although you can book them together and services are timed to connect).

Discounts are available when travelling at off-peak times, e.g. Super Saver Fares with a reduction of 50 per cent and Saver Fares with a 25 per cent discount. 'Golden Age' passengers (men over 65 and women over 60) qualify for a 25 per cent discount on production of identification.

Children under two travel free if they don't occupy a seat, and there are reductions of one-third for children aged between 3 and 12. You can take one large and one medium-size suitcase per person on coach services, and excess baggage incurs a small fee. Bicycles can be carried for a flat fee of $10 per journey, irrespective of the length of the trip (you must remove the pedals and wrap the chain, e.g. in newspaper).

Each of the main coach lines offers a travel pass allowing unlimited travel for a fixed period. Newmans, for example, offers a Flexi-Pass sold in blocks of time, e.g. 15 hours' travel for $164, 20 hours' for $214, 40 hours' for $410 and 60 hours' for $585. Passes can be topped up, like a pre-paid telephone card.

You can obtain a copy of coach timetables from InterCity Travel centres (for InterCity Coachlines) in cities and large towns, Visitor Information Network (VIN) centres or by calling the numbers listed above.

An economical way of travelling for young people is backpackers' buses, which operate throughout New Zealand (similar to those in Australia). Backpackers' buses are operated by a number of companies, of which Kiwi Experience and Magic Bus are the best known. Services operate on a pass basis, whereby once you've purchased a ticket, you can switch buses and stop off along the route, whether for a few hours or for a few days. Sporting and adventure activities are also sometimes offered along the way, such as white-water rafting and kayaking. These services tend to be cheap and cheerful, and are targeted at those aged between 18 and 35. You must pay extra for accommodation, although this is usually low-cost and there's also the option of camping. See the Backpackerbus website (🖥 www.backpackerbus.co.nz) for details of travel passes and trips. Booking is essential in summer.

Taxis

Taxis are plentiful in most cities and towns in New Zealand. They're usually ordinary saloon cars (or minibuses) painted in distinctive colours, which vary with the town or city. You can pick one up at a taxi rank or order one by telephone; they cannot normally be hailed in the street and will pick you up only if they're stopping to drop a passenger (so you'd better be quick!).

All taxi fares are metered, with a minimum charge of $3, and you pay only the amount showing on the meter and aren't expected to tip (Americans please note!).

An extra charge is made for telephone bookings, items of luggage, and when travelling during the evening and at weekends, when taxis are most in demand, due to the curtailment of bus services. There's also a surcharge for waiting and for journeys to and from airports (around $1).

Ferries

As a country consisting mainly of two large islands, the North and the

Ferry terminal, Auckland

South, separated by the Cook Strait, New Zealand is highly reliant on ferry services between the two.

The principal service, the Interislander, is highly efficient and employs two roll-on-roll-off ferries most of the year, the Arahura (the larger) and the Aratere (the newer), which carry passengers, vehicles and railway carriages. They sail between Wellington in the North Island and Picton in the South Island, taking around three hours. (The ferry route is 96km/60mi, although the Strait is only 20km/12mi wide at its narrowest point). Purbeck, a freight vessel, also operates across the Strait, as does a fast ferry, The Linx.

The number of daily sailings varies between summer and winter. In summer (December to April) there are four on Sundays and Mondays and five on all other days, but in winter the service is usually reduced to two or three crossings per day, as one of the vessels is taken out of service for maintenance. Summer timetables vary only slightly from year to year: ships leave Wellington at around 8am, 9.30am, 3.30pm and 5.30pm, and Picton at 5.30am, 11.30am, 1.30pm, 7pm and 9pm.

It isn't essential to book for the Interislander ferry except at busy times, such as the beginning of school holidays, although it's cheaper, as discounted tickets can be purchased only in advance. If you turn up without a ticket, you must pay the full fare, even if you're travelling off-peak. Bookings can be made up to six months in advance (☎ freephone 0800-802 802 or visit 🖳 www. interislander.co.nz) and there's a wide range of fares, offers and conditions.

The Interislander offers three fares types: Easy Change, Saver Change and Web Saver. The Easy Change fare, for example, is $70 return for an adult, or $325 for two adults, two children and a family car. A full list of fares is on the website.

Interislander ferries depart from the Interisland terminals in Wellington and Picton, both of which are well signposted. There are buildings at both terminals where tickets can be purchased and where foot passengers can check in their luggage for the journey rather than carry it on board. There are also car parks and car hire facilities (if you have a hire car or are staying on the other island for a short time only, it's cheaper to leave your car on one island and hire another when you arrive). A free bus service (the Interislander Shuttle Bus) runs between Wellington railway station and the Interisland terminal, including one bus timed to connect with the evening train to Auckland. At Picton, shuttle buses operate from the Interisland terminal to the station to meet the arrival and departure of trains, which run directly to Christchurch.

The latest check-in time is 30 minutes before departure for foot passengers and one hour for those with vehicles. Foot passengers may take only two pieces of luggage weighing a maximum of 30kg and no more than 200 'linear' centimetres in size (a combination of the height, width and breadth).

Interislander ferries are well equipped, with a cinema, telephones, several bars, children's nursery and play areas, Visitor Information Network (VIN) centres and a number of eating places, including fast food outlets. There are also fruit machines – something of a novelty in a country where gambling is tightly controlled. For a supplement you can use the club class lounge at the terminal, which provides free drinks and snacks, newspapers and an oasis of peace before boarding the ship (children under 18 aren't permitted!).

In addition to the Interislander, there are several smaller ferry services linking the two main islands, as well as serving smaller islands.

Holiday & Visitors' Passes

A variety of travel passes is available for travel within New Zealand. Among the best is the InterCity Travel Pass New Zealand (⌨ www.travelpass.co.nz), which offers two passes. Travelpass 2-in-One combines national coach travel on Intercity or Newmans coach lines and the Cook Strait ferry crossing, allowing you to travel between the North and the South Islands. The price for an adult ranges from $387 for five days' travel (travel days need not be consecutive) to $845 for 15 days' travel. Travelpass 3-in-One is as above, but with one train journey; the price for an adult ranges from around $490 for five days' travel to $900 for 15 days' travel. Extra days for either pass cost $53 per day.

If you wish to travel around New Zealand by train you can buy a 7-day Scenic Rail Pass (⌨ www.tranzscenic. co.nz). Travel is unlimited and you can choose your route and stop off wherever you like. The approximate costs are shown below.

7-Day Pass	Adult	Child
South Island	$265	$160
South Island with Ferry	$300	$210
All Services	$310	$205
All Services with Ferry	$360	$215

Roads

In the absence of a comprehensive rail system, the road network is the mainstay of public and private transport in New Zealand, extending to 92,207km (57,295mi), of which around 65 per cent is sealed (tarmac). The country has no national motorway (freeway) network, and motorways are short, e.g. in and around cities such as Auckland and Wellington, although more are planned. Most New Zealand roads have just one lane in each direction, but they're invariably well surfaced and maintained, even when they pass through areas with difficult terrain (which is frequently). All New Zealand roads are toll-free, but that's set to change: the Orewa-Puhoi motorway will be a toll road (due to be built by 2009), and new roads planned around Auckland are also likely to be toll roads.

New Zealand has the second-highest rate of vehicle ownership in the world (after the US), at around 700 per 1,000 people. The reason for this devotion to the motor vehicle is that driving is the most convenient way of getting around the country, and many places aren't accessible by public transport, or services are infrequent. A car is essential if you live in a rural area – unless you plan to live like a hermit.

Even in Auckland and Wellington, people make use of their cars a great deal, as traffic congestion and parking aren't (yet) bad enough to make driving a headache. However, traffic density is increasing, along with the resultant pollution, which is an important issue in this environmentally-minded nation; and the government and motoring associations are now considering traffic reduction measures for Auckland. Motoring is more expensive than taking a coach or train, but cheaper than flying, particularly over long distances (unless your car journey includes an overnight stop).

The travel brochures portray motoring in New Zealand as an idyllic pursuit, where roads are traffic-free most of the time and the scenery breathtaking. To some extent this is true in rural areas, particularly outside the main tourist season, when it's possible to drive for miles without seeing another motorist (or having to crawl behind a caravan). However, it disguises the dangers that lurk along the country's roads.

In New Zealand, where traffic drives on the left, there's a restriction on importing and registering left-hand drive cars, e.g. from the US or the European mainland. If you wish to import a left-hand drive car, you should first make enquiries with Land Transport New Zealand (see below). Left-hand drive cars aren't usually allowed to be registered for ordinary daily use.

Roads in New Zealand are divided into three main categories: motorways, state highways and secondary roads. Motorways are found only in the major cities, where they provide a direct route from the suburbs into the centre. They usually consist of two or more lanes in each direction (although motorways entering Auckland have three lanes in each direction) and are known by names rather than numbers: for example, in Auckland the Northern, Southern and North-western motorways radiate from the city centre in their respective directions,

and the Wellington Urban Motorway runs northwards from the city centre. Motorways are identified by signs with white lettering on a green background, and junctions are numbered.

In 2004 a new system was introduced which numbers junctions according to their distance in kilometres from a given point of the motorway (usually the start), rather than in numerical order. For example, junction 10 would be 10km (6mi) from the given point.

State highways are major trunk roads with usually just one lane in each direction, on which you can expect to average around 55 to 65kph when travelling cross-country. They're red on maps and identified by a shield symbol, on both road signs and maps. There are eight principal state highways in New Zealand as shown below.

Secondary routes are yellow on most maps and denoted by a shield symbol on maps and road signs. They're identified by a two-digit

Highway	Route
No.1	Awanui-Auckland-Wellington-Picton-Christchurch-Invercargill
No.2	Auckland-Tauranga-Gisborne-Napier-Wellington
No.3	Hamilton-New Plymouth-Palmerston North
No.4	Te Kuiti-Wanganui
No.5	Putaruru-Napier
No.6	Blenheim-Invercargill (via the Southern Alps)
No.7	Greymouth-Waipara (near Christchurch)
No.8	Timaru-Milton (inland route)

soon be increased to 16 (the 15 age limit dates back to the days when the school leaving age was 15 and school-leavers were often required to drive vehicles on farms). However, 15-year-olds are entitled only to a Learner Licence and don't receive a Full Licence until at least two years later. The driving licence system in New Zealand is unique in having three stages: Learner Licence, Restricted Licence and Full Licence, each of which has to be passed by prospective drivers.

A Learner Licence is issued after you've passed a theoretical and practical test. With a Learner Licence, you can drive a car only when accompanied by an experienced driver, and the car must display 'L' plates. Learner Licence drivers under the age of 20 are subject to additional restrictions, including a lower blood/alcohol limit (30mg of alcohol per 100ml of blood, which in practice means they cannot drink and drive at all – see **Drinking & Driving** below).

The second stage, the Restricted Licence, is issued after a minimum of six months as a learner driver and an additional practical test. With a Restricted Licence, you can drive alone but can carry no passengers other than your spouse and/or dependants (the only ones considered brave enough?), and you cannot drive at night. The Full Licence is the third and final stage, awarded after

number and in most cases the first digit indicates that the road starts or finishes (as the case may be) on the state highway with the same number. All other roads are unclassified and unnumbered and indicated by white lines on most maps, but have no special identification or road signs. They're usually of reasonable quality and sealed (i.e. with a tarmac surface), unless they're specifically marked on a map or signposted as 'unsealed' or 'not tar sealed', which means that they're gravel or compacted earth. They're passable by standard two-wheel-drive cars in good weather and four-wheel-drive vehicles at any time.

Driving Licence

The minimum age for driving in New Zealand is 15, although this may you've held a Restricted Licence for six months if you're aged 25 or over, or for 18 months if you're under 25, and after passing further theoretical and practical tests. To obtain a Full Licence therefore takes at least a year, and it costs over $115 (**excluding** driving lessons). You require an eyesight test to obtain a New Zealand driving licence.

If you already have a driving licence, it can be used in New Zealand for up to a year, provided it's written in English. If it isn't, it must be accompanied by an international driver's permit, which you can obtain from a motoring organisation in your home country. After a year, your foreign driving licence must be exchanged for a New Zealand licence. If your driving licence was issued in Australia, Canada, the European Union, Norway, South Africa, Switzerland or the US, you may be eligible for exemption from the practical driving test, but must take a theory test. Driving licence holders from other countries must take a practical test.

Licences are printed on paper and are valid until your 80th birthday, after which they're renewable every two years, subject to a driving assessment and a medical examination. You're required to carry your driving licence or car papers with you when driving in New Zealand.

Before taking to the road in New Zealand, you should familiarise yourself with the official guide to road rules and regulations, known as the Road Code, which is New Zealand's best-selling book (amazingly, considering that nobody reads it!). It's also available on a CD-ROM, which includes details of driving tests, practice tests, first-aid information and demonstrations of how to manoeuvre a vehicle.

Drinking & Driving

It's estimated that a large proportion of road accidents in New Zealand are due to drunken driving (and a fair number due to drunken walking), which is acknowledged as one of the country's most pressing social problems. It's still socially acceptable in New Zealand to drive after a 'few drinks' and the limited

licensing hours for 'hotels' (pubs) often encourage people to travel in search of a drink when their local pub is closed on a Sunday or they live in a 'dry' area.

Drunken driving is endemic at all levels, from older drivers, who consider they're experienced enough to drive after drinking, to bravado youngsters who may even encourage their mates to drive when drunk. Drunk drivers in New Zealand are often very drunk indeed. One driver who ended up in court on a drunk driving charge was reported to have so much alcohol in his body that a medical expert at his trial reckoned he should have been 'brain dead'.

Police and TSS officers can breathalyse drivers at any time without a reason, and drivers involved in accidents, however minor, are routinely breathalysed. Random breath tests are common, and roadblocks can be set up or moved at a moment's notice. All motorists stopped are tested, and a reading above 400mcg of alcohol per litre of breath leads to a blood test, after which, if you're still over the limit, you're charged with drunken driving. The alcohol limit for motorists in New Zealand is 80mg per 100ml of blood (0.08 per cent), similar to the UK but higher than many other European countries. For motorists under 20 years of age the limit is 30mg.

In recent years, the government has made great efforts to reduce drinking and driving through public education campaigns and stricter laws. These have had some effect, although drunken driving remains a serious problem and is one of the main causes of accidents. It's estimated that at least 20 per cent of drivers killed on the roads each year were over the legal limit.

⚠ **Caution**

Drunk driving is a serious offence, and motorists caught driving over the legal limit can be fined up to $1,500 or be imprisoned for up to six months.

The penalty for a third offence can be a fine of up to $6,000, a two-year prison sentence and a minimum one-year disqualification from driving. Drunk driving causing injury or death carries fines of between $10,000 and $20,000. Your car can also be confiscated, although this usually applies only to repeat offenders. Each year, over 30,000 New Zealanders are convicted of drunken driving, although few are jailed.

The latest threat on New Zealand's roads is driving under the influence of drugs. Although there are no official figures, a significant number of drivers are believed to be under the influence of illegal drugs (mainly cannabis) when driving, and the government plans to introduce roadside drug testing when a reliable test is available.

Wellington

3.

YOUR DREAM HOME

When you've chosen the region or town for your dream home in New Zealand, you need to decide on the type of property that will best suit your requirements, weigh up the purchase options and assess the fees associated with buying. There's an overwhelming choice of property for sale and in mid-2007 it was a buyers' market in many areas (although increasing numbers of New Zealanders are renting, unable to afford to buy a home after steep property price increases over the past several years). As when buying property anywhere, it's never wise to be in too much of a hurry. Have a good look around in your chosen region and obtain an accurate picture of the types of property available, their relative values and what you can expect to get for your money. However, before doing this you should make a comprehensive list of what you want (and don't want) from a home, so that you can narrow the field and save time on wild goose chases.

To reduce the chances of making an expensive error when buying in an unfamiliar region, it's often prudent to rent a house for a period (see **Renting before Buying** on page 95), taking in the worst part of the year (weather-wise). This allows you to become familiar with the region and the weather, and gives you plenty of time to look around for a home at your leisure.

Wait until you find something you fall head over heels in love with and then think about it for a week or two before rushing headlong to the altar. One of the advantages of buying property in New Zealand is that there's usually another 'dream' home around the next corner – and the second or third dream home is often even better than the first. However, don't dally endlessly, as good properties at the right price don't remain on the market for ever.

RESEARCH

A successful purchase is much more likely if you thoroughly investigate the various regions, the types of property available, prices and relative values, and the procedure for buying property Down Under.

The secret of successfully buying a home in New Zealand is research, research and more research.

It's all too easy to fall in love with the beauty and ambience of New Zealand and to sign a contract without giving it sufficient thought. If you're uncertain, don't allow yourself to be rushed into making a decision, by fears of an imminent price rise or because someone else is supposedly interested in a property (estate agents sometimes maintain that this is the case, whether it is or not, in order to panic you into a purchase). It's vital to do your homework thoroughly and avoid the 'dream sellers' (often fellow countrymen) who will happily prey on your ignorance and tell you anything in order to sell you a property. Many people make expensive (and even catastrophic) mistakes when buying homes in the Antipodes, usually because they do insufficient research and are in too much of a hurry, often setting themselves ridiculous deadlines such as buying a home during a short holiday, although they wouldn't dream of acting so rashly when buying a property in their home country!

It isn't uncommon for buyers to regret their decision after a few months or years and wish they had purchased a different kind of property in a different region (or even in a different country!).

If possible, you should take advice from people who already own a house in New Zealand, from whom you can usually obtain invaluable information (often based on their own mistakes). Much of this advice is included in this book, but you'll really believe it if you hear it 'from the horse's mouth'! You should also read books especially written for those planning to live or work in or New Zealand (such as *Living and Working in New Zealand*, also published by Survival Books). It helps to study specialist property magazines and newspapers (see **Appendix B** for a list) and to visit property exhibitions such as those organised in the UK. There are also a number of websites where you can obtain information and advice from other expatriates (see **Appendix C**).

☑ **SURVIVAL TIP**

Bear in mind that the cost of investing in a few books or magazines (and other research) is tiny compared with the expense of making a big mistake. Nevertheless, don't believe everything you read!

AVOIDING PROBLEMS

The problems associated with buying property abroad have been highlighted in the last decade or so, during which the property market in many countries has gone from boom to bust and back again. From a legal viewpoint, New Zealand is one of the safest places in the world in which to buy a home, and buyers have a high degree of protection under local law, irrespective of whether they're citizens or foreign non-residents. Nevertheless, you should take the usual precautions regarding offers, agreements, contracts, deposits and obtaining proper title to a property.

The most common problems experienced by buyers Down Under include:

● Buying in the wrong place. Do your homework (see **Regions** on page 50, **Location** on page 57 and **Research** above) and rent first (see **Renting Before Buying** on page 95). The wrong decision regarding location is one of the main causes of disenchantment among foreigners who have purchased property in New Zealand.

● Buying a home that's difficult or impossible to sell. If there's a chance that you'll need to sell in the short to medium term, it's important to buy a home that will be easy to sell. A property with broad appeal in a popular area (particularly a waterside property) usually fills the bill; it will need to be very special to sell quickly in a less popular area. A modest, reasonably priced property is likely to be much easier to sell than a large, expensive home, particularly one needing restoration or modernisation. In most areas there's a small market for renovated rural property. There are usually many buyers in the lower price ranges, but they become much scarcer above around $500,000 unless a property is exceptional, i.e. outstandingly attractive, in a popular area and with a superb situation. In some areas, even desirable properties remain on the market for many months or even years.

● Buying a house and plot that's much larger than you need because it seems to offer such good value. Although buying a house with umpteen rooms and several acres of land may seem like a good investment, bear in mind that, should you wish to

sell, buyers may be thin on the ground (see above). You should think carefully about what you're going to do with a large house and garden. Both will require a lot of maintenance, and your heating costs might be high if the property is in a cool region (i.e. much of the South Island). After you've installed a swimming pool, tennis court and croquet lawn, you still have a lot of change left out of even a couple of acres. Do you like gardening or are you prepared to live in a jungle? Can you afford to pay a gardener? Of course you can always plant an orchard or vineyard, create a lake or take up farming!

Don't, on the other hand, buy a property that's too small; when you have a home in New Zealand, you'll inevitably discover that you have many more relatives and friends than you realised!

- Paying too much. Foreign buyers, particularly the British, are often tempted to pay more than the true market value of a property because it's so cheap compared to a similar property in their home country and they're reluctant to negotiate for fear of losing it. Some Antipodean vendors and agents take advantage of this tendency by asking inflated prices. Before buying a property from an agent advertising in the foreign press, check the prices of similar properties offered by New Zealand agents to ensure that it's good value.

- Grossly underestimating restoration and modernisation costs. A tumbledown house for $100,000 can seem a steal, but renovation can cost as much as a new building, as well as taking time and creating headaches.

- Buying a property for business, e.g. to convert to holiday flats, and being too optimistic about the income. The letting season can be just 20 weeks or less in some areas, which means that it's difficult or impossible to cover the cost of maintaining a home from letting income, let alone make a living (see **Chapter 9**).

- Not having a survey done on an old property. As surveys aren't a matter of course in New Zealand, many people assume they aren't necessary – often with disastrous consequences (see **Inspections & Surveys** on page 118).

- Not taking legal advice. Another common assumption among foreign

buyers Down Under is that the estate agent handling a sale will look after their interests and ensure that they don't run into problems, which isn't necessarily the case (see **Legal Advice** below).

● Not including the necessary conditional clauses in a contract. As above, the agent or seller's solicitor handling the sale won't necessarily safeguard your interests by inserting provisos in the purchase contract (see **Contracts** on page 202).

● Taking on too large a mortgage. Lenders are offering larger and longer mortgages, which can tempt buyers into borrowing more than they can afford to repay (see **Chapter 4**).

Legal Advice

Many people who buy homes in New Zealand don't obtain independent legal advice, and most of those who experience problems have taken no precautions whatsoever. Of those that do take legal advice, many do so only after having paid a deposit and signed a contract or, more commonly, after they've run into problems.

☑ SURVIVAL TIP

The most important thing to do before buying property in New Zealand (or indeed anywhere) is to obtain expert, independent legal advice from someone who's familiar with local law.

As when buying property in any country, you should never pay any money or sign anything without first obtaining legal advice from an experienced lawyer in a language in which you're fluent. You'll find that the small cost (in comparison to the price of a home) of obtaining legal advice is excellent value, if only for the peace of mind it affords. Trying to cut corners to save a few dollars on legal costs is foolhardy in the extreme when a large sum of money is at stake.

You may be able to obtain a list of lawyers who speak your language and are experienced in handling New Zealand property sales, either in New Zealand or in your home country, e.g. British buyers can obtain a list from the Law Society in the UK. Specialist lawyers advertise in international property newspapers and magazines.

There are professionals speaking various languages in all areas of New Zealand (reflecting the cultural melting pot that the country is), and many expatriate professionals (e.g. architects and surveyors) also practise there. However, don't assume that a fellow countryman will offer you a better deal or do a better job than a local person (the contrary may be true). It's wise to check the credentials of all professionals you employ, whether Kiwi or foreign.

It's never wise to rely solely on advice proffered by those with a financial interest in selling you a property, such as a builder or estate agent, although their advice may be excellent and totally unbiased.

Finance

You should have your finance in place before you start looking for a property and, if you need a mortgage, obtain a mortgage guarantee certificate from a lender that guarantees you a mortgage at a certain rate, which is usually subject to a valuation (see **Mortgages** on page 142). If you're buying a property for restoration, most lenders won't make a loan against a property that they consider is uninhabitable (e.g. lacking access or sanitation) and they may require 'proof' that the restoration costs won't exceed 40 per cent of the purchase price (in which case a little inventiveness may be required on your part!); you might also be required to use local-registered builders, which is recommended in any case. You'll also need a 10 per cent deposit plus the fees and taxes associated with buying (see **Fees** on page 109).

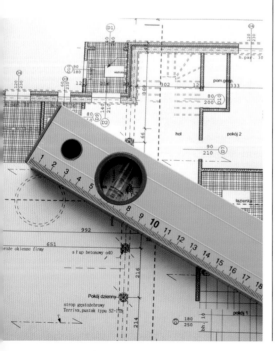

TYPES OF PROPERTY

Most New Zealand families live in detached homes on an individual plot, known as a 'section'. This dates back to the pioneering days when the authorities divided great tracts of land into sections for house building. Each section was a quarter of an acre and the phrase 'quarter-acre paradise' was coined to describe the typical New Zealand home as well as the country itself. A quarter of an acre (or its metric equivalent, approximately 1,000m^2) is still the standard plot size in New Zealand, although many sections have been divided and a second property built in the garden, or in some cases the original house has been demolished and several new properties built in its place, although there are minimum plot sizes in some areas.

Most New Zealand properties are single-storey bungalows (although they're usually called 'houses'), although two-storey houses are becoming more popular. If a property is described as a 'villa', don't expect a palace complete with columns, marble floors and a sunken bath complete with asp, as Kiwi villas are usually modest homes made of wood with a corrugated iron roof (see below)! Semi-detached properties, terraced houses (known as townhouses) and apartments aren't as common as detached properties in most of New Zealand. The suburbs of most main cities have large townhouses from the Victorian area, many of which have been lovingly restored, and in recent years new smaller townhouses have been built. Apartments are largely confined to city centres.

> Apartment living went out of fashion in the '80s when many people moved out to the suburbs, although it's becoming fashionable again and apartments in the central areas of Auckland and Wellington are highly sought-after.

Thankfully, there are hardly any high-rise apartment blocks in New Zealand, which does, however, boast a unique type of housing called a 'unit'. This is a single building containing a number (often four or six) of smaller properties, each having its own plot and therefore being part house, part apartment.

New Zealand homes aren't usually built to the same standards as is common in Europe, and construction methods are similar to those used in Australia and many parts of the US. Brick and stone are less common than elsewhere, except in more expensive properties, although cheaper properties may have a single wall in brick or stone to add a touch of 'elegance'. Older properties tend to feature exterior wooden weather-boards (often made of Kauri wood) an corrugated iron roofs (instantly identifiable from the noise when it rains!). As hardwood has become expensive owing to environmental constraints, however, construction of new properties is usually a ('soft') timber frame filled with plywood panels, which are sprayed with fibre cement and painted to give the impression of rendered brickwork. Modern roofs tend to be made of textured steel or concrete tiles, rather than corrugated iron. An advantage of this type of construction is that there's a significant cost saving over brick and stone properties, and repair and maintenance costs are also lower.

Although many European immigrants regard New Zealand home construction as 'flimsy', the materials used are adequate for the climate. In addition, New Zealand is officially situated within an earthquake belt (it has been affectionately dubbed the 'shaky isles' or 'quaky isles'), where 'flimsier' construction has the benefit of being more flexible in the event of a quake, easier to repair, and also less likely to cause you serious injury if it comes tumbling down around your ears! Earthquakes, or rather tremors, are fairly frequent throughout New Zealand, although most are too minor to be noticed and on average a serious

little smaller than American homes but roomier than properties in most of Europe.

Most homes – except for the oldest, unrenovated properties – are well equipped and fitted. Fitted kitchens with cupboards and built-in appliances are standard, and many newer properties have a utility or laundry room. Newer properties are likely to have a bathroom attached to the principal bedroom as well as a main bathroom (often known as a family bathroom). Bedrooms often have fitted furniture, and some homes have walk-in wardrobes. Some modern builders proudly boast that all you need to bring with you when you move in is a lounge suite and a bed!

If you find an older property that hasn't been renovated, it will be in stark contrast to a modern home: leaky tin roofs, gaps in the windows and even holes in the weather-boarding are fairly common. It's wise to tread warily if you're offered a house at a tempting price that's described as 'needing TLC' (tender loving care), which is usually a euphemism for a ruin!

earthquake happens only once every 210 years.

The design and layout of New Zealand properties is fairly standard throughout the country. A typical home has a hall, kitchen, living area, dining area (which may be combined with either the living area or the kitchen), bathroom and three bedrooms.

Unless you're buying an individual, architect-designed property (rare, except at the top end of the market) the layout of the homes is monotonously predictable – it often seems as if every house in New Zealand was built from the same set of plans! Homes are, however, functional and quite spacious. New Zealand homes are, on average, a

Leaky Building Syndrome

This sounds like a joke but is far from being one. Leaky building syndrome (LBS) is the name for the problems affecting an estimated 10,000 to 90,000 New Zealand homes built in the last 20 years or so, particularly those constructed in a 'Mediterranean style', i.e. with flat or sloping roofs with minimal eaves and a white or beige plaster finish, designed to give a flavour of Greece or Spain (despite New Zealand's much wetter climate).

The leaky building crisis began to surface in New Zealand in the late '90s, although it wasn't the first country to be affected: the US and Canada suffered problems in the mid-'90s. LBS is the result of using poorly-tested building materials and methods, rushing construction and the failure of the authorities to check building standards properly. Buildings affected take in water through the exterior finish. The finish is known in the building trade as monolithic plaster, but although it looks like plaster, it's actually a synthetic material which is sprayed on the outside of timber-framed houses.

The leaking monolithic plaster is only the beginning of the problem, however. After water has penetrated the 'plaster', it can soak into the wooden structure of the house. The timber in modern houses is often untreated, which ties in with New Zealand's 'clean and green image', but this is proving to be a disadvantage because when the wood gets wet, it rots. Steel-framed buildings and those made of treated timber can also be affected if they remain wet long enough, causing extensive damage to the fabric and structure of the home. An unfortunate side effect of LBS is a risk to human health, because some of the moulds that grow on damp timber and other building materials can cause breathing and skin problems.

⚠️ **Caution**

The regions with the highest number of leaky buildings are those which have seen the most rapid growth over the past two decades: Auckland, Bay of Plenty, Christchurch, Dunedin, Nelson, Queenstown and Wellington.

Some experts recommend that people avoid buying or renting buildings with a monolithic plaster finish. Certain buyers have taken this advice to heart and refuse to consider any home built between around 1988 and 2002 in the Mediterranean style, with monolithic cladding (fibrous plaster or stucco), a flat roof, no eaves and untreated timber, even if it has no sign of leaks or potential problems.

To remedy LBS, it's often necessary to remove a building's cladding and replace the structural timber. The average cost is estimated to be just under $200,000 per home, but it can be over $500,000 and, in any case, cheaper to knock down the building and start again. The total cost of resolving New Zealand's LBS problem is thought to be anywhere between $1bn and $5bn. But the question of compensation to the owners of leaky buildings is proving to be controversial.

Even when an owner is entitled to recompense (e.g. from the builder for poor or shoddy workmanship or the council for failing to check the work properly), it can take a long time for cases to be resolved. The government instigated the Weathertight Homes Resolution Service to try to secure compensation for owners of leaky homes, but it hasn't always managed to gain the confidence of those using it and some owners have opted to go to court to resolve their problems. As a result, the government has recently amended its approach and, in spring 2007, the Weathertight Homes Resolution Services Act 2006 (known as the WHRS act) came into force, providing quick, flexible, cost-effective solutions to leaky home disputes, as an alternative to the courts.

The WHRS act is administered by two government agencies: Weathertight Services at the Department of Building and Housing, which receives and assesses claim applications, and provides guidance, information and mediation; and the Weathertight Homes Tribunal, supported by the Ministry of Justice, which is a judicially independent tribunal that adjudicates claims. In August 2007, the Building and Construction minister announced that as well as claiming damages to repair their homes, owners of leaky buildings could claim general damages, including compensation for mental distress or anxiety.

⚠ Caution

Some owners of leaky homes have been so traumatised by their situation that they've contemplated suicide and in October 2007, the *New Zealand Herald* **reported that over 40 had been put on suicide watch.**

For further information and details of the latest developments in the LBS saga, see the Department of Building and Housing website (💻 www.dbh.govt.nz/leaky-buildings-and-weathertightness).

Even with the new legislation, the problem of leaky buildings doesn't look set to be resolved in the near future. Some of the first wave of repairs carried out to affected buildings have proved ineffective and the problems are reappearing. Some reports estimate that up to half of the repairs done to date will turn out to be substandard. As a result, it's strongly recommended that property buyers have a professional inspection (with specific reference to signs of water damage and potential leaks) if they suspect there's a leakage problem or if the building has been repaired in order to cure one.

Obvious signs of leaky buildings include:

- mould on the inside or outside of exterior walls;
- cracks or gaps in the exterior cladding;
- draughty windows or doors;
- rotten woodwork;
- watermarks around doors or windows.

RENTING BEFORE BUYING

Unless you know exactly what you're looking for and where, it's best to rent a property for a period to reduce the risk of making a costly mistake, particularly when you're planning to buy in an unfamiliar area.

Renting is particularly important for those planning to establish a business in New Zealand, when it isn't recommended to buy a home until you're sure that your business will be a success. Renting long-term before buying is particularly prudent for anyone planning to live in New Zealand permanently. If possible, you should rent a similar property to the one you're planning to buy, during the time(s) of year when you plan to occupy it. The advantages of renting include the following:

- It allows you to become familiar with the weather, the amenities and the local people, to meet other foreigners who have made their homes in New Zealand and share

their experiences, and to discover the cost of living for yourself.

- It 'buys' you time to find your dream home at your leisure.
- It saves tying up your capital and can be surprisingly inexpensive in many regions. You may even wish to consider renting a home in New Zealand long-term (or 'permanently'). Some people let their family homes abroad and rent one in New Zealand for a period (you may even make a profit!).

On the other hand, the disadvantages of renting should be taken into consideration, including the following:

- Annual property price increases in many areas are higher than interest rates (although this is much less certain in the current property market), which means that you may be better off putting your money into a property than investing it while you rent.

- Taking a long-term rental before buying means moving house (one of life's most stressful experiences) twice within a year or two.

- You may not find the type of rental property you want, which may influence your experience of living in a particular area and possibly in New Zealand generally. For example, most rental properties are apartments, and rural homes are rarely available for rent.

☑ **SURVIVAL TIP**

If you're looking for a long-term rental property, you may need to rent a holiday apartment for a week or two to allow yourself time to find one that suits you.

Rented Accommodation

Renting rather than buying a home is usually the better choice for anyone who is staying in New Zealand for just a few years or less, when buying isn't usually practical, and for those who don't want the expense and restrictions involved in buying and owning a home. If you're a migrant, it's sensible to rent for a period before buying, particularly if you're unsure of where you'll be living or working. There's a likelihood that you'll change jobs or regions within your first few years in New Zealand (a common occurrence) or even decide to return home. Renting also allows you to become familiar with a neighbourhood, the people and the weather before deciding whether you want to live there permanently.

Rental property of all sizes and descriptions is available in New Zealand, although only some 25 per cent of property is rented (including just 10 per cent of new properties). However, in recent years there has been an increased tendency among New Zealand households to rent rather than buy (following steep increases in property prices in the early years of the 21st century), particularly in Auckland (which accounts for nearly 40 per cent of the rental market), where rental properties are in short supply. Rented property in towns and cities consists mainly of apartments and flats, although houses are available to rent. Unless a newspaper advertisement specifically states that a property is a house or cottage, you should assume that it's an apartment.

Two-bedroom apartments are the most highly sought-after property in the main towns and cities.

Finding a Rental Property

Your success or failure in finding a suitable rental property depends on many factors, not least the type of property you're looking for (a one-bedroom apartment is easier to find than a four-bedroom detached house), how much you want to pay and the area where you wish to live. Good rental accommodation is in short supply in the major cities, with the possible exception of luxury homes with astronomical rents. There are sometimes 20 to 30 applicants for each vacant property in popular suburbs, particularly for homes with three or more bedrooms, and you may have to take what you can get. Most people settle for something in the outer suburbs and commute to work.

There are a number of ways to find a rental property, including the following:

● Ask acquaintances, friends and relatives to spread the word, particularly if you're looking in the area where you already live. A lot of rental properties are found by word of mouth, particularly in Auckland, where it's difficult to find somewhere with a reasonable rent unless you have connections (many rental properties change tenants without even coming onto the open market).

● Check the advertisements in local newspapers and magazines.

● Visit estate agents and letting agents. All cities and large towns have estate agents who also act as letting agents for owners (look under 'Real Estate Agents' in the yellow pages). Obtain rental lists from agents or have them emailed or faxed to you at your workplace. You can also contact agents via the internet.

● Look for advertisements in shop windows and on notice boards in company offices, shopping centres, supermarkets, and universities and colleges.

● Check newsletters published by churches, clubs and expatriate organisations, and their notice boards.

● Use the internet. This is particularly useful before you arrive in New Zealand, as it gives you a chance to inspect the market, find out what's available and where, and earmark your preferred area and type of property. However, in today's current rental market don't expect any

properties you see online still to be available when you arrive in New Zealand!

To secure accommodation advertised in local newspapers, you must be quick off the mark, particularly in the cities. Buy the newspapers as soon as they're published and start telephoning 'at the crack of dawn'. You must be available to inspect properties immediately or at any time. Some rental properties are 'open' for inspection at certain times, e.g. Saturday mornings from 10 to 10.30am, so if you're particularly interested in a property make sure you're on time to look at it – agents and landlords tend not to wait for latecomers.

Finding a property to rent in Auckland is like trying to find one in London or New York, where the best properties are usually let through personal contacts. Some people go to any length to rent a property, including offering to pay above the asking price, to pay six months' rent in advance or to sign a contract for two or three years.

> Many rental properties are let on a first-come, first-served basis. When inspecting a property, take enough money (or your cheque book) with you so that you're in a position to pay a deposit straight away if you want to secure the property.

You should (ideally) not rent anything without viewing it first. New Zealand landlords and agents are notoriously inventive in their descriptions (although legislation has been introduced to try to curb this) and they can make even the shabbiest, most tumbledown 'villa' sound like the poshest place in town. If you use an agency or estate agent to find a rental property, he will usually charge at least one week's rent as commission.

It's possible to arrange to rent a house or flat before your arrival in New Zealand, and several immigration consultants (and even some travel agencies) can arrange rentals for you. Bear in mind that properties obtained through these sources are often more expensive than those obtained locally. Another drawback of renting from abroad is that it's difficult to assess a property accurately from thousands of miles away and the location may prove to be inconvenient (although it may look ideal on a map).

Rental Costs

The main divide in rental costs is between Auckland and Wellington on the one hand and the rest of the country on the other. In these two cities you pay significantly more to rent a property, particularly in the better areas. There isn't a great deal of difference elsewhere, and the national average rent of around $200 per week has remained unchanged in the last few years (three-bedroom houses rent for an average of $250 per week). The typical rent for a two-bedroom

City	2-Bedroom	3-Bedroom
Auckland	310	385
Christchurch	215	310
Dunedin	185	265
Gisborne	145	195
Hamilton	185	260
Napier	180	250
Nelson	190	260
Otago	260	300
Palmerston North	160	210
Tauranga	205	270
Wellington	240	310

unfurnished apartment ranges from $150 per week in cheaper areas, such as Dunedin and Rotorua, to between $350 and $500 per week in central Auckland or Wellington. The weekly rent for a three-bedroom unfurnished apartment ranges from $250 in Dunedin to between $450 and $650 in central Auckland. Anything with a sea view will cost up to 50 per cent more, particularly in Auckland (there are lots of glorious views in New Zealand, but sea views are the only ones for which landlords charge extra). Basic properties are at a premium in any town with a university and may actually cost more than a good quality property elsewhere.

Most landlords prefer to let their properties for at least 12 months at a time and some won't let for less than this period; those who do tend to charge a higher rent, particularly for lets of less than six months.

Approximate weekly rents for unfurnished properties are shown above.

If you find a rental property through an estate agent or rental agency, you must usually pay a fee equal to one week's rent.

Rental Contracts

When renting property in New Zealand, it's usual to sign a tenancy agreement, although the Department of Building and Housing issues a standard agreement for landlords and tenants. If your landlord uses this agreement and you're happy with the details, it isn't usually necessary to have it checked by a lawyer, as the terms and conditions are simple and written in non-legal language (other countries please take note!).

Most tenancy agreements are on a periodic basis, which means that the tenancy continues indefinitely until either party gives notice. A tenant is required to give only 21 days' notice to end a tenancy, but a landlord must give 90 days' notice, except in exceptional circumstances, such as when he wishes to move into the property himself (in which case he need only give 42 days' notice). It's possible to have a tenancy agreement for a fixed period, in which case the tenancy lasts for the period agreed at the outset only, although it can be extended by agreement.

When you take up a tenancy, you must pay a bond to the landlord,

which is usually the equivalent of one or two weeks' rent, although legally it can be up to four weeks'. The bond isn't held by the landlord but by the Bond Processing Unit of the Tenancy Services Centre (Department of Building and Housing), and the landlord must pay your bond to the Unit within 23 working days of receiving it. At the end of the tenancy, the Bond Processing Unit refunds your bond less the cost of any damage (for which you're responsible under the standard tenancy agreement). Rent is usually paid fortnightly.

The landlord must pay rates and home insurance, although your belongings may not be covered under the landlord's policy and you may need to take out separate insurance for these (see page 183).

If you have a dispute with your landlord, the Tenancy Services Centre will advise you on your rights and responsibilities and help resolve the problem. The biggest causes of disputes in rented property, apart from tenants' failure to pay the rent on time, is landlords who don't maintain their premises (although they're legally required to) and problems with neighbours (who may also be the same landlord's tenants) in, for example, an apartment block.

Hotels, Motels & Bed & Breakfast

Hotels and motels aren't a cost-effective, long-term solution for house hunters, but there's sometimes little choice if you need accommodation for a short period. Bed and breakfast accommodation is also available in many cities and towns, and you may be able to negotiate a good rate for a long stay.

Hotels

In New Zealand the term hotel can be confusing for the newcomer. As in Australia, a public house or a bar is usually called a hotel, when in fact it doesn't provide accommodation. (It may keep a bedroom or two 'for rent', to satisfy a quaint old law that says hotels must offer accommodation, but you aren't expected to ask to stay there!)

However, you'll be pleased to hear that New Zealand has a plethora of 'proper' hotels with accommodation ranging from the humble to the luxurious. Standards and service are usually high, and an increasing number of hotel staff have completed the nationally-recognised 'Kiwi Host' customer service workshop. Most guide books contain a selection of hotels and other kinds of accommodation, among the best known of which are the *AA Accommodation New Zealand Guide* and *Friars Guide to Accommodation with Dining*.

Many businesses have adopted the Qualmark Rating system (🖥 www.qualmark.co.nz), similar to the Michelin star rating or the key rating systems in the UK. The system awards stars on a scale of one to five, where one star indicates that the property meets minimum requirements and is clean and comfortable, and five stars indicate that the accommodation is the best available in its class. Properties participating in the system display a sign with the Qualmark system logo (a capital Q in navy and green) together with the number of stars awarded. Properties are inspected annually.

Motels

Motels are found throughout New Zealand, even in quite remote areas, and although they're rarely located in prime positions they're usually easily accessible, on or near major roads. City motels are usually in the suburbs with good access to public transport. One unique feature of a New Zealand motel is that most accommodation is more like an apartment than a hotel room, with one or two bedrooms, a living area, kitchenette and a full-sized bathroom.

> **Motels are so well equipped that New Zealanders frequently use them as holiday bases and not just for one- or two-night stays.**

Some have restaurants, bars and swimming pools on site, although they aren't generally as well served as hotels. A refreshing change is that chain motels (which can be soulless in other countries) are often family-run in New Zealand and, while of a consistent standard, also offer genuinely friendly, personal service.

Another feature of motels is that they frequently operate 'all-in' pricing, which means that you pay a fixed room rate irrespective of how many people occupy it. You're unlikely to find more than $5 or $10 difference between the rate for a single room and a double or family room, which makes motels economical for families (less so for singles).

The main motel chains in New Zealand are Best Western, Budget, Flag and Golden Chain. Expect to pay $75 to $400 per night for a motel room or suite.

> The Motel 'bible' in New Zealand is Jason's *Motels and Motor Lodges*, and the Motel Association has a comprehensive website (💻 www.nzmotels.co.nz).

Bed & Breakfast

New Zealand has a long tradition of providing bed and breakfast accommodation (the country's largest category of tourist accommodation), usually known as guest houses, which in rural areas are often on working farms. Prices are similar to those of cheaper hotels, although guest houses offer a more individual service. However, there has been a trend toward more up-market B&Bs in

recent years, and many are now quite luxurious – with prices to match.

The price of guest house accommodation usually includes a hearty breakfast, which isn't normally the case in a hotel, so the price is more reasonable than it looks. Expect to pay around $60 to $120 per night for a room. Not all guest house rooms have en suite facilities, but owners usually allow guests access to most of the facilities of their home, so in many ways a guest house is often better served than a hotel. In modest guest houses you may find that the facilities are rather worn or 'homely', but if you need anything such as extra blankets or pillows, you need only ask your host.

You can find guest houses through local tourist offices and VIN centres, via the Federation of Bed and Breakfast Hotels (don't take the term 'hotels' too literally), 52 Armagh Street, Christchurch (☎ 06-358 6928, 💻 www.nzbnbhotels.com, where you can download the Federation's brochure), and from books such as *The New Zealand Bed and Breakfast Book* (💻 www.bnb.co.nz), published annually, or *The Bed and Breakfast Directory of New Zealand*. There are also dozens of websites where you can book B&Bs.

ESTATE AGENTS

When looking for a house to purchase, you can visit local estate agents (known as real estate agents in New Zealand), look for a private sale in the small ads in local newspapers, or tour the area looking for 'For Sale' signs. The easiest option is to visit an estate agent (or a number). There are 'family' estate agents and a number of large national chains, including Bayleys ( www.bayleys.co.nz) and Harcourts (⌨ www.harcourts.co.nz). If you wish to see what's available before you arrive in New Zealand, the vast majority of agents have websites. The Real Estate Institute of New Zealand includes details on its website (⌨ www.reinz.org.nz) from a number of agents in different parts of the country. The larger estate agents also publish property newspapers or magazines advertising properties for sale. For example, Harcourts publishes a 'Blue Book' series, which you can buy in a number of countries or download from the website (see above).

All estate agents in New Zealand must be licensed and registered with the Real Estate Agents Licensing Board. You can check by contacting them at PO Box 1247, Wellington (☎ 04-520 6949). Don't deal with anyone who isn't registered, because if they cannot meet the standards for registration it's unlikely that they will abide by any other standards either. However, the fact that an agent is licensed shouldn't be taken as a guarantee that he's reputable. It's illegal for an estate agent to mislead you deliberately, but it's often impossible to prove that they've done so.

In New Zealand, estate agents' fees are entirely the responsibility of the vendor, and the buyer doesn't pay anything (although of course the fees are in effect 'built in' to the price of a property). This underlines the fact that the agent is working for the seller, not for you, so you cannot expect him to do you any favours. (In fact, most estate agents are working for themselves, i.e. trying to earn as much money as possible!).

Before visiting an agent, you should have a good idea of the kind of property you're looking for (e.g. a house or an apartment), the price you can afford to pay and where you wish to live. The agent should then be able to give you a list of properties which fit that description. You should avoid the temptation to look at properties which are outside the areas you've chosen or which cost more than you can afford (agents **always** send you details of properties outside your stated price range!). If a property you view seems suitable, you'll be pressed to make a decision quickly.

When you see a property you like, don't hesitate to haggle over the price, which is standard practice, even when the seller or an agent says that the price is firm or gives the impression that other buyers are keen to snap it up.

Usually, an offer of between 3 and 8 per cent under the asking price is 'acceptable', but there's nothing to say you cannot offer less if you think the price is too high or the vendor is anxious to sell. To get an idea of whether asking prices are realistic, you can check with Quotable Value (🖥 www.qv.co.nz) – not to be confused with the document of the same name – New Zealand's largest valuation and property information company, which publishes monthly tables of average property prices on a region-by-region basis. Some estate agents publish regular surveys and reports on the state of the New Zealand property market and current prices. For information, contact the Real Estate Institute of New Zealand (🖥 www.reinz. org.nz).

Purchase Restrictions

There are certain (limited) restrictions on property purchase in New Zealand by individuals who aren't permanent residents of the country. For further information, see **Purchase Restrictions** on page 22.

Viewing

If possible, you should decide where you want to live, what sort of property you want and your budget before visiting New Zealand. Obtain details of as many properties as possible in your chosen area and make a shortlist of those you wish to view (it's also wise to mark them on a map). Most Antipodean agents expect customers to know where they want to buy within

a 30 to 40km (20 to 25mi) radius, and some even expect them to narrow their choice down to certain towns or villages. If you cannot define where and what you're looking for, at least tell the agent, so that he knows that you're undecided. If you're 'window shopping', say so. Many agents will still be pleased to show you properties, as they're well aware that many people fall in love with (and buy) a property on the spot.

> **You should make an appointment to see properties, as agents don't like people simply turning up.**

If you make an appointment, you should keep it or call and cancel it. If you're on holiday, it's acceptable to drop in unannounced to have a look at what's on offer, but don't expect an agent to show you properties without an appointment. If you view properties during a holiday, it's best to do so at the beginning so that you can return later to inspect any you particularly like a second or third time.

You should try to view as many properties as possible during the time available, but allow sufficient time to view each property thoroughly, to travel and get lost between houses, and for breaks for sustenance. Although it's important to see enough properties to form an accurate opinion of price and quality, don't see too many in one day (between four and six is usually enough), as it's easy to become confused about the merits of each property. If you're shown properties that don't meet your specifications, tell the agent immediately. You can also help the agent narrow the field by telling him exactly what's wrong with the properties you reject. Agents vary enormously in their efficiency, enthusiasm and professionalism. If an agent shows little interest in finding out exactly what you want, you should go elsewhere.

It's wise to make notes of both the good and bad features of each property, and take lots of photographs of those you like, so that you're able to compare them later at your leisure (but keep a record of which photos are of which house!). It's also shrewd to mark each property on a map so that, should you wish to return, you can find them without getting lost (too often). The more a property appeals to you, the more you should look for faults and negative points; if you still like it after stressing all the negative points, it must have special appeal.

PROPERTY PRICES

In general, property prices in New Zealand are slightly lower than those in most of western Europe due to its small population and low demand, low cost of land and generally low construction costs. There is, however, a huge gulf between Auckland and the rest of the country. Property is much more expensive there, mainly because most of the best paid jobs are to be found there. Auckland also has one of the best climates in New Zealand and is the first choice of the majority of immigrants. Wellington is the country's second-most expensive city for property purchase. Price variations are less marked in the rest of the country.

After falling in the early 21st century, interest rates have been raised steadily in recent years (to around 10 per cent) in an attempt to curb inflation. House prices rose by 50 per cent in the '90s but doubled between 2000 and 2007 in most areas. However, after frantic activity in the first half of 2007, the market slowed considerably on the back of interest rate rises and amid fear that homes were over-valued (by up to 50 per cent, according to some reports). In autumn 2007, the property market remained stable and the steep rises seen in the early years of the 21st century had slowed or stopped altogether.

> Advertised prices are usually around 3 to 8 per cent above a property's true market value and substantially above its rateable value.

Apartments are often as expensive as houses and townhouses (or even more so), as they're invariably located in city centres, whereas most houses are in suburbs or the country. See also **Cost of Property** on page 22. When calculating your budget, you should also allow for lawyer's fees (see **Conveyance** on page 149) and bear in mind that banks charge a mortgage processing fee equal to 1 per cent of the mortgage amount and require a deposit (usually $500 minimum) on application.

NEGOTIATING THE PRICE

When buying a property, it usually pays to haggle over the price, even if you think it's a bargain. Don't be put off by a high asking price, as most sellers are willing to negotiate. In fact, sellers generally presume buyers will bargain and rarely expect to receive the asking price for a property (although some vendors ask an unrealistic price and won't budge a cent). In popular areas, asking prices may be unrealistically high (up to double the real market price), particularly to snare the unsuspecting and ignorant foreign buyer. It's a good idea for your peace of mind to obtain an independent valuation (appraisal) to determine a property's market value. If a property has been realistically priced, you shouldn't expect to obtain more than a 5 or 10 per cent reduction.

Timing is of the essence in the bargaining process. Generally the longer a property has been for sale and the more desperate the vendor is to sell, the more likely a lower offer will be accepted.

Some people will tell you outright that they must sell by a certain date and that they will accept any reasonable offer. You may be able to find out from neighbours why someone is selling, which may help you decide whether an offer would be accepted. If a property has been on the market for a long time, e.g. longer than six months in a popular area, it may be overpriced. If there are many desirable properties for sale in a particular area or developments that have been on the market a long time, you should find out why, e.g. there may be a new road, railway or airport planned.

Before making an offer, you should find out as much as possible about a property, such as the following:

- when it was built;

- whether it has been used as a permanent or a holiday home;

- how long the owners have lived there;

- why they're selling (they may not tell you outright but may offer clues);

- how keen they are to sell;

- how long the property has been on the market;

- the condition of the property;

- the neighbours and neighbourhood;

- local property tax rates;

- whether the asking price is realistic.

For your part, you must ensure that you keep any sensitive information

Waterfront apartments, Auckland

from a seller and give the impression that you have all the time in the world (even if you must buy immediately). All this 'cloak and dagger' stuff may seem unethical, but you can be assured that if you were selling and a prospective buyer knew you were desperate and would accept a low offer, he certainly wouldn't be in a hurry to pay you any more!

If you make an offer that's too low you can always raise it, but it's impossible to lower an offer once it has been accepted (if your first offer is accepted without haggling, you'll never know how low you could have gone!). If an offer is rejected, it may be worth waiting a week or two before making a higher offer, depending on the market and how keen you are to buy a particular property. Obviously you'll be in a better position if you're a cash buyer and able to close quickly. Cash buyers in some areas may be able to negotiate a considerable price reduction for a quick sale, depending on the state of the local property market and how urgent the sale is.

If you make a low offer, it's wise to indicate to the owner a few negative points (without being too critical) that merit a reduction in price. Note, however, that if you make a very low offer, an owner may feel insulted and refuse to do business with you!

> ☑ **SURVIVAL TIP**
>
> Be prepared to walk away from a deal rather than pay too high a price.

If you want to buy a property purely as an investment, shopping around for a 'distress sale' (i.e. where the owner simply must sell) may result in the best deal. However, if you're seeking an investment property it's wise to buy in an area that's in high demand, preferably with both buyers and renters. For the best resale prospects, it's usually best to buy in an area or community (and style) that's attractive to local buyers.

An offer should be made in writing, as it's likely to be taken more seriously than an oral offer.

BUYING AT AUCTION

If you enjoy the thrill of betting, you may wish to consider buying a property at auction. Before doing so, however, you should:

- ascertain the true market value of the property. The best way to do this is to check the selling prices of similar properties in the immediate area.

- arrange your finance. You'll probably be expected to pay a 10 per cent deposit as soon as your bid is successful and sign a contract within a day or two (if not immediately).

- inspect the property thoroughly. Never buy unseen no matter how low the price. If it seems too good to be true, it probably is!

You could consider making a pre-auction bid of around 20 to 30 per cent less than its market value. Prices fetched at auction are notoriously unreliable, and sellers who are 'jittery' may (legally) agree to a deal before the auction, in which case you could have yourself a bargain!

Only a small proportion of domestic properties in New Zealand are offered for sale at public auction, although it's becoming more popular. These are usually properties whose value isn't easily determined, such as unique luxury properties and those requiring major renovation. Properties repossessed from those who have failed to meet their mortgage repayments are also sold at auction.

FEES

In addition to the fees listed below, you usually need to pay utility connection, reconnection, registration or transfer fees for electricity, gas, telephone and water (see **Utilities** on page 237). You must also consider the running costs of a property, which include a caretaker's or management fees if you leave a home empty or let it, community fees for a unit or other communal property, garden, pool and property maintenance, contents insurance (see page 115), local property taxes, and standing charges for utilities (electricity, gas, telephone, water). Annual running costs usually average around 2 to 3 per cent of the cost of a property.

Purchase costs are modest in New Zealand, rarely more than around 4 or

5 per cent of the purchase price. The main fees are as follows:

- **Land transfer registration fee** – around $150 and sometimes included in the legal fees (see below);

- **Lawyer's fees** – Conveyance by a lawyer (the only professional allowed to charge for conveyance) can cost anything from $400 to $2,000, so it's worth shopping around and haggling over the cost.

- **Mortgage fees** – Banks charge a mortgage processing fee equivalent to 1 per cent of the mortgage amount.

- **Land Information Memorandum (LIM)** – This is an optional document obtainable from the local council and contains information about a property's zoning and boundaries, building consents given, etc. Costs vary greatly according to the council, and may be higher if you require an LIM urgently; you can pay anything from $2 to $1,500, but the usual cost is between $200 and $300.

- **Inspection or survey fee:** Although it isn't compulsory to have a building inspection or structural survey carried out, it's often wise, particularly when you're buying an old detached house. You should allow between $500 and $750 for a structural survey.

- **Building insurance:** It's invariably a condition of lenders that properties are fully insured against structural and other damage. It may be necessary to insure a property from the day you sign the purchase contract.

BUYING OFF PLAN

Buying 'off pan' means buying a property that hasn't yet been built, which involves certain risks (in New Zealand as in other countries). The practice is becoming more common in New Zealand, but you should always check the procedure with a lawyer. Before you commit yourself to an off-plan property purchase or pay any money, it's vital you do your homework on the property, the development and the developer. In some areas, there's a wide variety of off-plan property available (often confusingly similar) and it's easy to be carried away by a developer's and/or estate agent's sales pitch. You may be put under pressure to pay a deposit immediately and told

that there are queues of other clients waiting to buy the property. While this may be true, the chances are that you'll be able to find a similar property elsewhere and it may be better and/or cheaper.

Once you've found a property you like, you must do the following:

- Obtain as much information as possible about the developer. First impressions are important so look carefully at the quality of the show house and brochures, and how professional the sales representatives are. However, remember that it's easy to produce glossy brochures and stunning show

houses, but not so easy to build 50 top-quality apartments! Find out about the developer's reputation by looking at previous projects, asking around, doing internet searches (sometimes just typing the developer's name in a search engine brings up a wealth of sites listing problems!) and using internet forums.

- Ask for as much information about the property as possible. This includes architect's plans of the property itself and the development as a whole; price lists for the different types of property; lists of materials and specifications; and whether it's possible to make changes to the property (e.g. room distribution, fittings and colours).

- Check the list of specifications and find out exactly what they include. The list should include the materials used for floors, roofing and pipes etc; colours of walls, doors, windows and tiles; bathroom fittings; whether fitted wardrobes are installed; and kitchen fittings (if appliances are provided, the brand names should be listed).

- Check development plans for the area by enquiring at the local planning department. This is very important if the area surrounding the construction site is undeveloped – never assume it will remain so. Many people have bought off plan assuming that their property would have privacy and/or uninterrupted views only to find this wasn't the case.

- Ask if the developer intends to make any changes to the plans, layout or fixtures and fittings during construction.

- If the property forms part of a large complex with several construction stages, ask for evidence that the developer intends to complete all of them (e.g. planning permission or financing). If the developer decides not to build all stages, your property may end up without a swimming pool, gardens or other facilities.

- Check the exact location of the property you're planning to buy in relation to other constructions. In order to secure a sale, a sales representative will happily 'promise' you sea views or a north-facing balcony when in fact your view may be partially (or completely) obstructed by and your balcony in the shade of other buildings.

- Check that the developer has opened a trust account (all money from purchasers must be deposited in a trust account that cannot be touched until completion).

- Ask for a list of intended by-laws for the finished development. In some cases, developers register by-laws that restrict the use of communal elements to the owners of certain properties. For example, a roof garden may be only for owners of top-floor apartments or a parking area only for owners on the ground-floor. Such by-laws can greatly affect resale potential.

- Study the plan of the property in detail. On an architect's scale

drawing it's difficult to imagine the actual size of the property and the rooms. The finished product is often smaller than you imagined, particularly the bedrooms. Compare the measurements with your current home and the show house. Also check the size of the gardens and pool, and decide whether they're adequate for your needs – pools are often far too small for the number of properties they serve.

☑ SURVIVAL TIP

Find out about the other buyers and what sort of community the development will have, and check whether your neighbours will be mainly holidaymakers or residents.

- Ask about other plans for the development such as sports facilities and shopping centres. Developers are quick to promise all sorts of extras but should provide evidence of these such as architect's plans and planning permission.

- Enquire about progress reports. Developers are notoriously lax about providing information on the progress of building work, which can be difficult to obtain unless you visit the site yourself periodically. In fact, some developers don't allow buyers to visit the site! The best developers provide monthly reports with photographs.

Don't sign or pay anything when looking round a development for the first time. Give yourself a cooling-off period and look at alternatives.

BUYING WITHOUT LAND

In some cases, developers purchase a quarter-acre plot complete with a house, remove the house and put it up for sale without land. All you need to do is find yourself a plot and have your new home delivered to the site and installed there. This method of buying a house is much less common than it used to be, but it's still used and can be a way of buying a home cheaply. The main points are not to buy a house until you have somewhere to site it, and to make sure that the plot has services (e.g. water and electricity) available. Also confirm the cost of moving the house and reinstalling it, which may exceed the cost of the house itself! The job needs to be done by specialist builders and hauliers, who literally cut the house into two or three sections and move it to your plot.

Lifestyle Plots

In New Zealand, the term 'lifestyle plot' or 'block' refers to a kind of smallholding – a plot of (often) undeveloped land, usually in the country. Buyers of lifestyle plots tend to be independent, rustic types who yearn for a more rural (back-to-nature) way of life. They often build their own home on the plot (or have one built) and may keep horses or ponies or a few farm animals in addition to growing their own vegetables. Lifestyle plots are available in many areas and are usually temptingly cheap.

When buying a lifestyle plot, the main points to check are that mains services are available nearby and the cost of connecting them, and that the land is suitable for agricultural purposes, e.g. the quality of the soil and whether water is available for irrigation. If you plan to keep animals, good fencing (preferably post and rail) should be included, as the cost of fencing a large plot can be high.

⚠ **Caution**

You should check any development plans for the area, as there have been a number of cases where buyers planning a life of seclusion have found some years later that their plot adjoins an industrial park or is divided by a main road.

You can expect to pay around $275,000 for a small lifestyle plot (around 5 acres/2ha) or up to $750,000 if it's within commuting distance of Auckland (the practice of working in Auckland and commuting to a 'farm' in the country has become popular in the last few years). A plot twice this size (if you think you can manage it – 10 acres is **an awful lot of land**!) might cost between 50 and 100 per cent more, depending on the location, aspect, topography, climate, surrounding development (or lack of it), etc..

RESALE HOMES

Buying 'resale' doesn't necessarily mean buying an old home. There can be many advantages in buying a modern resale home rather than a brand new one, including better value, an established development with a range of local services and facilities in place, more individual design and style, no 'teeting troubles', furniture and other extras included in the price, a mature garden and trees, and a larger plot. With a resale property you can see exactly what you'll get for your money, and the previous owners may have made improvements or added extras such as a swimming pool that may not be fully reflected in the asking price.

The possible disadvantages of buying a resale home depend on its age and how well it has been maintained. They can include a poor state of repair and the need for renovation or refurbishment, inferior build quality and design, no warranty (i.e. with a home that's more than ten years old), insect infestations, LBS (see page 92), and (in the case of a community property) the possibility of incurring high assessments for repairs.

COMMUNITY PROPERTIES

Properties in New Zealand with elements (whether a building, amenities or land) shared with other properties are here referred to as community properties. Community properties include units (apartments and flats) and single-family homes (semi-detached or detached) on a private estate with communal areas and facilities. Owners of community properties own not only their homes, but also a share of the common elements of the building or development, including foyers, hallways, passages, stairs, lifts, patios, gardens, roads, and leisure and sports facilities (such as swimming pools and tennis courts).

When you buy a community property you automatically become a member of the community of owners.

Advantages

The advantages of owning a community property include increased security; lower property taxes than detached homes; access to a range of sports and leisure facilities; lots of social contact and the companionship of close neighbours; no garden, lawn or pool maintenance; fewer of the responsibilities of home ownership; and the opportunity to live in an area where owning a single-family home would be prohibitively expensive, e.g. a beach front or town centre.

Disadvantages

The disadvantages of community properties may include excessively high community fees (see below); restrictive rules and regulations (see below); a confining living and social environment and possible lack of privacy; noisy neighbours (particularly if neighbouring properties are let to holiday-makers); limited living and storage space; expensive covered or secure parking (or insufficient off-road parking); and acrimonious owners' meetings where management and factions may try to push through unpopular proposals.

Checks

Before buying a community property it's advisable to ask current owners the following questions:

● Do they like living there?

● How noisy are other residents?

● Would they buy there again (why or why not)?

● Is the community well managed?

● What are the regular fees (levies) and restrictions?

● Are any additional fees due imminently (e.g. to pay for major repairs or painting the façade)?

● How healthy is the community's reserve fund?

● If the property is new, how quickly have construction and/or minor defects been corrected by the developer?

Community meeting minutes are a valuable source of information and you should ask for these for the last four or five years and read them carefully. Not only do they give a good idea of the community's finances, but they also how the community is managed and how well (or badly) the residents get on.

Community Fees

Owners of community properties must pay community fees for the upkeep of communal areas and for communal services. Charges are calculated according to each owner's share of the development or apartment building and **not** whether they're temporary or permanent residents.

Fees go towards road cleaning; 'green zone' maintenance (including communal and possibly private gardens); cleaning, decoration and

maintenance of buildings; employing a strata manager, a building manager or caretaker; communal lighting in buildings and grounds; water supply (e.g. swimming pools, gardens); insurance; administration; and maintenance of lifts. Always check the level of regular and additional charges before buying a community property; if necessary, owners can be charged an additional amount to make up any shortfall of funds for maintenance or repairs (see below). Fees are usually billed quarterly and adjusted at the end of the year when actual expenditure is known and the annual accounts have been approved by the committee. If you're buying an apartment from a previous owner, ask to see a copy of the fees for previous years and the minutes of the last annual general meeting, as owners may be 'economical with the truth' when stating community fees, particularly if they're high. You should obtain receipts for the previous five years (if applicable).

Community fees vary considerably according to the communal facilities provided, but as a rule of thumb expect to pay around 1 per cent of the purchase price per year for an apartment in a well equipped building in a city. Fees for luxury complexes or developments with high upkeep (e.g. extensive gardens and several swimming pools) are invariably higher, but high fees aren't necessarily a negative point (assuming you can afford them), provided you receive value for money and the community is well managed and maintained. **The value of a community property depends to a large extent on how well the development is maintained and managed.**

Community Rules

Community rules allow owners to run a community in accordance with the wishes of the majority, while at the same time protecting the rights of the minority. Rules usually govern such things as noise levels; the keeping of pets (not usually permitted); letting; exterior decoration and plants (e.g. the placement of shrubs); rubbish disposal; the use of swimming pools and other recreational facilities; the activities of children (e.g. no ball games or cycling on community grounds); parking; business or professional use; use of a communal laundry room; the installation and positioning of satellite dishes; and the hanging of laundry. Check the rules and discuss any restrictions with residents.

☑ SURVIVAL TIP

In some off-plan communities, developers draw up community rules that favour particular properties (or the developers themselves). Before committing yourself to an off-plan purchase, ask to see the proposed community rules.

are more like country estates or luxury hotels with prices starting at over $500,000. Before buying a retirement home, you should visit a number of villages and talk to residents, as they vary enormously in quality, variety of amenities and styles, and cost. There's a large demand for homes in retirement developments and villages, and they usually sell quickly.

Facilities may include a billiards room, bowling green, craft room, croquet lawn, garage, heated outdoor or indoor swimming pool (or both), landscaped gardens, library service, lifts, lounge/dining area, bar, gardens, restaurant, spa complex, sun room and tennis courts, and guest suites that can be booked for visitors. In some villages, home cleaning is included and meals may also be provided (called 'assisted living'). One of the most important features of retirement homes is that help is on hand 24 hours a day, either from a live-in warden or caretaker or via an alarm system linked to a control centre. A nurse and maintenance man are usually on call and there are visiting doctors and dentists. Many retirement villages provide 24-hour, seven-days-a-week emergency care and some also have nursing homes.

RETIREMENT HOMES &SHELTERED HOUSING

For those who are retired or nearing retirement age (e.g. over 55), purpose-built retirement homes and sheltered housing are available in most areas of New Zealand. Retirement villages vary in size and offer different levels of accommodation, from self-contained independent living apartments, cottages or townhouses to serviced apartments, hostels and nursing homes. Most villages offer a luxurious lifestyle, safety and security, and a supportive environment, and some

Initial (ingoing) costs of buying a retirement home include the purchase of an apartment or a lease to the property, fees (see page 109), and incidental costs associated with drafting agreements or contracts. As in other countries, some retirement homes are leased (e.g. for 30 years or until you die) rather than owned freehold. Running (ongoing) costs include weekly/monthly fees for facilities, insurance, maintenance, rates and services.

There are several potential problems with owning a home in a retirement village. A 'deferred management fee' may be payable on leaving the village (e.g. when you die), which is usually a percentage of the original purchase price. In some villages, leases must be sold by the village administration and, when an apartment or lease is put up for sale, fees must usually be paid until it's sold. This leaves owners (or their families) open to abuse, and some retirement villages deliberately allow apartments to remain empty so that they can charge fees (of up to $1,250 a month!) without providing any services. Other common problems include restricted access to services, financial disputes and poor management.

INSPECTIONS & SURVEYS

It isn't compulsory or usual in New Zealand to have a building inspection or structural survey carried out, but when you've found a property that you like, you should not only make a close inspection of its condition, even if it's a fairly new building, but also ensure that 'what you see is what you get'. In many rural areas, boundaries aren't always clearly drawn – often because the title hasn't been brought in line with recent changes in local topography, e.g. the growth or clearance of woodland. If you're shown a property with a large plot, the vendor or agent may wave his arms and declare airily: 'This is all yours; it's included in the price'. The truth may be rather more complicated!

The extent of the inspection you carry out (or commission) will depend largely on whether a property is derelict and in need of complete restoration, partly or totally renovated, or a modern home. You should ensure that a property over ten years old is structurally sound, as it will no longer be covered by a warranty. Although New Zealand has good building standards, you should never assume that a building is sound, as even quite new buildings can have serious faults.

Doing your own Checks

There are a number of checks you can carry out yourself, including the following:

- If you buy a waterside property, you should ensure that it has been designed with floods in mind, e.g. with electrical installations above flood level and tiled floors.

☑ **SURVIVAL TIP**

Check whether there are any airfields nearby – public or private; you don't want your rural idyll spoiled by droning light aircraft or, worse, buzzing microlights.

Check the local crime rate by asking neighbours and contacting the nearest police station in order to assess whether any existing security measures, such as shutters and locks, are likely to be adequate or whether you'll need to install additional systems, such as an alarm or window bars, which will affect not only your budget but also the appearance of your property. However, bear in mind that neighbours may be reluctant to tell you if burglary and vandalism are prevalent, and the local police may have different standards of comparison from your own!

Check the condition of any walls, fences or hedges and find out who they belong to and therefore who is responsible for their upkeep.

- If you're planning to make extensions or alterations (e.g. the addition of a swimming pool or stables) that may require planning permission, make enquiries whether such permission is likely to be granted.

- When it comes to examining the building itself, check the outside first, where they may be signs of damage and decay, such as bulging or cracked walls, damp, missing roof tiles, rusty or insecure gutters and drainpipes, dry or wet rot in beams and other woodwork, and doors and windows that no longer hinge, lock or fit properly. Plants growing up or against walls can cause damp, and the roots of trees or shrubs close to a building can damage foundations (look for telltale cracks). Use binoculars to inspect the roof and a torch to investigate the loft, noting any cracks or damp patches using a camera and notepad. If you see a damp patch on the outside, check whether it runs right through the wall when you go inside. In an area that's liable to flooding, storms and subsidence, it's wise to check an old property after heavy rainfall, when any leaks should come to light.

- If the soil consists of clay, the ground surrounding a house can 'shrink' after a long dry period. Large trees can create the same effect by drawing water out of the soil (eucalyptus are notably adept at this). This shrinkage can cause cracks in walls and, in extreme cases, subsidence.

cost of extending the service to the property, as it can be very expensive in remote rural areas (see **Utilities** on page 237). If a property has a well or septic tank, you should have it tested (see **Septic Tanks** on page 122). Also check whether a property is due to be (or could be) connected to mains drainage and sewerage.

- Mains water, sewerage, electricity, gas and telephones may not be in place in some country areas, where generators, solar energy and wind power may be alternatives. **If a house doesn't have electricity or mains water, it's important to check the cost of extending these services to it, which can be high.** Many rural properties get their water from a spring or well, which is usually fine, but you should check the reliability of the water supply, as wells can and do run dry!

- Check the quality of the water in the area of the property; for example, is it hard or soft and what is the nitrate content? (See also **Water** on page 241.)

- Locate the stop cock for the mains water supply, if there is one, and test the pressure (preferably in summer during a dry spell). Ask where the meter is and check it.

- If the property has a swimming pool, check that planning permission was granted for its construction, as it isn't unusual for owners to construct pools without permission, in which case you could be obliged to demolish it or fill it in. Check also the type of pool structure, which

- In the case of a property that has been restored, if work has been carried out by registered local builders, ask to see the bills. If the current (or a previous) owner did the work himself, it's essential to consult an expert to ascertain whether it has been done well or botched. You should also make sure that any major changes or additions had planning permission; if not, you could be obliged to demolish them – at your own expense.

- Test the electrical system, plumbing, mains water, hot water boiler and central heating systems as applicable. Don't take anyone's word that these work, but check them for yourself and, at the same time, find out how these systems work.

- If the property doesn't have electricity or mains water, check the nearest connection point and the is rarely specified in purchase documents, and its condition and that the filtration and other cleaning systems work as they should. If you know little or nothing about swimming pools, it's worthwhile getting an expert to make the checks for you. The small cost of an inspection should be set against the potentially astronomical cost of repairing an unsound pool. If repairs are required, these may be paid for by the vendor or covered by a reduction in the price of the property. Make sure that a pool has an approved safety system, especially if you plan to let the property (see **Swimming Pools** on page 123); if there isn't a safety system, take into account the cost of its installation. More generally, consider the location of the pool, the local climate and your inclinations, and ask yourself how often you're likely to use it and whether its maintenance will be more trouble and expense than it's worth.

- If a building has a 'ventilation space' beneath the ground floor, check that this hasn't become blocked by plants or been filled with debris; if it has, this could have caused ground-level wooden floors to rot and damp to rise up walls.

It's strongly recommended that, if possible, you visit a property or area in the winter, as not only do some house prices fall when the tourist season ends, but media images rarely hint at how cool and damp it can be in the winter in parts of New Zealand. Such a visit may also reveal problems that weren't apparent at another time (e.g. that the DIY shop you were banking on for materials and tools is closed until the spring, which can be the case in remote areas).

> ☑ **SURVIVAL TIP**
>
> Although you can make basic checks yourself, they're no substitute for a professional inspection, the cost of which is a small price to pay for the peace of mind it provides. If you would have a survey carried out on a similar property in your home country, you should have one done in New Zealand.

Professional Survey

Although a survey isn't legally required as part of the purchasing process in New Zealand, it's strongly recommended before committing to a purchase. Some local buyers simply ask a builder friend to come along with them when visiting a property, or ask a local builder for a quote before buying (perhaps the cheapest and easiest way), but as a foreigner you're recommended to commission at least a valuation and preferably a full survey, especially if you're planning to buy an old building.

If you decide that you'll need a survey before buying a property, it's worth making enquiries at an early stage to ascertain who is best qualified to help you, what type of survey reports they offer and how much they charge. You can expect that a competent surveyor won't be available immediately.

Survey Report

You should receive a written report (within a few days of the survey) on the condition of a property, including anything that could affect its value or your enjoyment of it in the future, an estimate of its current and possibly future value and an estimate of the cost of any necessary renovation or repair work. Some surveyors will allow you to accompany them, and some will produce a video of their findings in addition to a written report.

Discuss with your surveyor in advance exactly what will be included in his report and, more importantly, what will be excluded (you may need to pay extra to include certain checks and tests). An inspection can be limited to a few items or even a single system only, such as the wiring or plumbing in an old house.

The report should first identify and establish that the property and land being offered for sale are, in fact, in the vendor's name and that the land 'for sale' matches the land registry plan. Although this is normally the role of a lawyer, your surveyor has a duty to check it, as a greater or lesser amount of land can affect a valuation.

You may be able to make a 'satisfactory' survey a condition of the preliminary purchase contract, although a vendor may refuse or insist that you carry out a survey before signing the contract. You may, however, be able to negotiate a satisfactory compromise with the vendor.

☑ **SURVIVAL TIP**

Use your survey results to negotiate a better price for the property: point out what needs repairing or renovating and its estimated cost, and propose that the seller reduces the price by this amount.

SEPTIC TANKS

If a property is connected to a mains sewerage system, you're fortunate! Most rural properties and many in small towns aren't on mains drainage and therefore have individual sewerage systems, which normally consist of a septic tank. Before committing yourself to a purchase, have the septic tank checked or, if there isn't one, ask a specialist to assess your requirements and the likely cost of installing a system. Contact your town hall for a list of approved specialists authorised to carry out an inspection or a feasibility study. Even if they don't need replacing, old septic tanks may be in need of drainage, repair or new pipes. Modern regulations demand, for example, long overflow pipes, which may need to be extended by up to 10m (33ft); this may not be possible within the property's boundaries, and you may need to enter negotiations with a neighbour. Make sure also that a septic tank is large enough for the property in question, e.g. 2,500 litres for two bedrooms and up to 4,000 litres for five bedrooms.

If a property has neither mains drainage nor a septic tank, you must check that one can be installed. If you need to install a septic tank, you should check the following:

- that there's enough available land, bearing in mind that the drains for a septic tank must be installed a certain minimum distance from the boundaries of a property (e.g. 3 to 5m/10 to 16ft), and must cover a certain area depending on the size of the tank (generally at least 85m²/915ft²);

- whether there are rivers, canals or other water courses (including underground springs and waterways) that might affect the siting of a tank and soak-away and the type of soak-away – for example, a septic tank mustn't be less than 35m from a well;

- whether the ground is marshy or rocky, in which case installation could be difficult and/or expensive;

- whether the land slopes upwards away from the house, which may mean that waste water must be pumped up to the soak-away – another additional expense;

- whether there's access to the site for a lorry (delivering the tank and subsequently emptying it) and a digger to install the soak-away;

- whether you need to obtain approval from the local council and/or regional authorities for the installation and have it checked once installed.

It's essential to check these things before purchasing a property. The cost of installation can be between $3,000 and $7,000, depending on the size of tank and the type of installation.

SWIMMING POOLS

It's common for foreign buyers to install a swimming pool at a home in New Zealand, which will greatly increase your rental prospects and the rent you can charge if you plan to let. (Many self-catering holiday companies won't take on properties without a pool.) However, you should calculate the cost of installing and maintaining a swimming pool and assess whether it's worthwhile, especially if you don't intend to let the property.

There are many swimming pool installation companies or you can even buy and install one yourself. There are also various types of pool, each with advantages and disadvantages. Above-ground pools are the cheapest but can be unsightly. A 15m long oval pool can be installed for as little as $3,500, and smaller 'splasher' pools can cost less than $750, although elaborate pools can cost $8,500 or more.

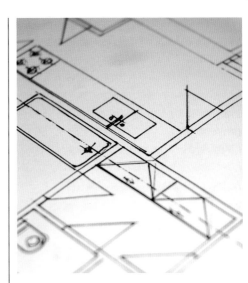

In-ground pools come in three general types: moulded fibreglass (or 'one-piece') pools, which can simply be 'dropped' into a hole in the ground and cost around $13,000 for a reasonable-size moulding; panelled pools, which can be bought in kit form and put together without professional help and cost from around $7,000; and concrete block pools, which normally require professional installation and are therefore usually the most expensive option, costing from around $25,000 for a 10m x 5m pool.

Note that you sometimes need planning permission to install a pool and need to comply with safety regulations. The Fencing of Swimming Pools Act of 1987 requires that all domestic pools in New Zealand be fenced, to protect children from drowning. A new standard for such fencing is to be issued in late 2007 or early 2008; details of requirements can be obtained from any recognised pool installation company, but also check yourself with your local and/or state authorities.

Pools require regular maintenance and cleaning, which is also expensive (heating a pool, particularly an outdoor one, can cost a fortune, especially in cooler regions). If you have a holiday home or let a property, you'll need to employ someone to maintain your pool (you may be able to get a local family to look after it in return for using it).

RENOVATION, RESTORATION & BUILDING

Property renovation and restoration is a major pastime in New Zealand, where tens of thousands of people spend their evenings and weekends rebuilding, extending or redecorating their homes (when they've finished rebuilding, extending or redecorating their holiday homes, that is!). It may be something you wish to consider – there are plenty of older properties in need of renovation in New Zealand, and they're often offered at tempting prices.

It isn't particularly expensive to renovate a property in New Zealand, as the basic materials (weather-boarding and corrugated iron) are plentiful and cheap. The main difficulty is likely to be finding somebody to do the renovation for you. As most New Zealanders are avid 'DIYers', there's a shortage of people to do odd jobs and small property repairs. On the other hand, if you're keen on DIY yourself, it could be the ideal solution. However, you should note that property in need of renovation is sometimes in a serious state of decline, with a rotten wooden frame or weather-boarding and a leaking tin roof (see **Leaky Building Syndrome** on page 92).

⚠ **Caution**

Even if you intend to do much of the work yourself, you should take advice from a surveyor or builder regarding whether a house is worth saving before committing yourself to a purchase

---

If you intend to buy an old building, you should check that it isn't registered with the Historic Places Trust, as extensions and renovations to such properties are strictly controlled. Even many timber buildings which appear to have little or no historical interest are protected in this way, as they're considered part of New Zealand's heritage.

Don't, whatever you do, believe an agent who says that a property will 'make a charming home with a little work'. Also bear in mind that you're unlikely to make a profit if you decide to sell a property you've renovated and that you could make a substantial loss, as it's easy to spend more than you could ever hope to recoup in 'added value'.

It's vital to check a property requiring renovation or restoration before committing yourself to a purchase. Most importantly it must have sound walls, without which it's cheaper to erect a new building! Almost any other problem can be fixed or overcome (at a price), though a sound roof that doesn't leak is highly desirable. Don't believe a vendor or agent who tells you that a roof or anything else can 'easily' be repaired or patched up, but obtain expert advice from a local builder or architect. As well as a new roof (or extensive repair), old buildings often need a damp-proof course (condensation and damp can be a problem), timber treatment, new windows and doors, insulation, a modern kitchen and bathroom, re-wiring and central heating. In addition, many older properties have iron or steel plumbing pipes, which are susceptible to leaks and corrosion and expensive to replace.

Mains water, sewerage, electricity, gas and telephones may not be in place in some country areas, where generators, solar energy and wind power may be alternatives. **If a house doesn't have electricity or mains water, it's important to check the cost of extending these services to it, which can be expensive.**

☑ **SURVIVAL TIP**

Many rural properties get their water from a spring or well, which is usually fine, but you should check the reliability of the water supply, as wells can and do run dry!

If you're planning to buy a waterside property, you should also check the frequency of floods. If they're commonplace, you should ensure that a building has been designed with floods in mind, e.g. with electrical installations above flood level and solid tiled floors.

Any new building or significant addition to an existing building must comply with town planning regulations. Consent for the work can be obtained from your local council, who will send a building inspector to advise you on what you may and may not do and monitor the work.

If you decide to build a house or renovate or extend an existing one, you should hire a builder who's a member of the Registered Master Builders Federation (☎ 0800-269 119, 🖥 www.masterbuilder.org.nz); Federation members offer a seven-year guarantee. The Certified Builders Association of New Zealand also guarantees that its members are qualified builders (☎ 0800-237 843, 🖥 www.certifiedbuilders.co.nz). Both associations strongly advise customers against paying any builder before work has been completed.

Lady Knox geyser, Rotura, North Island

4.
MONEY MATTERS

One of the most important aspects of buying a home in New Zealand and living there (even for short periods) is money management, which includes transferring and changing money, opening a bank account and obtaining a mortgage. Whether or not you plan to live Down Under, you may also incur local taxes, which are covered in Chapter 7.

If you're planning to invest in property or a business in New Zealand that's financed with funds in a foreign currency (e.g. GB£ or US$), it's important to consider both the present and possible future exchange rates. If you need to borrow money to buy property or for a business venture Down Under, you should carefully consider where and in what currency to raise finance. Bear in mind that if your income is paid in a foreign currency it can be exposed to risks beyond your control when you live in New Zealand, particularly regarding inflation and exchange rate fluctuations. On the other hand, if you live and work in New Zealand and are paid in local currency, this may affect your financial commitments abroad.

If you own a holiday home or investment property in New Zealand, you can employ a local accountant or tax adviser to look after your financial affairs there, e.g. receive your bank statements, ensure that your bank is paying your standing orders (e.g. for utilities and property taxes) and that you have sufficient funds to pay them, and declare and pay your local taxes. If you let a home in New Zealand through a local company, it may perform the above tasks as part of its service.

You should ensure that your income is (and will remain) sufficient to live on, bearing in mind possible devaluations (if your income isn't paid in local currency), rises in the cost of living (see page 28), unforeseen expenses such as medical bills and anything else that may reduce your income (such as stock market crashes and recessions!).

It's wise to have at least one credit card when visiting or living in New Zealand(Visa and MasterCard are the most widely accepted). Even if you don't like credit cards and shun any form of credit, they do have their uses, for example no-deposit car hire; no pre-paying hotel bills (plus guaranteed bookings); obtaining cash 24 hours a day; simple telephone, mail-order and internet payments; greater security than cash; and, above all, convenience. Note, however, that not all Antipodean businesses accept credit cards.

CURRENCY

The New Zealand unit of currency is the New Zealand dollar, affectionately known as the 'Kiwi dollar' or just the 'Kiwi' (New Zealanders gave up their British-style pounds, shillings and pence in 1967). It hasn't always been one of the world's strongest currencies but has a reputation for stability, although it fell to a 12-year low against the US$ in 1998 as a result of the crisis in world (particularly Asian) financial markets. Its fortunes have revived in recent years and it has strengthened significantly against the US$ in the 21st century (although so have many other currencies). You cannot spend foreign currency in New Zealand, although there are a few duty-free and tourist shops that accept Australian and US dollars (at an unfavourable exchange rate).

The New Zealand dollar is divided into 100 cents. Banknotes are issued in denominations of 5, 10, 20, 50 and 100 dollars (there's no $1 bill), and coins are minted in 1 and 2 dollars, 50, 20, 10 and 5 cents. (The 5 cent coin is colloquially known as the 'pest'.) The cent is identified by the symbol ¢, although occasionally you'll see it expressed as a decimal, e.g. $0.75, or values of more than a dollar expressed as cents, e.g. 115¢, neither of which is officially correct. Until 1992, Her Majesty Queen Elizabeth II appeared on all New Zealand banknotes, but she was then 'retired' (despite protests from many people) and now appears only on the $20 note. Famous New Zealanders have been installed on other notes: Lord Rutherford ('Father of the Atom') on the $100, Apirana Ngata

(a Maori statesman) on the $50, Kate Sheppard (a suffragette) on the $10 and Sir Edmund Hillary (one of the first men to climb Mount Everest) on the $5 note.

It's wise to obtain some New Zealand currency before your arrival in the country. However, because international *bureaux de change* don't usually handle coins, the smallest unit of currency you'll be able to obtain outside New Zealand is $5. Ask for a selection of $5, $10 and $20 notes, which are the most useful. Many shops, taxi drivers and small businesses are reluctant to accept $50 and $100 notes; legally they cannot reject any notes (or coins), but if you proffer a $100 note, they're likely to have no change. These notes also attract the most scrutiny, as they're more likely to be the target of forgers, although counterfeit currency isn't a serious problem in New Zealand.

IMPORTING & EXPORTING MONEY

Exchange controls operated in New Zealand between 1938 and 1984 but were then abolished and there are now no restrictions on the import or export of funds. It's possible to transmit funds to New Zealand without being hindered by bureaucratic procedures, and a New Zealand resident is permitted to open a bank account in any country and to export unlimited funds from New Zealand. However, you must make a declaration if you wish to import more than $10,000 in cash (in which case you might be asked why!).

When transferring or sending money to (or from) New Zealand, you should be aware of the alternatives. One way is to send either a personal cheque or a bank draft (cashier's cheque), both of which should be sent by registered post. Money shouldn't be treated as having been paid until the cheque or draft has cleared the system, which is usually within seven days of receipt.

☑ **SURVIVAL TIP**

A safer method of transferring money is to make a direct transfer or a telex or electronic transfer between banks.

A direct transfer involves a process similar to sending a cheque or bank draft and usually takes at least seven days (but can take much longer). A telex or electronic transfer can be completed within a few hours. However, bear in mind that (because of the time difference) banks in New Zealand close for the day before they open in Europe or the US, so it will be at least the next day before funds are available in New Zealand. The transfer process is usually faster and less likely to come unstuck when it's between branches of the same or affiliated banks (in any case, delays are more likely to be overseas than in New Zealand). The Commonwealth Bank of Australia, which has branches in Europe and the US, can transfer funds almost instantaneously to its branches in New Zealand, although its branch network there (around 130) isn't the most extensive.

NZ Post can transfer, send and receive money within New Zealand and abroad. For domestic transactions, money order certificates costing $3 are available for amounts up to $1,000 and for larger amounts electronic money orders can be purchased for $5. For the transfer of money to and from overseas, NZ Post uses the services of Western Union, which charges around $74 for sums up to $1,000. Further information is available on ☎ freephone 0800-005 253.

The cost of transfers varies considerably – not only commission and exchange rates, but also transfer charges (shop around and compare rates). Usually the faster the transfer, the more it costs. Transfer fees also vary with the amount being transferred, and there are usually minimum and maximum fees. For example, banks in the UK charge from £5 to process a cheque for up to £50, and up to £40 for a cheque worth the equivalent of £10,000 (most banks in the UK charge in the region of £10 to £45 for electronic transfers). In emergencies, money can be sent via American Express offices by Amex card holders.

☑ **SURVIVAL TIP**

When you have money transferred to a bank in New Zealand, ensure that you give the name, account number, branch number and bank sort code or, better still, the IBAN number, which contains all the relevant bank details (though not your account number). Bear in mind that the names of some New Zealand banks (and towns) are strikingly similar, so double check your instructions.

If you plan to send a large amount of money to New Zealand or overseas for a business transaction such as buying property, you should ensure that you receive the commercial rate of exchange rather than the tourist rate. Check charges and rates in advance and agree them with your bank (you may be able to negotiate a lower charge or a better exchange rate). If you send a cheque or bank draft to New Zealand, it should be crossed so that it can be paid only into an account with exactly the same name as shown on the cheque.

Most banks in major cities have *bureaux de change*, and there are banks and *bureaux de change* with extended opening hours at both Auckland and Wellington international airports, plus other airports when international flights arrive (which may be just a few times a week). At *bureaux de change* you can buy and sell foreign currencies, buy and cash travellers' cheques, cash personal cheques, and obtain a cash advance on credit and charge cards. There are private *bureaux de change* in the major cities and tourist resorts with longer business hours than banks, particularly at weekends, e.g. they open on Saturdays from 9.30am to 12.30pm when banks are closed, and there are 24-hour, automatic, money-changing machines in some major cities (e.g. outside the Downtown Airline Terminal, Auckland). Most *bureaux de change* offer competitive exchange rates and low or no commission (but always check) and are easier to deal with than banks. If you're changing a lot of money, you may be able to negotiate a better exchange rate. Note, however, that the best exchange rates are usually provided by banks. The New Zealand dollar exchange rate against most major international currencies is displayed in banks and listed in daily newspapers.

If you're visiting New Zealand, it's safer to carry travellers' cheques than cash. Travellers' cheques in major currencies, including US$ and £ sterling, are easily exchanged in New Zealand but aren't usually accepted by businesses, except perhaps some luxury hotels, restaurants and shops, which usually offer a poor exchange rate. Some banks exchange travellers' cheques free of commission, although their charges are usually built into the (inferior) exchange rate, so always compare the net amount you'll receive. Keep a separate record of cheque numbers and note where and when they were cashed. American Express provides a free, three-hour replacement service for lost or stolen travellers' cheques at any of their offices worldwide, provided you know the serial numbers of the lost cheques. Without the serial numbers it can take three days or longer. Most companies provide freephone telephone numbers for reporting lost or stolen travellers' cheques in New Zealand, e.g. American Express (☎ freephone 0800-442 208). You can also buy foreign currency travellers' cheques from any New Zealand bank, which charge a minimum commission fee of $5 or 1.25 per cent. Shop around, as fees can vary, particularly on larger amounts.

There isn't a lot of difference in the cost between buying New Zealand currency using cash, travellers' cheques or a debit or credit card. However, many people simply take cash when travelling overseas, which is asking for trouble, particularly if you have no way of obtaining more cash locally, e.g. with travellers' cheques or a debit or credit card. **One thing to bear in mind when travelling anywhere, is *never* to rely on only one source of funds!**

☑ SURVIVAL TIP

One of the quickest (it takes around ten minutes) and safest methods of transferring cash is via a telegraphic transfer, e.g. Moneygram (☎ UK 0800-666 3947, 🖳 www.moneygram. com) or Western Union (☎ UK 0800-833 833, 🖳 www.westernunion.com), but it's also one of the most expensive, e.g. commission of 7 to 10 per cent of the amount sent!

Western Union transfers can be picked up from a post office in New Zealand just 15 minutes after being paid into an office abroad. Money can be sent via American Express offices by Amex cardholders.

BANKS & BUILDING SOCIETIES

There are officially just two kinds of financial institution in New Zealand: registered banks and what are euphemistically known as 'other financial institutions'. The main exception is the Reserve Bank of New Zealand (🖳 www.rbnz.govt.nz), which doesn't fit into either of these categories and is the country's central bank, performing a role similar to the Bank of England or the Federal Reserve Bank in the US. It has a range of functions, including managing the money supply, supervising commercial banks, implementing the government's financial policy, controlling the exchange rate, providing a banking service to the government and acting as a registrar for government stocks.

Savings banks in New Zealand were traditionally mutual organisations owned by their members or investors, which concentrated on accepting personal savings and granting mortgages for residential property. In this respect they were much like building societies in the UK and savings and loan organisations in the US. However, deregulation in the financial sector during the '80s allowed commercial banks to enter this market. With their greater financial clout and marketing expertise they've managed largely to take it over, and as a result many savings banks have either converted to registered banks or been taken over by them.

Changes in the banking system over the last few years have meant that most individuals and businesses in New Zealand carry out their banking, including savings, loans, mortgages and day-to-day transactions, with one of the registered banks. Banks operating in this sector include Australia New Zealand Bank (ANZ,  www.anz.com/nz) and ASB ( www.asbbank.co.nz), formerly the Auckland Savings Bank. Not surprisingly, ASB is strongest in Auckland but it's also popular in the rest of the country and is routinely rated New Zealand's number one major bank in terms of customer satisfaction. Other major registered banks include the Bank of New Zealand (BNZ,  www.bnz.co.nz), which is New Zealand's largest bank in terms of assets and, despite its name, wholly Australian-owned; the National Bank ( www.nationalbank.co.nz); and Westpac NZ ( www.westpac.co.nz)'

It's estimated that only around 12 per cent of the New Zealand banking market is operated by indigenous banks. Note that the New Zealand banking operations of Australian banks are completely separate, so customers of Australian Westpac, for example, cannot access their Australian accounts at Westpac in New Zealand, or vice versa.

Some banks are mainly telephone and internet-based, e.g. TSB ( www.tsb.co.nz). PSIS is a financial institution owned by its customers, which offers banking services administered by the Bank of New Zealand, although it isn't a bank and as such isn't a member of the Banking Ombudsman scheme

nor subject to supervision by the Reserve Bank. The large insurance group AMP ( www.amp.co.nz) also offers banking services, and the New Zealand Post Office offers banking services at post shops under the name Kiwibank. Other financial institutions that aren't registered banks include merchant banks and leasing companies, which mainly serve the business sector. They aren't authorised to accept deposits from the public and, in any case, registered banks offer a more comprehensive range of services to the public and business community. Finance companies aren't registered banks, but provide consumer credit such as loans and hire purchase (or time purchase as it's also known in New Zealand). There are also many

international banks in New Zealand but most of these are located in the financial district of Wellington and don't have extensive branch networks around the country.

All New Zealand banks are efficient and highly automated. You'll find that staff, who are generally friendly and informal, work behind low counters or desks rather than armoured glass. This isn't to say that banks in New Zealand aren't robbed (they sometimes are), but little cash is shuffled across bank counters (or used in shops and other businesses), as most withdrawals are made by automated teller machine (ATM).

Normal banking hours in New Zealand are from 8.30 or 9am until 4.30pm, Mondays to Fridays, although banks may stay open for half an hour later one evening a week (which is the exception rather than the rule). Banks don't open at weekends and are closed on public holidays, although *bureaux de change* open at weekends.

Most registered banks offer a range of non-banking services, such as insurance, including life insurance, and pensions. Charges and premiums are usually competitive compared with similar products available from other sources, such as insurance brokers. However, it's important to shop around, as some banks sell only their own products or those from certain companies, rather than choosing the best deal from the whole range

available (which an independent broker should do).

Opening an Account

You can open a New Zealand bank account from outside the country or after your arrival. To open an account while overseas, you need to find the nearest office of a New Zealand bank, e.g. by looking in the telephone directory or asking your bank for assistance. You probably won't find a great deal of choice, but there are branches of the major New Zealand banks in most major cities in Europe, North America and Asia. You don't usually need to visit a branch in person, as an account can be opened by telephone or post. Note that most banks require an opening balance of at least $200 ($500 in some cases).

Different banks require different documentation, so you should check exactly what's required beforehand; typically you'll need two forms of identification, your IRD number (see page 171) and possibly statements from your current or previous bank. Note that if you don't have an IRD number when you open an account, you'll be charged resident withholding tax (RWT) on interest at 39 per cent. If you think that you might need an overdraft, loan or mortgage in New Zealand in the future, you should obtain a reference from your overseas bank manager to the effect that your account has been maintained in good order.

Current Accounts

The normal account for day-to-day transactions in New Zealand is a current or cheque account. You receive a cheque book within a week of opening your account, even though cheques are becoming less widely used in New Zealand, where most people pay with debit or credit cards in shops and settle their regular household bills by direct debit. There are no cheque guarantee cards in New Zealand, which is why you may be asked to produce a driving licence or credit card as proof of identity when paying by cheque. Not surprisingly, many shops and businesses won't take personal cheques (there may be a notice to this effect), which they're entitled to do (even the British High Commission doesn't accept them!).

The design of cheques is basically the same as that in most other countries; you enter the name of the payee, the date, the amount in words and figures, and sign it. All cheques should be crossed, so that they can be paid only into a bank account in the name of the payee and cannot be cashed. The use of a cheque incurs cheque duty of 5¢, which is automatically deducted by your bank (remember this when reconciling cheques you've written with the amounts that appear on your bank statement).

Cheque clearing in New Zealand is highly efficient, and a cheque paid into your account is usually credited the next day (occasionally the same day if it's at the same branch or bank). A cheque drawn on your account and given to someone else may also be debited from your account on the same or next day, and there isn't a delay of between three and ten days as in some other countries. Nevertheless, when paying a cheque into your account, it's probably best to wait a few days to spend the money, just in case the drawer didn't have sufficient funds to cover the cheque (in which case the cheque will be returned to you by post, which may take a couple of days). You should assume that a cheque drawn on your account will be debited from it on the same day.

To stop a cheque, contact your bank. If your cheque book or EFTPOS card(s) is lost or stolen, inform your bank immediately.

> Account statements are usually provided monthly, although you can ask to have them sent weekly. It's also possible to obtain details of your most recent transactions, request a mini-statement or make a balance enquiry at an ATM, commonly referred to as a cash dispenser.

Although you can withdraw cash from your account at any branch of your own bank by writing a cheque, it's much easier to use an EFTPOS card (see **Debit Cards** opposite) in an ATM. It's also possible to pay cash or cheques into your account at some machines.

Savings Accounts

You can open a savings (or deposit) account with any registered bank. Over the last few years, registered banks have become more competitive in this sector and have largely taken over the functions of the savings banks. In most cases you can choose from a range of savings accounts with interest rates varying according to the amount deposited, the period for which the money must be left on deposit, and the notice which must be given before you can withdraw it. An account with a minimum deposit period is known as a term deposit account, with terms ranging from one month to five years (the longer the term, the higher the interest paid). The interest rate may fluctuate according to the bank rate, be fixed for the entire term, or escalate (where the rate of interest paid rises annually, irrespective of general interest rates).

Registered banks offer a range of investments in addition to regular savings accounts, including stocks and shares, bonds and securities. Although you can also buy these through a stockbroker, banks offer competitive fees, particularly for small transactions. You don't need to use your own bank, and may be able to find a cheaper stock and share service elsewhere (e.g. via the internet).

Bank Charges

As in many countries, banks in New Zealand make charges for most transactions. Most banks charge a monthly fee for some accounts of at least $5, unless you meet certain conditions, such as maintaining a minimum monthly balance. Electronic transaction and cheque fees are around 50¢, and staff-assisted transactions cost around $2.50. Most banks also charge around $1.50 for the use of another bank's ATM.

In order to reduce your bank charges, the Citizens' Advice Bureau (☎ 0800-367 222, 🖳 www.cab.org.nz) offers the following advice:

● Reduce the number of transactions you make, e.g. when you pay with an EFTPOS card (see **Debit Cards** below)

- Use electronic banking, which is cheaper than over-the-counter transactions.

- Ask if there's a flat-fee option, which may be cheaper if you have a lot of monthly transactions, and negotiate the best deal with your bank.

All regular bills such as electricity, gas, telephone, mortgage and rent, can be paid automatically by direct debit from your bank account. The creditor or your bank will provide the necessary form for you to complete and return to them. You're protected against loss as a result of error or fraud in the system, although, like most bank transactions in New Zealand, direct debits usually attract bank charges (both for set-up and per debit).

Debit Cards

When opening a bank account, you should request an 'electronic funds transfer at point of sale' (EFTPOS) card, also known as a debit card, which can be used to pay for goods and services, with payments debited from your account, usually on the same day. The use of debit cards is widespread in New Zealand, much more so than in many European countries, and most garages, hotels, restaurants and even small shops accept them. An EFTPOS card can also be used to withdraw cash from ATMs throughout the country and overseas, for which you need a personal identification number (PIN), which is usually sent automatically and separately from the card itself.

Guard your EFTPOS card and PIN carefully; if the card is lost or stolen, inform your bank immediately so that it can be cancelled. It's common practice in New Zealand for people to give their EFTPOS card and PIN to other people (e.g. partners, children or friends) to enable them to withdraw money on

their behalf. Note, however, that if a card is misused the bank will hold you responsible for any debits charged to the card, whether you authorised them or not. If your card is lost or stolen, you won't be responsible for any more than a token amount (and even then it isn't usually charged), provided you've used your card properly and informed your bank as soon as you discovered it was missing.

You aren't usually charged a fee when using an EFTPOS card in a shop or other outlet, although it's legal for shops to charge a fee to cover their costs. Those that do must display a notice advising you of the fee, which is usually 50¢ or $1. When using an EFTPOS card to withdraw cash from a cash dispenser, you aren't usually charged a fee if the cash dispenser belongs to your own bank. Many banks have arrangements with other banks whereby their EFTPOS cards can be used in other banks' ATMs, although where this is possible you may be charged a fee of up to $3.

Credit & Charge Cards

New Zealanders are enthusiastic users of credit and charge cards, although many prefer debit cards, where payments are immediately debited from their account. Credit and charge cards are issued by most banks (although some will give you a credit card only if you have a certain type of account with them, e.g. a mortgage loan), are accepted almost anywhere (small shops may not accept them), and can be used to withdraw cash from ATMs or over the counter at banks, although this service costs from $1.50 to $4 and interest is charged from the day of the withdrawal. To use a credit or charge card in an ATM you require a PIN.

Most international credit and charge cards are widely accepted in New Zealand, including American Express, Diners Club, MasterCard and Visa, plus the local Bankcard, which is also widely accepted in Australia. Annual fees are between around $20 and $100.

Most credit cards offer loyalty schemes with various bonuses, such

as frequent flyer points with Qantas or Air New Zealand, or cash rewards ('cashback'). These loyalty schemes are extremely popular, particularly those offering air miles, and in late 2001, BNZ was forced to change its GlobalPlus scheme from one point per $1 spent to one point per $2 spent, as it was becoming too expensive for the bank!

⚠ **Caution**

Some large store groups in New Zealand issue their own charge cards, to which you can charge purchases made in their stores and associated shops. However, you should note that they usually charge a significantly higher interest rate than most credit cards.

Credit card fraud is a huge problem in New Zealand. If you lose your credit or charge card, you must report it to the issuer immediately by telephone. The law protects you from liability for any losses when a card is lost or stolen, unless it has been misused with your consent (e.g. by a friend), in which case you're liable.

Overdrafts & Loans

To apply for an overdraft or loan you must have a permanent address in New Zealand and a regular income. The amount of a loan or overdraft, the interest rate and (in the case of a loan) the period of repayment depend on your financial status, which a bank appraises using a credit scoring system. You can expect banks to be cautious (or even to refuse you altogether) unless you've lived in the same place for at least three years. Some banks offer a 'buffer' overdraft (e.g. $100 or $200) automatically to new customers, which is intended to cover you against minor overspending, but if you want a permanent overdraft facility you must usually pay a set-up fee (e.g. $20 to $50) and will incur high interest rates on the amount overdrawn.

It pays to shop around for a loan, as interest rates vary considerably with the bank, the amount and the period of the loan. Don't neglect banks other than your own, as it isn't necessary to have an account with a bank to obtain a loan. Ask friends and colleagues for their advice. If you have collateral, e.g. New Zealand property, or you can get someone to stand as a guarantor for a loan, you'll be eligible for a secured loan at a lower interest rate. A life insurance policy can be used as security for a bank loan and can be limited to cover the period of the loan.

It's also possible to take out payment protection insurance, which covers your payments in the event of illness or death, and may qualify you for a lower interest rate. To compare the interest rate on different loans, check the annual percentage rate (APR). Borrowing from finance companies, such as those advertising in newspapers and magazines, is usually much more expensive than borrowing from banks.

A popular form of loan in New Zealand is a 'revolving loan', which operates like a large permanent overdraft facility, except that you must make a fixed repayment each month, according to your income. You can borrow up to a set multiple of the monthly payment; e.g. if you can repay $200 per month, a lender may allow you to borrow up to 20 ($4,000) or 30 times ($6,000) this amount. The advantage of such a scheme is that you have access to loan finance whenever you need it, and don't need to borrow the entire sum all at once. As you make repayments, the money you've repaid again becomes available for you to borrow, up to your limit. The disadvantage is that it's easy to be constantly in debt! A revolving loan can also be linked to a mortgage (see **Types of Mortgage** below).

MORTGAGES

Mortgages (home loans) are available from New Zealand banks, mortgage brokers and some direct response (i.e. via telephone or internet) lenders. Generally, there's little difference between the interest rates charged, although there's a wide variety of mortgage plans with different repayment methods, terms (i.e. periods) and fees (see below), so it's worth shopping around for the best deal. Mortgage brokers are increasing in popularity and account for around a third of the market. If you decide to use the services of a mortgage broker, ensure that he's a member of the New Zealand Mortgage Brokers Association, whose members must have professional indemnity insurance and work with at least six different lenders. You can contact the Association at PO Box 303-353, Takapuna, Auckland (☎ 09-912 1000, 🖳 www.nzmba.co.nz).

Generally, New Zealand financial institutions are accommodating when it comes to granting mortgages and put a great deal of effort into gaining your business. Banks are keen for you to take out a mortgage with them and

many offer competitive deals. Some banks don't even require you to attend an interview at their local branch but offer mortgages by telephone or via the internet. All you need to do is telephone a freephone number (or complete an online questionnaire) and provide details of the property you wish to purchase and your personal details, and you'll receive an 'in principle' decision virtually immediately. The main direct response mortgage companies are BankDirect and AMP Banking. Telephone mortgage companies are highly competitive (although they offer a 'no frills' service) and are particularly suitable if you know exactly what kind of mortgage you require. If you don't, you'd be wise to visit your local bank, where staff will explain the different types of mortgage on offer.

There are no fixed lending criteria in New Zealand, although generally the maximum mortgage you can obtain is where the repayments are no more than 30 per cent of your net income (which is combined for a couple). It's sensible, however, to take out a mortgage on which the repayments constitute no more than 20 to 25 per cent of your income. The most you can usually borrow is 90 per cent (some lenders set the limit at 80 per cent) of the value of a property, although a high percentage mortgage may be based on the lender's own valuation (rather than what you're actually paying for the property) and you may be required to take out mortgage guarantee insurance (which guarantees that the lender gets his money back if you default on your repayments). It's customary in New Zealand for a property to be held as security for a loan taken out on it, i.e. the lender takes a first charge on the property.

> Mortgages can be obtained for any period up to 25 years, although the trend nowadays is for people to take 20 or even 15-year mortgages. The reason for this is that many New Zealanders take out a second mortgage in order to pay for their children's education or a holiday home before they retire. Although the repayments on a shorter mortgage are higher, you pay much less interest in the long term.

Types of Mortgage

The two main kinds of mortgage offered in New Zealand are a 'table mortgage' (equivalent to a repayment mortgage in other countries), where you make equal repayments of capital and interest throughout the period of the loan, and an interest-only mortgage, where you pay only the interest on the sum borrowed and are required to repay the original capital at the end of the term. Most lenders require you to take out an insurance policy to guarantee repayment of a loan, and in this way an interest-only mortgage is similar to an endowment mortgage offered in some other countries. Some lenders allow you to take out an interest-only mortgage without insurance, which makes the repayments temptingly low, but unless you make lots of money (or come into a big inheritance or win the lottery) during the period of the mortgage, you may need to sell your home at the end of the term in order to repay the capital! A third kind of mortgage that's sometimes offered is a 'straight line' mortgage, where you repay capital and interest throughout the term but repayments reduce over the years as the amount of capital owed reduces.

The interest rate on a New Zealand mortgage is either 'floating', so that it varies with interest rates generally, or fixed for the period of the loan, the repayment period being adjusted accordingly. A recent trend is for lenders to offer mortgages that are fixed (usually at a 'bargain' rate) for a period, such as one to five years, and then revert to a floating rate. These offer a temptingly cheap way of getting a foot on the property ladder, provided you budget for the fact that your repayments are likely to increase after the fixed-rate period expires, depending on how interest rates change in the meantime. In October 2007, floating mortgage interest rates ranged from 9.5 to 10.5 per cent or up to 1 per cent lower with a one to five-year fixed rate period. You can compare mortgage rates on the Consumer.org.nz website (🖥 www.consumer.org.nz).

☑ **SURVIVAL TIP**

As you work your way through the mortgage maze, you should bear in mind that banks and financial institutions in New Zealand are experts at dressing up mortgages in a user-friendly way and creating a variety of seemingly too-good-to-be-true packages. Your mortgage can, however, only be either a table, straight line or interest-only mortgage, with either a fixed or floating rate – no matter what fancy marketing name may be given to it. Make sure that you compare interest rates and calculate how much you're going to have to repay.

A New Zealand mortgage usually provides a high degree of flexibility. Many lenders allow you to convert from one type of mortgage to another, increase or decrease your payments, take a payment 'holiday' for a few months, or repay part of the capital early (thus reducing your repayments or the term of the mortgage). It's even possible to transfer your mortgage to another property. In fact, provided you keep making repayments, you're likely to find your lender accommodating.

Should you need to, it's usually quite easy to re-mortgage your property and gain access to some of the equity you've built up in it (assuming that property prices have risen since you purchased it!). It's also possible to have a mortgage linked to a revolving loan facility (see **Overdrafts & Loans** above), where the difference between the capital borrowed and the value of your property can be advanced for other uses, such as home improvements, a car purchase or a holiday. This is a cheap way of borrowing, as the mortgage interest rate is usually much lower than that for a loan, although interest on a mortgage cannot be claimed as a tax allowance in New Zealand. Many New Zealanders use one of these methods to finance the purchase of a holiday bach or crib (a glorified shed), which, because of their often flimsy construction (even more so than most New Zealand homes), don't qualify for a full mortgage.

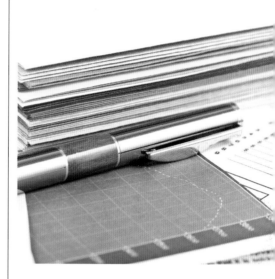

Conditions & Fees

When applying for a mortgage, you must provide proof of your income and outgoings, such as other mortgage payments, rent, other loans and regular commitments (e.g. bills). Proof of income includes three months' pay slips for employees; if you're self-employed, you require an audited copy of your trading accounts for the past three years. Once a loan has been agreed in principle, a lender will provide you with an offer outlining the terms. If you decide to accept the offer, you must usually pay a deposit (likely to be at least $500). If the property purchase doesn't go ahead (for any reason), the deposit should be refundable, although many lenders charge a 'discontinued application fee', which is deducted from the deposit, so it isn't wise to accept a mortgage offer unless you're certain you want to go ahead with a property purchase.

All lenders charge an 'application' fee, usually 1 per cent of the mortgage amount or from $150 to $600 (you won't be charged all of this sum if your application is rejected); there's usually a minimum fee and there may also be a maximum, although many mortgage lenders will negotiate the fees. It isn't usually necessary to have a survey unless you're borrowing over 80 per cent of the value of a property.

If you fail to maintain your mortgage repayments, your property can be repossessed and sold at auction, although this rarely happens in New Zealand, as most lenders are willing to arrange lower repayments when borrowers get into financial difficulties. It's best to contact your lender immediately if you have repayment problems, rather than wait until a huge debt has accumulated. You may be offered the chance to transfer to another type of mortgage or may be able to re-mortgage entirely and gain access to some of the equity in your property.

Foreign Currency Mortgages

It's possible to obtain a foreign currency mortgage, e.g. in Japanese yen, Swiss francs or US dollars, all currencies which, with their historically low interest rates, have provided huge savings for some borrowers in the last few decades. However, you should be cautious about taking out a foreign currency mortgage, as interest rate gains can be wiped out overnight by currency swings. A number of New Zealanders took out Swiss franc loans in the '80s and were unable to maintain their payments when the value of the NZ$ plummeted against the Swiss franc. Most mainstream lenders advise against taking out foreign currency home loans unless you're paid in a foreign currency.

When choosing between a local currency loan and a foreign currency loan, be sure to take into account all costs, fees and possible currency fluctuations. If you have a foreign currency mortgage, you must usually pay commission charges each time you transfer money into a foreign currency to meet your mortgage repayments, although some lenders do this free of charge.

Whatever type of home loan you choose, take time to investigate all the options and bear in mind that mortgage advice offered by lenders can be misleading and isn't to be trusted. One way of finding the best deal is to contact an independent mortgage broker. You should note, however, that brokers earn their living from fees paid by lenders and therefore may not always be impartial. Wherever you obtain advice, always ensure that it's impartial (ask whether an adviser is being paid a commission by a lender).

> **☑ SURVIVAL TIP**
>
> The conditions for foreign currency loans are much stricter than for local currency loans, e.g. they're generally granted only to high-earners (e.g. a minimum of $100,000 a year) and are usually for a minimum of $200,000 and a maximum of 60 per cent of a property's value.

Abel Tasman National Park, South Island

Bluff Hill, Napier, North Island

5.

THE PURCHASE PROCEDURE

This chapter details the purchase procedure for buying a home in New Zealand. It's generally straightforward – hence the brevity of the chapter – although (as in all countries) there are possible pitfalls for the unwary.

It's wise to employ a lawyer before paying any money or signing a contract and, if necessary, have him check anything you're concerned about regarding a property that you're planning to buy.

When you find a house you wish to buy, you must make a formal offer in writing, and most estate agents have a standard form for this purpose. A formal offer has to be made even if you wish to pay the advertised price. The conditions of the offer – e.g. the approval of finance (e.g. a mortgage), a satisfactory independent valuation, a satisfactory title search, the sale of another home – must be specified in the offer. Unless you've agreed to pay the asking price, there then follows a bargaining process which concludes when both parties have agreed a price for the property. During this process, there's no need to draft a new offer each time you raise the proposed price; the offer can be signed and countersigned a number of times until agreement is reached.

Because the time between viewing a property and signing a contract can be short, you should have your finances arranged before you start looking. Most banks will give you an 'in principle' decision on a mortgage before you've found a suitable property and issue you with a mortgage guarantee certificate. This allows you to make an offer in the knowledge that, assuming the property is in order and your financial circumstances haven't changed, you'll be lent the required amount of money.

CONVEYANCE

Conveyance (often called conveyancing) is the legal term for the process of buying and selling properties and transferring ownership via the title deed. There are two main stages of conveyance: the first leads to the exchange of contracts; the second leads to the completion of the sale, when you become the new owner.

Property conveyance in New Zealand is usually done by a lawyer, but it's straightforward and you can do it yourself (although most choose not to). Irrespective of whether you employ a professional or do your own conveyance, the following should be done before a purchase:

- Verifying that a property belongs to the vendor or that he has legal authority to sell it;

- Checking for the existence of any clauses in the deeds restricting the use, development and possibly appearance of the property (known as restrictive covenants);

- Checking that there are no encumbrances or liens, e.g. mortgages or loans, against the property or any outstanding debts such as local taxes or utility bills – or that these are cancelled by the vendor before completion (i.e. a conditional clause to that effect is inserted into the contract – see page 152);

⚠ Caution

You must ensure that any debts against a property are cleared before you complete a purchase – a new owner is liable for any debts on a property once it's sold.

- Enquiring about any planned developments that may affect the value of the property (like a new airport runway or motorway at the bottom of the garden);

- Ensuring that planning or building permits are in order (e.g. for water, electricity and sewerage connection). You should also check the drainage or sewerage service diagrams for a home.

- Ensuring that legal title is obtained and arranging the necessary registration of ownership and payment of taxes such as stamp duty.

Conveyance by a lawyer, who's the only professional permitted to charge for the service, normally costs between $600 and $2,000. The fee may include the land transfer registration fee of $128 (see page 109).

There's no fixed scale of conveyance charges, as this was abolished in 1984, so it's worth shopping around and haggling over the cost. It's possible to find a lawyer who will do the job for as little as $400.

Once you've instructed a solicitor to act on your behalf in a property purchase, the process is usually swift (Land Information New Zealand is efficient) and it's rare to discover hidden horrors, such as dozens of relatives laying claim to a property.

Cross-leasing

One peculiarly local concept in property purchase is cross-leasing (also known as X-leasing). This usually applies in a situation where the previous owner of a section has leased part of it for the construction of another home (e.g. the one you're planning to buy). In this case, your ownership of the land is leasehold rather than freehold, usually for the balance of a period such as 100 years, at a nominal rent. To all intents and purposes your title to an X-leased section is as secure as freehold; your lawyer will explain if there are any conditions that you need to be aware of.

Land Information Memorandum

You should also ask your lawyer to obtain a Land Information Memorandum (LIM) report from the local council (see page 122), which describes the title of the land, outlines the official boundaries and buildings, the changes allowed to these buildings and flood risks. This useful document (particularly for future reference) can cost anything from $2 to $1,500 ($200 to $300 is usual) depending on the property and the details included, so you should check the cost in advance. Application for a LIM must be made in writing to the local council and it's usually issued within ten working days.

Care should be exercised, however, because LIMs have a reputation for being unreliable. This isn't so much because the information they contain is inaccurate, as because it's incomplete. Once you receive a LIM, you (or

your solicitor) should therefore visit the local council to confirm that they don't have other information about the property. To discover even more about a property that interests you, you can buy the government's *Quotable Value* (*QV*), which reveals the prices other properties in the area are being sold for, for around $5. Another $4 will tell you how much the particular property sold for previously, while $50 buys a hazard report.

CONTRACT

As soon the price is agreed, you must sign a sales contract, which commits you to go through with the purchase, on certain conditions, e.g. you aren't obliged to go ahead with the purchase if you find out that a new road is about to be built through the living room (see **Conditional Clauses** below), but you cannot back out because you decide that you don't like the house or cannot afford it, unless you pay compensation. You also cannot subsequently reduce the price you've agreed to pay.

Many estate agents try to make purchasers sign a contract as soon as a sale is agreed, i.e. the day you view the property and say that you want it.

⚠ Caution

You shouldn't sign a contract before taking legal advice and confirming that the title is clear.

If you feel obliged to sign a contract before the conveyance checks are complete, you should ask your lawyer to insert a clause in the contract to the effect that the contract is null and void if any problems arise. However, there's no legal requirement to sign a contract immediately, so don't allow yourself to be pressured into signing. It's usually better to pass up a property if, for example, the agent says that another party is keen to sign (which may in any case be a bluff), rather than buy a property that you aren't sure about.

The advantage of the New Zealand system over, say, that in the UK is that the seller cannot accept a higher offer after he has signed a contract with you (i.e. gazump you), although most estate agents will try to push up the price before pressing the highest bidder to sign a contract.

A deposit of 10 per cent is required when a sales contract is signed. This is usually non-refundable, but most contracts include a clause requiring its return if the title to the property isn't clear or the land is subject to government requisition (compulsory purchase).

When buying a property in New Zealand, it's the exception rather than the rule to have a structural survey carried out. The main exception is if you're borrowing more than 80 per cent of the value of the property, when the lender usually insists that a survey and valuation are carried out to protect their interests. Nevertheless, particularly if the property is of a type susceptible to leaky building syndrome (see page 92), you're strongly advised to have a survey carried out before committing yourself to a purchase.

Conditional Clauses

Contracts often contain conditional clauses, such as the sale being conditional on a good survey report or on finance being obtained (see below). Conditions usually apply to events out of the control of the vendor or buyer, although almost anything agreed between the buyer and vendor can be included in a contract. If any conditions aren't met, the contract can be suspended or declared null and void and the deposit returned. However, if you fail to go through with a purchase and aren't covered by a clause in the contract, you forfeit your deposit or might even be compelled to complete a purchase.

When signing a contract to buy a home or land on which you require a loan, you should include a clause regarding your ability to obtain finance. This makes the contract 'subject to finance'; if you cannot obtain finance within the time specified in the contract, e.g. 7 to 14 days, it becomes null and void and you won't have to proceed. Without a finance clause, you could be sued by the vendor for failing to buy the property. If you cannot arrange finance in the specified time, you can ask for an extension to the completion date, but you may be liable for penalty interest.

If any fixtures or fittings, such as carpets, curtains or furniture, are included in the purchase price, you should have them listed in an addendum to the contract.

FINAL CHECKS

Before completion it's wise to carry out the following checks on the property:

- Verify that the property is in the same condition as when you offered to buy it. If its condition has deteriorated, you may seek compensation from the seller.

- Verify that items including on the fixtures and fittings inventory are still present (and haven't been replaced by inferior, possibly second-hand, items) and in good condition/working order.

- Check that any agreed repair or restoration work has been carried out.

6.

MOVING HOUSE

This chapter contains information about shipping your belongings and immigration and customs procedures, plus checklists of the tasks to be completed before or soon after arrival in New Zealand, and suggestions for finding local help and information.

SHIPPING YOUR BELONGINGS

The cost of removing the contents of an average three-bedroom property from Europe or North America to the Antipodes is usually from around GB£7,500 to £10,000 (US$15,000 to $20,000), depending on the country or region you're moving from and the part of New Zealand you're moving to (e.g. a house in the suburbs of Auckland or a remote retreat in the South Island). Removal companies usually take care of the paperwork and ensure that the correct documents are provided and properly completed (see **Customs** on page 159). Major international moving companies generally provide a wealth of information and can advise on a wide range of matters regarding an international relocation. It's also wise to check the procedure for shipping your belongings to New Zealand with the relevant embassy or consulate in the country where you live.

It's recommended to use a major shipping company with a good reputation. For international moves it's best to use a company that's a member of the International Federation of Furniture Removers (FIDI) or the Overseas Moving Network International (OMNI), with experience in New Zealand. Members of FIDI and OMNI usually subscribe to an advance payment scheme providing a guarantee: if a member company fails to fulfil its commitments to a client, the removal is completed at the agreed cost by another company or your money is refunded. Some removal companies have subsidiaries or affiliates in New Zealand, which may be more convenient if you encounter problems or need to make an insurance claim.

You should obtain at least three written quotations before choosing a company, as costs can vary considerably. Moving companies should send a representative to provide a detailed quotation. Most companies will pack your belongings and provide packing cases and special containers, although this is naturally more expensive than packing them yourself. Ask a company how fragile and valuable items are packed and whether the cost of packing cases, materials and insurance (see below) is included in a quotation. If you're doing your own packing, most shipping companies will provide packing crates and boxes. Shipments are charged by volume, e.g. the cubic metre in Europe and the cubic foot in the US.

If you're flexible about the delivery date, shipping companies will quote a lower fee based on a 'part load', where the cost is shared with other deliveries. This can result in savings of 50 per cent or more compared with an individual delivery. Whether you have an individual or shared delivery, obtain the maximum transit period in writing; otherwise you may need to wait months for delivery!

Be sure fully to insure your belongings during removal with a well established insurance company. Don't insure with a shipping company that carries its own insurance, as its rates are usually high and it may fight every penny or cent of a claim. Insurance premiums are usually 1 to 2 per cent of the declared value of your goods, depending on the type of cover chosen. It's prudent to make a photographic or video record of valuables for insurance purposes.

Most insurance policies provide cover for 'all risks' on a replacement value basis. Note, however, that china, glass and other breakables can usually be included in an all-risks policy only when they're packed by the removal company and insurance usually covers total loss or loss of a particular crate only, rather than individual items (unless they were packed by the shipping company).

If there are any obvious breakages or damaged items, they must be noted and listed before you sign the delivery bill. If you need to make a claim, be sure to read the small

print, as some companies require clients to make a claim within a few days, although seven is usual. Send a claim by registered post. Some insurance companies apply an 'excess' of around 1 per cent of the total shipment value when assessing claims. This means that if your shipment is valued at $30,000, there's no point in making a claim for less than $300.

If you're unable to ship your belongings directly to New Zealand, most shipping companies will put them into storage and some allow a limited free storage period before shipment, e.g. 14 days, after which you may be charged between $60 and $100 per month for an average container, excluding insurance, although prices (and the quality of storage facilities) vary greatly.

⚠ Caution

If you need to put your household effects into storage, it's imperative to have them fully insured, as warehouses have been known to burn down!

Make a complete list of everything to be moved and give a copy to the removal company. Don't include anything illegal (e.g. guns, bombs or drugs) with your belongings, as customs checks can be rigorous and penalties severe.

Provide the shipping company with detailed instructions of how to find your Antipodean address from the nearest main road and a telephone number where you can be contacted. If your New Zealand home has poor or impossible access for a large truck, you must inform the shipping company (the ground must also be firm enough to support a heavy vehicle). Note also that, if furniture needs to be taken in through an upstairs window (e.g. to an apartment), you may need to pay extra. You should also make a simple floor plan of your new home with rooms numbered and mark corresponding numbers on furniture and boxes as they're packed, so that the removal company will know where everything is to go and you can leave them to it.

After considering the shipping costs, you may decide to ship only selected small items of furniture and personal effects, and buy new bulky items of furniture Down Under. If you're moving abroad permanently, take the opportunity to sell, give away or throw out at least half of your possessions; it will cut down your removal bill, clear your mind and make life simpler, and you'll have the added pleasure of buying new furniture that suits your new house.

Bear in mind when moving home that everything that can go wrong often does, so allow plenty of time and try not to arrange the move from your old home on the same day as the new owner is moving in; that's just asking for fate to intervene! See also **Pets** on page 34, **Customs** on page 159 and the **Checklists** on page 165.

PRE-DEPARTURE HEALTH CHECK

If you're planning to take up residence in New Zealand, even for part of the year only, it's wise to have a health check (including general health, eyes, teeth, etc.) before your arrival, particularly if you have a record of poor health or are elderly. If you're already taking medicine regularly, you should note that the brand names of medicines vary from country to

country, and you should ask your doctor for the generic name. If you wish to match medication prescribed abroad, you'll need a current prescription with the medication's trade name, the manufacturer's name, the chemical name and the dosage. Most medicines have an equivalent in other countries, although particular brands may be difficult or impossible to obtain in New Zealand.

It's possible to have medication sent from abroad, when no import duty or value added tax is usually payable. If you're visiting a holiday home in New Zealand, you should take sufficient medication to cover your stay, but make sure that when you travel you carry a letter from your doctor describing the medication and your condition to show to customs officials. It's also wise to take some of your favourite non-prescription medicines, such as pain killers, cold and flu remedies and lotions, as they may be difficult or impossible to obtain in New Zealand or may be much more expensive. If applicable, take a spare pair of spectacles or contact lenses, dentures and hearing aid with you.

IMMIGRATION

When you arrive in New Zealand, your passport and other papers will be inspected by an immigration officer and (provided everything is in order) you'll be given permission to enter and remain for the purpose and the period for which you've applied. It's worth noting that visitors can be refused entry (even with a valid visa) if an immigration officer believes that they could be a threat to public security or health, i.e. a visa doesn't automatically grant right of entry. Visitors arriving from countries that come under the visa waiver scheme can apply for a visitor permit on arrival using the New Zealand Passenger Arrival Card that's provided on aircraft and ships (see **Customs** below). Bear in mind that you may be expected to produce other documents to support your claim for entry, such as a return ticket and/or evidence of funds. New Zealand immigration officials are usually fairly amiable, although certain Asian visitors, young people on working holidays (who rank highly as potential illegal immigrants) and those coming from notorious drug areas such as Asia or South America may be subjected to 'scrutiny'.

☑ SURVIVAL TIP

Immigration officials may be curt and/or rude. Stay calm and always answer questions politely – being rude or curt in return will only prolong the entry process.

Whatever your appearance and the nature of your visit, you should carry evidence of your funds (or access to funds) and proof of why you're entering New Zealand and why you need to leave (e.g. to return to work or study overseas).

Take care how you answer seemingly innocent questions from immigration officials (immigration officials **never** ask innocent questions), as you could find yourself being refused entry if you give incriminating answers. Whatever the question, never imply that you may remain in New Zealand longer than the period permitted or for a purpose other than that for which you've been granted permission. For example, if you aren't permitted to work in New Zealand, you could be asked, "Would you like to work in New Zealand?" If you reply, "Yes", even if you have no intention of doing so, you could be refused entry.

If you arrive in New Zealand at a location which isn't an authorised customs airport or seaport, you're required to report to an immigration officer within 72 hours of your arrival and must meet the usual visa requirements. The harbour master or airfield owner will tell you where to report.

CUSTOMS

The New Zealand Customs Service carries out checks at all points of entry into the country to enforce customs regulations, which apply to everyone entering the country, whether residents, visitors or migrants. There are no concessions, even for visitors from Australia, despite the 'close economic agreement' with New Zealand (apparently they aren't that close!). Before your arrival in New Zealand you'll be given a New Zealand

Passenger Arrival Card, which you must complete and give to customs when you arrive. This card includes a declaration stating whether you have any banned, restricted or dutiable goods (i.e. above your duty-free allowance – see below). Most ports of entry operate a two-channel system: red for those with goods to declare and green for those with nothing to declare. If you think you have goods that must be declared (i.e. that are prohibited or restricted or above your duty-free allowance – see below) or aren't sure, you should go through the red channel. If you don't make a declaration, you may be subject to a random check.

Prohibited & Restricted Goods

In addition to the usual items such as drugs, pornography, guns and explosives (which you cannot import without permission), anything with plant or animal origins may be prohibited or subject to import restrictions under New Zealand's 'Biosecurity' laws.

⚠ **Caution**

Breaches of the strict New Zealand Biosecurity laws result in an instant $200 fine and the possibility of an additional fine of up to $100,000 for an individual ($200,000 for a corporation) and of up to five years in prison.

Food, plants, dried flowers, seeds and potpourri mustn't be imported into New Zealand under any circumstances. You can be fined for importing an apple or kiwi fruit, even if it came from New Zealand in the first place!

There are also restrictions governing the following:

● animals or items made from animal feathers, fur, horns, skin, tusks, etc;

● equipment used with animals, including riding tackle;

● biological specimens;

● garden tools, furniture and ornaments;

● lawn mowers, strimmers, etc;

● tents and camping equipment;

● golf clubs;

● vacuum cleaners, brooms and brushes;

● wicker and cane items;

● bicycles;

● walking and gardening boots.

The above are often subject to inspection, cleaning and fumigation procedures, for which you may be charged a fee, if not an outright ban. It therefore isn't recommended to import any of these items into New Zealand. If you wish to, you should obtain advice from customs in advance and declare them on arrival.

On your Arrival Card you're asked to declare whether you've been camping

or hiking in forest or parkland in the previous 30 days, and whether you've been in contact with animals other than domestic cats and dogs. You must also list the countries you've visited within the previous 30 days.

Pets and other animals shouldn't be imported into New Zealand without authorisation from customs. Should you wish to take your pet to New Zealand, you should entrust the job to a specialist pet shipping service. You require a health certificate provided by a vet in your home country and your pet must undergo a period of quarantine after it arrives in New Zealand (exemptions apply under certain conditions to pets imported from Australia, Hawaii,

Norway, Singapore, Sweden and the UK). The good news is that you won't be charged duty on your pet.

If you bring prescribed medicines with you, you should carry a prescription or letter from your doctor stating that the medicine is being used under a doctor's direction and is necessary for your health. You should carry medicines in their original containers. You must also make a declaration if you wish to import more than $10,000 in cash.

Information

If you're in any doubt about whether anything you wish to import into New Zealand is banned or restricted, you should make inquiries at a New Zealand embassy, consulate or high commission, or directly to the New Zealand Customs Service (☎ freephone 0800-428 786 or 04-473 6099, 💻 www.customs.govt.nz) or contact the New Zealand Customs office at your point of entry:

- **Auckland:** Customhouse, 50 Anzac Avenue, PO Box 29 (☎ 09-359 6655).

- **Auckland International Airport:** PO Box 73 003, Mangere (☎ 09-275 9059).

- **Christchurch:** 6 Orchard Road, PO Box 14 086 (☎ 03-358 0600).

- **Dunedin:** 32 Portsmouth Drive, Private Bag 1928 (☎ 03-477 9251).

- **Invercargill:** Business Centre, Ground Floor, Menzies Building, 1

Esk Street, PO Box 840 (☎ 03-218 7329).

- **Lyttelton:** 5th Floor, Shadbolt House, Norwich Quay, PO Box 40 (☎ 03-328 7259).
- **Napier:** Dungevan House, 215 Hastings Street, PO Box 440 (☎ 06-835 5799).
- **Nelson:** 10 Low Street, PO Box 66 (☎ 03-548 1484).
- **New Plymouth:** 54-56 Currie Street, PO Box 136 (☎ 06-758 5721).
- **Opua:** PO Box 42 (☎ 029-602 1669).
- **Tauranga:** 27-33 Nikau Crescent, PO Box 5014 (☎ 07-575 9699).
- **Wellington:** Head Office, The Customhouse, 17-21 Whitmore Street, PO Box 2218 (☎ 04-473 6099).
- **Whangarei:** PO Box 4155 (☎ 029-250 9305).

Duty-free Allowances

Apart from personal effects (such as clothing), everyone aged over 17 entering the country is allowed certain duty-free allowances which include:

- 200 cigarettes or 250g of tobacco or 50 cigars or a combination of all three not weighing more than 250g;
- 4.5 litres of wine or beer;
- a 1.125-litre bottle of spirit or liqueur.

You may also import other goods (e.g. gifts) valued up to $700. New Zealand law allows you to purchase duty-free goods at a New Zealand airport on arrival, although if you exceed your allowance you can be charged customs duty plus goods and services tax (GST) at 12.5 per cent. If you're entering the country to take up residence, you can also import used household effects and a car, although it's unlikely you'll be bringing these when you arrive at the airport! New Zealanders are entitled to the same allowances if they've been out of the country and living abroad for at least 21 months.

EMBASSY REGISTRATION

Nationals of some countries are required to register with their embassy or consulate after taking up residence in New Zealand, and most embassies like to keep a record of their country's citizens who are resident in New Zealand (it helps to justify their existence).

FINDING HELP

One of the biggest difficulties facing new arrivals in New Zealand is how and where to obtain help with day-to-day problems – for example, paying utility bills, enrolling a child in school or simply disposing of rubbish. This book will go some way towards answering your questions – as will our sister book *Living and Working in New Zealand* – although you'll also need detailed local information. How successful you are in finding this depends on your employer, the town or area where you live (e.g. those who live and work in a major city are much better served than those living in rural areas), your nationality and English proficiency, even your sex.

You may find that acquaintances, colleagues and friends can help, as they're often able to proffer advice based on their own experiences and mistakes – although you may have none of these on your arrival in the country! However, their advice may be irrelevant to your situation – or even inaccurate.

The government of New Zealand provides a reception area with information on accommodation and job-finding help, and there's a wealth of settlement programmes for migrants. Citizens' advice bureaux (CABs), local council offices and tourist offices are excellent sources of reliable information on a wide range of subjects. Some companies may have a department or member of staff whose job is to help new arrivals, or they may contract this job out to a local company. Women living in or near a city or major town are able to turn to many women's clubs and organisations for help (men aren't so well served). There are numerous expatriate associations, clubs and organisations in the major cities and large towns (including 'settlers' or 'friendship' associations) for immigrants from most countries, providing detailed local information on all aspects of life, including health services, housing costs, schools, shopping and much more. Women living in country areas will find a good network of support provided by Country Women's Institutes.

Many organisations produce booklets, data sheets and newsletters, operate libraries, and organise a variety of social

Akaroa harbour, Banks Peninsula, South Island

events, which may include day and evening classes ranging from cooking to English classes. For a list of local clubs, look under 'Clubs and Associations' in the yellow pages. The Department of Immigration or local authority can put you in touch with clubs and societies in the city or area where you plan to live. Most embassies and consulates provide information bulletin boards (accommodation, jobs, travel, etc.) and keep lists of social clubs and societies, and many businesses (e.g. banks and building societies) produce books and leaflets containing useful information for newcomers. Libraries and bookshops usually have books about the local area (see also **Appendix B**).

MOVING IN

One of the most important tasks to perform after moving into a new home is to make an inventory of the fixtures and fittings and, if applicable, the furniture and furnishings, and check that these are in accordance with your contract – whether purchase or rental.

If your property was purchased, you should check that the previous owner hasn't absconded with any fixtures and fittings that were included in the price, e.g. carpets, light fittings, curtains, furniture, kitchen appliances, garden ornaments, plants or doors – even if you did a final check before completion (see page 165).

When moving into a long-term rental property, you must complete an inventory of its contents and a report on its condition. This includes the condition of fixtures and fittings, the state of furniture and furnishings, the cleanliness and state of the decoration, and any damaged or missing items. An inventory should be provided by your landlord or agent and may include every single item in a furnished property (even the number of teaspoons). The inventory check should be carried out in your presence, both when taking over and when terminating a rental agreement. If an inventory isn't provided, you should insist on one being prepared and annexed to the lease. If you find a serious fault after signing the inventory, send a registered letter to your landlord and ask for it to be attached to the inventory.

It's wise to obtain written instructions from the previous owner (or agent or current owner if you're renting) regarding the operation of appliances, heating and air-conditioning systems, maintenance of grounds, gardens and lawns and swimming pool, care of surfaces such as wooden or marble floors, and the names of reliable local maintenance men.

Check with your town hall regarding local regulation of such things as rubbish collection, recycling and on-road parking.

CHECKLISTS

Before Arrival

The following list contains a summary of the tasks that should (if possible) be completed before your arrival in New Zealand:

- Obtain a visa (if applicable) for all your family members (see **Chapter 1**). Obviously this **must** be done before your arrival.

- If possible (and applicable), visit New Zealand before your move to arrange schooling for your children and find a job.

- Arrange temporary or permanent accommodation.

- Arrange for the shipment of your personal effects (see page 155).

- Arrange health insurance for your family (see page 188). This is essential if you won't be covered by New Zealand's public healthcare scheme.

- Open a local bank account and transfer some funds (see page 131). You should also obtain some local currency before your arrival, which saves you having to change money immediately on arrival.

- Obtain an international driver's permit, if necessary.

- Obtain an international credit card (or two), which will prove invaluable during your first few months Down Under.

- Collect and update your records, including those relating to your family's education, employment (including job references), insurance (e.g. car insurance), and medical and professional history.

Don't forget to bring the above documents with you if relevant, plus bank account and credit card details, birth certificates, death certificate (if a widow or widower), divorce papers, driving licences, educational diplomas and professional certificates, employment references, insurance policies, marriage certificate, medical and dental records, receipts for any valuables you're bringing with you and student identity cards. You also need any documents that were necessary to obtain your visa, plus a number of passport-size photographs.

After Arrival

The following list contains a summary of tasks to be completed after your arrival in New Zealand (if not done before):

- On arrival at the airport or port, have your visa cancelled and passport stamped, as applicable.

- If you aren't importing a car, rent one for a week or two until you buy one locally. It's difficult or impossible to get around in rural areas without a car.

- Register with your local embassy or consulate (see page 162).

- If you plan to work in New Zealand, you need to obtain an Inland Revenue Department (IRD) number from your local Inland Revenue office.

- Open an account at a local bank and give the details to your employer (if applicable) and other local businesses, such as your landlord or utility companies.

- Join New Zealand's public healthcare system. This also applies to temporary residents if your home country has a reciprocal agreement.

- Arrange schooling for your children.

- Find a local doctor and dentist.

- Arrange whatever insurance is necessary (see **Chapter 8**), including health insurance (see page 188) and home contents insurance (see page 185).

Maori carving

Maybe the yacht will have to wait until next year...

7.
TAXATION

An important consideration when you're buying a home in New Zealand is taxation, as you may be liable for income tax, property tax and gift tax, even if you don't plan to live there permanently. It's advisable to obtain income tax advice before moving, as there are usually a number of things you can do in advance to reduce your tax liability, both in New Zealand and abroad. Be sure to consult a tax adviser who is familiar with the New Zealand tax system and that of your present country of residence. For example, you may be able to avoid paying tax on a business abroad if you establish residence and domicile in New Zealand before you sell it. On the other hand, if you sell a foreign home after establishing your principal residence in Australia, it becomes a second home and you may then be liable to capital gains tax abroad (this is a complicated subject and you should obtain expert advice). You should notify the tax authorities in your former country of residence that you're going to live permanently in New Zealand.

There's no wealth tax, capital gains tax, inheritance (estate) tax or local income tax in New Zealand (hurrah!). On the other hand, income tax is levied on all income (there's no exemption on the first few thousand dollars, as in many countries), including income derived from any money-making scheme, tax rates start at a whopping 19.5 per cent (see **Tax Rates** on page 173), there's a fringe benefits tax of between 49 and 64 per cent, and there's no tax exemption for mortgage interest or employment expenses (unless you're self-employed).

Note in particular that profit from the sale of property and land is subject to income tax if the principal purpose of purchasing it was to resell it or if your business is dealing in property.

In addition, gains resulting from certain investments, such as debentures and some preference shares, options and leases, may be taxable irrespective of whether the nature of the gain is capital or income.

INCOME TAX

Generally speaking, income tax in New Zealand is below average for a developed country. During the '90s most people saw their income tax reduced, but in the 21st century income taxes have increased. Most New Zealanders are resigned to paying taxes (tax evasion isn't a national sport as it is in some countries) and in any case the country has a system of pay-as-you-earn (PAYE) that ensures that tax is deducted at source from employees' salaries.

The tax system in New Zealand isn't particularly complicated. It's designed so that most people can prepare and file their own tax returns, although if you have many sources of income you may need to seek help from an accountant. The Inland Revenue Department (IRD) provides a comprehensive help service and publishes numerous fact sheets and brochures for taxpayers. The following helplines are available:

● Income tax and general enquiries – ☎ 0800-227 774 or 04-798 0779;

● Overdue tax and returns – ☎ 0800-227 771;

● Student loan repayments – ☎ 0800-377 778;

● Child support enquiries – ☎ 0800-221 221;

● Forms and stationery – ☎ 0800-101 035.

The IRD also has a comprehensive website (🖥 www.ird.govt.nz), which includes downloadable fact sheets and forms.

Liability

Your country of domicile determines whether you're liable to pay New Zealand income tax. New Zealand residents are taxed on their worldwide income, while non-residents are subject to income tax only on income derived from New Zealand. To determine 'domicile', the tax authorities apply what's known as the 'permanent place of abode test', although this is arbitrary and isn't enshrined in New Zealand tax law. Usually, anyone who is present in New Zealand for more than 183 days in a 12-month period is considered resident here and liable to pay taxes. You don't need to be a permanent resident to be liable, and the existence of financial and social ties (including bank accounts and club memberships) may be taken as evidence of domicile. In theory, you're exempt from New Zealand taxes if you aren't present in New Zealand for 325 days in a 12-month period. However, if you maintain a home in the country, you cannot be considered non-resident, no matter how brief your stay. If you decide to leave New Zealand, you should inform your local IRD office. Note that the 325-day time limit doesn't start

until the IRD has confirmed that you've ceased to become a resident!

Income subject to tax in New Zealand includes commissions, dividends, interest, profits or gains from a business, rents, royalties, salary and wages, and trust distributions.

Double Taxation

New Zealand has double-taxation treaties with 32 countries: Australia, Belgium, Canada, Chile, China, Denmark, Fiji, Finland, France, Germany, India, Indonesia, Ireland, Italy, Japan, Korea (South), Malaysia, the Netherlands, Norway, the Philippines, Poland, the Russian Federation, Singapore, South Africa, Spain, Sweden, Switzerland, Taiwan, Thailand, the UAE, the UK and the US.

> Despite their name, double-taxation treaties are designed to ensure that income which has been taxed in one treaty country isn't taxed again in another.

A treaty establishes a tax credit or exemption on certain kinds of income, either in the taxpayer's country of residence or in the country where the income is earned. Where applicable, a double-taxation treaty prevails over local law.

IRD Number

Before you start work in New Zealand, you should register with your local IRD office (☎ freephone 0800-227 774, 🖥

www. ird.govt.nz), which will issue you with an IRD or tax file number, which must be quoted on tax documents and when you open a bank account, for example. To apply for your IRD number you need to complete an IRD form and send a copy of your passport. IRD numbers are usually issued within five working days.

Tax Code

Every taxpayer in New Zealand is required to complete a Tax Code Declaration (form IR330) when they start employment and whenever there are any changes in their employment circumstances, e.g. if working hours are reduced. You should be given the form by your employer, who returns it to the IRD. The tax code for most employees is M. It's important that you fill in the form correctly, as the amount of tax you pay is based on the information provided.

Tax Return & Tax Bill

Recent changes in tax legislation have made tax calculations simpler and more accurate, and tax returns easier to complete. Until recently, everyone who earned an income in New Zealand had to file an income tax return annually with the Commissioner of the Inland Revenue Department. However, individuals who receive income from employment subject to PAYE or from interest and dividends subject to resident withholding tax

(RWT) are no longer required to do so.

> **⚠ Caution**
>
> **All individuals who derive income that isn't taxed at the time of payment or who run a business must file an annual return. The return, known as an IR3, is sent to you automatically each year.**

The New Zealand tax year runs from 1st April to 31st March, and returns must be filed by 7th July. The IRD then issues a tax assessment (i.e. a bill) showing the amount payable. Payments can be made in a variety of ways, including by cheque, by electronic payment or direct debit from your bank, by cash or cheque at any branch of the Westpac Trust bank, or online via the internet banking facility of any major New Zealand bank.

Personal Tax Summaries

Employees whose income tax is deducted at source by their employer under PAYE and who don't have any other income receive a Personal Tax Summary from the IRD based on information provided by employers. You may also receive a Personal Tax Summary if you receive family assistance payments, if you have a student loan and qualify for an interest write-off, or if you've paid too little or too much tax in the relevant year. The Personal Tax Summary shows whether you're entitled to a tax refund or have tax to pay. If you have tax to pay, you must pay it by 7th February or 7th April depending on your circumstances. If you're entitled to a refund, it will be paid when you've confirmed that you agree with the amount or within 30 days if the amount owing is less than $200.

Rebates

Before you're liable for income tax, you can deduct certain allowances (known as rebates) from your gross salary, which reduce your tax bill. Some rebates, such as the low earner rebate, are built into the PAYE rates but others, such as the housekeeper, childcare and donations rebates, must be claimed from the IRD. Key rebates include:

● **Child taxpayer rebate** ($156) – available for children under 15 or still at school;

● **Housekeeper rebate** ($310) – if you paid $940 or more for childcare or a housekeeper;

● **Donations rebate** ($630) – on charitable donations of $1,890 or more;

● **Low income earner rebate** – 4.5 per cent of net income up to $9,880 and 1.5 per cent of income between $9,880 and $38,000.

Tax rebates must be claimed by 30th September following the end of the relevant tax year. Expenses associated with employment (such as clothing or travel to work) cannot usually be claimed as a tax allowance in New Zealand. However, the self-employed can claim legitimate business expenses. Interest on a mortgage cannot be claimed as a tax allowance in New Zealand.

Tax Rates

It has become common practice in recent years for the rate of income tax to be adjusted annually in the July budget. There are three tax rates in New Zealand, which are listed below. It's important to note that earnings such as interest, rents, dividends and royalties is taxable as income in New Zealand, rather than separately as is the case in some other countries.

Resident Withholding Tax

Interest on bank and other savings accounts is paid after deduction of

Taxable Income	Tax Rate	Cumulative Tax
Up to $38,000	19.5%	$7,410
$38,001 to $60,000	33%	$14,670
Over $60,000	39%	

resident withholding tax (RWT) at a rate equivalent to the basic rate of income tax (19.5 per cent). If, however, you don't provide your IRD or tax file number (see page 171) to a bank when opening an account, it's taxed at the higher rate (39 per cent).

Businesses & Self-employment

Income tax for the self-employed and small businesses is broadly similar to that of wage and salary earners. You're sent a tax return (form IR3) at the end of your financial year, which you must complete and return by the seventh day of the fourth month following the end of your financial year. Therefore, if your financial year is the same as the tax year (April to March), your tax return must be filed by 7th July each year. You can apply to have a financial year that differs from the tax year. The self-employed are required to pay a proportion of their estimated tax on a monthly basis, which is based on their previous year's liability. When your tax return is submitted, the IRD reconciles the tax due with the sum already paid and issues a tax assessment for any tax payable or a refund if you've overpaid. Company tax is levied at a flat rate of 33 per cent, whether a company is resident or non-resident.

PROPERTY TAX

Property tax (rates) is levied by local authorities and is based on the rateable value (valuation) of properties. Bills are sent out at the beginning of the financial year and are payable by whoever occupies the property, whether it's the owner or a tenant. If you occupy a property for just part of a year, only a proportion of the tax is payable. The annual bill for an average family house is between $1,000 and $2,000. It isn't uncommon for residents, either individually or collectively, to appeal against their property valuation in order to obtain a tax reduction.

Property tax pays for local services such as street cleaning, lighting and subsidies paid to local public transport companies. It usually includes rubbish collection (although an extra charge is levied in some areas), recycling services and water, although in some areas such as Auckland, water is billed separately.

Auckland residents have been protesting for the last few years, because although water charges were recently excluded from their rates (most households pay over $800 per year), these weren't reduced!

GIFT DUTY

Gift duty (known as gift tax in other countries) is imposed at fixed rates on certain gifts, including property in New Zealand or elsewhere, if the donor was domiciled in New Zealand at the time of the gift. Gifts that aren't taxable include those made to charities, gifts for the maintenance or education of your immediate family, and gifts up to $2,000 per year to an individual, if they're made as part of the donor's normal expenditure, e.g. birthday and Christmas presents. The rates of gift duty are shown below.

FRINGE BENEFIT TAX

Fringe benefit tax (FBT) is payable by employers on the value of most fringe benefits paid to employees in New Zealand. The rate varies between 49 and 64 per cent. Benefits that attract FBT include company cars; low-interest loans; free, subsidised or discounted goods and services; and employer contributions to investment funds, insurance, health insurance and superannuation schemes. For further information, see the *Fringe benefit tax return guide* (IR425).

GOODS & SERVICES TAX

A goods and services tax (GST) is levied in New Zealand, which is essentially the same as the value added tax levied in European Union countries but isn't a sales tax as in the US.

GST is the second-largest component of tax revenue and is levied at a single rate of 12.5 per cent on most goods and services, although some are exempt (e.g. the letting of residential accommodation).

When you import goods into New Zealand, GST (and in some cases also customs duty) is assessed on their value, except in the case of certain exempt goods, including household goods and precious metals. Immigrants can import their possessions free of

Value of Gift	Rate of Duty
below $27,000	zero
$27,001 to 36,000	5% on amount over $27,000
$36,001 to $54,000	$450 plus 10% of amount over $36,000
$54,001 to $72,000	$2,250 plus 20% of amount over $54,000
over $72,000	$5,850 plus 25% of amount over $72,000

duty and tax, provided they've been owned and used before their arrival. This also applies to used cars, provided you meet the import criteria.

All businesses with a turnover of $40,000 or more within a 12-month period must register for GST with the Inland Revenue Department and levy GST on goods and services supplied – unless they're exempt (exempt services include financial services).

Similarly, businesses can reclaim GST paid on goods and services used in their business. A GST return must usually be filed every two months, although businesses with a turnover of less than $250,000 per year can choose to file a return every six months, and those with an annual turnover of over $24m must file monthly. For further information on GST contact the Inland Revenue on ☎ freephone 0800-377 776.

8.

INSURANCE

An important aspect of owning a home in New Zealand (or anywhere else) is insurance, not only for the home itself and its contents, but also for you and your family when visiting New Zealand. It's vital to ensure that you have sufficient insurance when visiting your home abroad, including building and contents insurance, third-party liability insurance, health insurance and travel insurance. This chapter deals with health, household, life, and holiday or travel insurance. Information about other types of insurance (e.g. car and third-party liability) can be found in *Living and Working in New Zealand* **(Survival Books – see page 283).**

New Zealand has an innovative approach to insurance, which is quite different from that in most western European countries, where state schemes pay benefits in the event of sickness, unemployment and other misfortunes. New Zealand's system isn't insurance based, and individuals aren't required to make contributions in order to benefit (although, as the substantial costs are funded by general taxation, they cannot be said to be free to taxpayers. New Zealand has also taken the concept of state insurance a step further than most other countries, and provides universal accident insurance to all citizens, residents and visitors (see **Accident Compensation Scheme** on page 192).

New Zealand's 'free' state insurance doesn't mean that you don't need to take out private insurance. The state schemes don't, by any means, cover every eventuality and neither are the benefits generous, meaning that private insurance is recommended, if not essential.

It's unnecessary to spend half your income insuring yourself against every eventuality from the common cold to being sued for your last cent, but it's important to insure against any event that could precipitate a major financial disaster, such as a serious illness or accident or your house falling down.

INSURANCE PROVIDERS

You can buy insurance from many sources, including traditional insurance companies selling through their own salesmen or independent brokers, direct insurance companies (selling directly to the public), banks and other financial institutions, and motoring organisations. An increasingly common trend in New Zealand is for banks to offer property, life and even motor insurance to their customers, which they do on an agency basis, i.e. they don't compare prices from various companies to find you the cheapest policy, although their premiums are usually competitive. There are numerous insurance companies to choose from, either providing a range of insurance services or specialising in certain sectors only. The major insurance companies have offices or agents (brokers) throughout the country, most of whom will provide a free analysis of your family or business insurance needs.

Two organisations offer useful information and advice about insurance: The Insurance Company of New Zealand, which publishes several guides to types of insurance (PO Box 474, Wellington, ☎ 04-472 5230, 🖥 www.icnz.org.nz), and the Citizens' Advice Bureau (CAB), which has offices in most large towns and cities (☎ freephone 0800-367 222, 🖥 www.cab.org.nz). New Zealand also has an insurance ombudsman, who handles complaints regarding insurance companies and services (PO Box 10-845, Wellington, ☎ 04-499 7612, 🖥 www.iombudsman.org.nz).

When buying insurance, shop till you drop. Obtain recommendations from friends, colleagues and neighbours (but don't believe everything they tell you!). Compare the costs, terms and benefits provided by a number of companies before making a decision. Premiums vary considerably (e.g. by 100 to 200 per cent), although you must ensure that you're comparing similar policies, and that important benefits haven't been omitted. Bear in mind that the cheapest policy isn't necessarily the best, particularly regarding the prompt payment of claims.

You should obtain a number of quotations for each insurance need, and shouldn't assume that your existing insurance company is the best choice for a new insurance requirement. Buy only the insurance that you **want** and **need** and ensure that you can afford the payments – and that your cover is protected if you're sick or unemployed.

Simply collecting a few brochures from insurance agents or making a few telephone calls could save you a lot of money. Note also that insurance premiums are often negotiable.

Brokers

If you choose a broker, you should use one who sells policies from a range of insurance companies. Some brokers or agents are tied to a particular insurance company and sell policies only from that company (which includes most banks). An independent broker should research the whole market and take into account your particular requirements, the various insurance providers' financial performance, what you can afford and the kind of policy that's best for you. He mustn't offer you a policy because it pays him the highest commission, which, incidentally, you should ask him about (particularly regarding life insurance).

Direct Insurance

In recent years many insurance companies have begun operating by 'direct response' (i.e. bypassing brokers), which has resulted in huge savings for consumers, particularly for car, building and home contents insurance. Direct response companies provide quotations over the telephone, and often you aren't even required to complete a proposal form. You should compare premiums from a number of direct response insurance companies with the best deals from brokers before choosing a policy.

INSURANCE CONTRACTS

> ⚠ **Caution**
>
> **Read insurance contracts carefully before signing them. If you don't understand everything, ask a friend or colleague to 'translate' it, or obtain professional advice.**

Policies often contain traps and legal loopholes in the small print. If a policy has pages of legal jargon and gobbledegook in **very** small print, you have a right to be suspicious, particularly as it's common practice nowadays to be as brief as possible, and write clearly and concisely in language which doesn't presuppose a doctorate in law. Note that an insurance certificate or schedule won't list all the applicable conditions and exclusions, which are listed only in the full policy document.

Many of the new direct response companies handle quotations, enquiries and claims by telephone on a paperless basis, so you may never see a form or document explaining your policy. This saves companies money, which they supposedly pass on to policyholders in the form of lower premiums, but it can leave you with inadequate protection. Take care how you answer questions in an insurance proposal form, because even if you mistakenly provide false information, an insurance company can refuse to pay out when you make a claim.

Most insurance contracts run for a calendar year from the date on which you take out a policy. All insurance policy premiums should be paid punctually, as late payment can affect your benefits or a claim, although if this is so, it should be noted in your contract or the policy itself. Before signing an insurance contract, you should shop around and take a day or two to think it over; never sign on the spot, as you may regret it later. With some insurance contracts, you may have a 'cooling off' period (e.g. 10 to 14 days) during which you can cancel a policy without penalty.

CLAIMS

Although insurance companies are keen to take your money, many aren't nearly so happy to settle claims. As in other countries, some insurance companies will do almost anything to avoid paying out in the event of a claim, and will use any available loophole. Fraud is estimated to cost the insurance industry millions of dollars a year (particularly motor insurance fraud), and staff may be trained to assume automatically that claims are fraudulent.

☑ **SURVIVAL TIP**

If you wish to make a claim, you must usually inform your insurance company in writing by registered letter within a number of days of the incident (possibly within 24 hours in the case of theft).

Don't send original bills or documents regarding a claim to your insurance company unless it's essential (you can send a certified copy). Keep a copy of bills, documents and correspondence, and send letters by recorded or registered post so that your insurance company cannot deny receipt.

Don't bank a cheque received in settlement of a claim if you think it's insufficient, as you may be deemed to have accepted it as full and final settlement. It's also unwise to accept the first offer, as many insurance companies try to get away with making a low settlement (if an insurer pays what you've claimed without a quibble, you've probably claimed too little!). When dealing with insurance companies, perseverance often pays off. Insurers are increasingly refusing to pay up on the flimsiest of pretexts, as they know that many people won't pursue their cases, even when they have a valid claim. Don't give up on a claim if you have a good case, but persist until you've exhausted every avenue.

HOME INSURANCE

Earthquake Insurance

New Zealand is within an earthquake zone, and minor (usually unnoticeable) tremors occur almost monthly, although records show that serious earthquakes occur, on average, only once every 210 years. As the consequences of a major earthquake would be catastrophic and no insurance company could possibly cover them, the New Zealand government assumes the responsibility of providing earthquake insurance. The Earthquake Commission operates an insurance scheme, which is funded through a small levy on property insurance policies. In the event that an earthquake devastates your property, the Earthquake Commission will pay you compensation up to a maximum of $100,000 for a property and $20,000 for contents. If your property is insured for less, you'll receive only the sum insured. The Earthquake Commission pays no compensation for boats, jewellery, money, vehicles or works of art.

This scheme ensures that, in the event of an earthquake, most property owners are compensated, even if the government goes bust as a result! Because $100,000 is unlikely to be sufficient to rebuild anything other than a very modest home, however, most insurance companies offer top-up insurance to cover the difference between the $120,000 paid by the government and the value of your home and contents, which is a must for owners of valuable properties. Further information is available from the Earthquake Commission, PO Box 311, Wellington (☎ 04-978 6400, 🖳 www. eqc.govt.nz).

Building Insurance

Buying a home is the biggest financial investment most people ever make. When buying a home, you're usually

responsible for insuring it before you even move in. If you take out a mortgage to buy a property, your lender usually insists that your home (including most permanent structures on your property) has building insurance from the time you sign the contract and legally become the owner. Even when it isn't required by a lender, you'd be extremely unwise not to have building insurance.

Building insurance usually includes loss or damage caused by aircraft or other vehicle impact, animals, falling trees or aerials, fire, flood, theft, malicious acts, oil leakage from central heating systems, earthquake, explosion, riot, storm and lightning, subsidence or landslide, and water leakage from pipes or tanks, and may also include cover for temporary homelessness (e.g. when your home has burned down). Some insurance companies also provide optional cover to include trees and shrubs damaged maliciously or by storms. Building insurance must be renewed each year, and insurance companies are continually updating their policies, so you must ensure that a policy still provides the cover you require when you receive a renewal notice.

Lenders fix the minimum level of cover required when you apply for a mortgage and usually offer to arrange the insurance for you, but you're usually free to make your own arrangements. If you arrange your own building insurance, it must of course meet the minimum requirement. Many people take the easy option and arrange insurance through their mortgage lender, which is generally the most expensive option.

Most insurers provide index-linked building insurance, where premiums are linked to inflation and building costs (if you insure through your mortgage provider, premiums are usually added to your monthly repayments). It's your responsibility, however, to ensure that your level of cover is adequate, particularly if you carry out improvements or extensions which substantially increase the value of your home. If your level of cover is too low, an insurance company is within its rights to reduce the amount it pays when a claim is made, in which case you may find that you cannot afford to have your house rebuilt or repaired should disaster strike.

☑ **SURVIVAL TIP**

If the property you're insuring is a second or holiday home, you must inform your insurance company, as a policy for a principal residence may not be valid.

The amount for which your home must be insured isn't the current market value but the cost of rebuilding it if it's destroyed. This varies according to the type of property and the area, e.g. from around $3 to $4 per $1,000 of rebuilding cost (per year) in an inexpensive area to $10 or more per $1,000 in the most expensive high-risk areas. Therefore insurance on a property costing $150,000 to rebuild costs from around $450 to $1,500 per year. There's usually no deduction for wear and tear, and the cost of redecoration is usually met in full.

Building insurance doesn't cover structural faults that existed when you took out the policy, which is why it's important to have a full structural survey carried out when you buy a property.

Insurance for 'non-standard' homes such as those with thatched roofs is usually higher. The highest level of cover usually includes damage to glass (e.g. windows and patio doors) and porcelain (e.g. baths, washbasins and WCs), although you may have to pay extra for accidental damage, e.g. when your son blasts a cricket ball through the patio window. Always ask your insurer what **isn't** covered and what it costs to include it (if required).

Premiums can usually be paid monthly (although there may be an extra charge) or annually. There may be an excess, e.g. $50 or $100, for some claims, which is intended to deter policyholders from making small claims. Some policies have an excess only for certain claims, e.g. subsidence or landslip (when your house disappears into a hole in the ground or over a cliff), which is usually $2,000 or $4,000. Owners of houses vulnerable to subsidence and those living in flood-prone areas are likely to pay higher premiums.

Many insurance companies provide emergency telephone numbers for policyholders requiring urgent advice. Should you need to make emergency repairs, e.g. to weather-proof a roof after a storm or other natural disaster, most insurance companies allow work up to a certain limit (e.g. $2,000) to be carried out without an estimate or approval from the insurance company, but check first.

Building insurance is often combined with home contents insurance (see below), when it's called home or household insurance, which is usually cheaper than taking out separate policies.

Contents Insurance

Home contents insurance is recommended for anyone who doesn't live in an empty house. Burglary is a major problem in some urban areas of New Zealand. Although there's a lot you can do to prevent someone breaking into your home, it's usually impossible or prohibitively expensive to make your home completely burglar proof. However, you can ensure you have adequate contents insurance and that your most precious possessions are locked in a safe or safety deposit box.

Types of Policy

A basic home contents policy covers your belongings against the same sort of 'natural disasters' as building insurance (see above). A basic policy may include garden contents, loss of oil and metered water, personal liability insurance (see below), replacement locks and temporary accommodation. However, a basic contents policy doesn't usually include items such as bicycles, cash, credit cards (and their fraudulent use), jewellery, musical instruments, sports equipment and certain other valuables, nor accidental damage caused by your family to your own property (e.g. putting your foot through the TV during a political party broadcast) or your home freezer contents (in the event of a breakdown or power failure), for which you may need to take out extra cover. Items such as computers and mobile telephones may need to be listed individually on your policy, and computers and other equipment used for business aren't usually covered (or

may be covered only for a prohibitive extra payment). For a higher premium you can insure against 'all risks', including accidental damage.

> ⚠ **Caution**
>
> **Most policies have a maximum amount they pay per item and/or a maximum amount per claim, e.g. $1,500 for each item of jewellery or work of art, or a total claim of $7,500.**

You can usually insure your belongings for their secondhand value (indemnity) or their full replacement value (new for old), except clothes and linen, for which wear and tear is assessed. The more popular form of contents insurance in New Zealand is replacement value, and it's best to take out an index-linked policy, where the level of cover is automatically increased by a percentage or fixed amount each year. Most policies have a maximum amount they pay per item and/or a maximum amount per claim, e.g. $1,500 for each item of jewellery or work of art, or a total claim of $7,500.

Some policies include legal expenses cover (e.g. up to $100,000) for disputes with employers, neighbours, shops, suppliers and anyone who provides you with a service (e.g. a plumber or builder). Most contents policies include public liability cover, e.g. up to $2m. If you have friends or lodgers living in your home, their belongings won't be covered by your policy.

Premiums

Your premium depends largely on where you live and your insurer. All insurance companies assess the risk of loss or damage (particularly from burglary) by location, based on your postcode. **Check before buying a home, as the difference between low and high-risk areas can be considerable.** Annual premiums, which start at around $400 in low-risk areas, can be several times this amount in high-risk areas.

As with building insurance, it's important to shop around for the lowest premium. If you're already insured, you may find that you can save money by changing insurers. However, watch out for penalties when switching insurers. Combining your home contents insurance with your building insurance (see above) is a common practice and is usually cheaper than insuring each separately. Having your building and contents insurance with the same insurer also avoids disputes over which company should pay what, which can arise if you have a fire or flood affecting both your home and its contents.

Security

Most insurers offer a no-claims discount or a discount (e.g. 5 or 10 per cent) for homes with burglar alarms and other high security features. In high-risk areas, good security is usually a condition of insurance. Beware of the small print in policies, particularly those regarding security, which insurers often use to avoid paying claims. You forfeit all rights under your policy if you leave doors or windows open (or the keys under a mat or flower pot), particularly if you've claimed a discount for impregnability. If there are no signs of forced entry, e.g. a broken window, you may be unable to claim for a theft (though there's an obvious solution to this problem). If you plan to leave your house empty for a long period, e.g. a month or longer, you may need to inform your insurer. **Always list all previous burglaries on an insurance proposal form, even if nothing was stolen.**

Sum Insured

Take care that you don't under-insure your house contents (including

anything rented such as a TV or video recorder) and that you periodically reassess their value and adjust your premium accordingly. Your contents should include everything you could take with you if you were moving house (i.e. everything except the kitchen sink). If you under-insure your contents, your claim may be reduced by the percentage by which you're under-insured. Some insurance companies offer policies called 'no-sum' or 'fixed-sum', where you aren't required to value all your possessions but are covered for a fixed amount depending on the number of bedrooms in your home. With this type of policy the insurance company cannot scale down a claim because of under-insurance. However, the fixed amount may be far below the actual value of your possessions and you're usually better off (in terms of insurance cover, not premium levels) calculating the value of the contents to be insured.

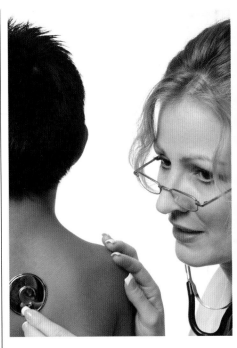

Claims

Take care when completing a claim form, as insurers have tightened up on claims and some will use any 'holes' in a claim to wriggle out of payment; few people receive a full settlement. Many insurers have an excess of $50 to $100 per claim (see above). Bear in mind also that, if you make a claim, you may need to wait months for it to be settled. Generally, the larger the claim, the longer you have to wait for your money,

although in an emergency a company may make an interim payment. If you aren't satisfied with the amount offered, don't accept it but try to negotiate a higher figure.

HEALTH INSURANCE

Health insurance is an important consideration for anyone planning to spend some time in New Zealand, whether a few weeks or months or permanently.

Everyone who is resident in New Zealand or a visitor from a country with which New Zealand has a reciprocal agreement is covered by the national healthcare scheme, which provides either free or reduced-cost medical treatment (see **Health** on page 32) However, while treatment under the state health scheme is considered adequate, many people also have private health insurance. The main purpose of this is to pay the cost of doctors' consultations, prescriptions and dentistry (which aren't covered by the state healthcare system), and also to pay for treatment in private hospitals, thus circumventing public hospital waiting lists. Private health insurance schemes also provide other benefits, such as cover for loss of earnings due to illness.

If you're living or working in New Zealand and aren't covered by the national healthcare scheme, it's risky or even foolhardy not to have private health insurance for you and your family. Whether you're covered by a local or foreign health insurance policy makes little difference (except perhaps in cost), provided you have the required level of cover, including international cover if necessary. If you aren't adequately insured, you could be faced with some extremely high medical bills. When deciding on the type of policy, ensure that the insurance scheme covers **all** your family's health requirements. If your stay in New Zealand is short, you may be covered by a reciprocal agreement, although this may cover you for emergencies only. **Make sure you're fully covered *before* you receive a large bill.**

When changing employers or leaving New Zealand, you should ensure that you have continuous medical insurance. For example, if you and your family are covered by a company health fund, your insurance probably ceases after your last official day of employment. If you're planning to change your health insurance company, ensure that no important benefits are lost. When changing health insurance companies, you should inform your old insurance company if you have any outstanding bills for which it's liable.

Nearly 50 per cent of New Zealanders have some form of private health insurance, which can be purchased from a variety of insurance companies, of which the largest is Southern Cross Healthcare, Private Bag 99-934, Newmarket, Auckland (☎ freephone 0800-800 181, 💻 www.southerncross.co.nz).

The cost depends on what's covered, your circumstances and which company you insure with. For a family of four, a hospital-only policy costs from $550 to $1,500 per year and a comprehensive policy from $600 to $4,000 per year. Private health insurance costs have rocketed in recent years as more people make claims to avoid waiting for treatment at public hospitals, and they're likely to continue increasing at a rate well above inflation, particularly for the elderly. The Consumers' Institute (🖥 www.consumer.org.nz) publishes helpful information on health insurance – including advice on whether you really need it!

If you make frequent trips for periods of up to three months, the cheapest insurance cover is usually provided by an annual travel policy (see page 193), although you must ensure that it provides adequate cover. When comparing the level of cover provided by different health insurance schemes, the following points should be considered:

- Does the scheme have a wide range of premium levels and are discounts or lower rates available for families or children?

- Is private hospital cover available and are private rooms available at local hospitals? What are the costs? Is there a limit on the time you can spend in hospital?

- Is dental cover included? What exactly does it include? Can it be extended to include extra treatment? Dental insurance usually contains numerous limitations and doesn't cover cosmetic treatment.

- Are there restrictions regarding hospitalisation, either in New Zealand or in other countries?

- What is the qualification period for benefits or services?

- What level of cover is provided outside New Zealand and what are the limitations?

- What is the cover regarding pregnancy, hospital births and associated costs? What is the position if conception occurred before joining the insurance scheme?

- Are medicines included?

- Are convalescent homes or spa treatments covered when prescribed by a doctor?

- What are the restrictions on complementary medicine, e.g. acupuncture, chiropractic, massage, naturopathy and osteopathy? Are they covered? Must a referral be made by a doctor?

- Is life insurance or a disability pension included, possibly as an option?

- Are possible extra costs likely, and if so, what for?

- Are spectacles or contact lenses covered, and if so, how much can be claimed and how frequently?

- Is the provision and repair of artificial limbs and similar health aids covered?

Dental Insurance

Except for school children and those on low incomes (in an emergency), dental treatment isn't provided free under the state healthcare system. It's possible to take out insurance to cover dental costs, although it's unusual to have full dental insurance in New Zealand, as the cost is prohibitive. The cost of dental insurance varies,

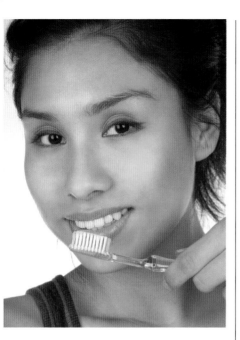

and cosmetic treatment is excluded. The amount paid by a health insurance policy for a particular item of treatment is usually fixed, and depends on your level of insurance. A detailed schedule of refunds is available from insurance companies.

International Health Policies

It's possible to take out an international health insurance policy, which may be of particular interest to people living in New Zealand temporarily, or those whose work involves a lot of travel or who work part of the time overseas. Some policies offer members a range of premiums, from 'budget' to 'comprehensive' cover. All policies offer at least two fee scales, one including North America (and possible other high-cost areas), the other excluding North America. Most policies include a full refund of ambulance, emergency dental treatment, home nursing (usually for a limited period), hospital, outpatient and repatriation charges. All policies include an annual overall claims limit, usually from $200,000 to $2m.

Some comprehensive policies provide a fixed amount for general medical costs (including routine doctors' visits) and maternity, optical and elective dental expenses. Premiums range from around $1,750 to over $5,000 per year, depending on your age, level of cover and the areas covered (if North America is covered,

depending on the state of your teeth and what treatment is covered. Most people find that it's cheaper not to have dental insurance, but to put a little money aside for dental costs and pay bills from their own pocket.

However, some cover may be included in general health insurance policies, which can be purchased from medical insurance companies and from dentists. Basic dental care such as check-ups, X-rays and cleaning are usually included in the standard premium, and some companies offer more comprehensive dental cover as an optional extra. Some international health policies (see below) include basic dental care, and most offer optional (or additional) dental cover, although there are many restrictions, premiums are much higher). If you don't require permanent international health insurance, you should consider a policy which provides limited or optional cover when you're overseas.

ACCIDENT COMPENSATION SCHEME

If you have an accident at work or on the roads, you'll be compensated by the government-run Accident Compensation Corporation (ACC), irrespective of who was to blame or whether you've yet paid any contributions (see below). The Accident Compensation Scheme is financed through income tax and (unlike most other state benefits) separate levies

on earnings; however, entitlement to benefits isn't based on contributions as it would be with a commercial insurance scheme. Note that, as the ACC isn't a social security scheme, continuing to pay into the social security scheme in your home country (which you're usually entitled to do) doesn't exempt you from paying the ACC levy on your earnings in New Zealand.

Employee ACC contributions, known as the 'earner's levy', are used to pay compensation for accidents occurring outside the workplace. They're fixed annually and deducted from your salary by your employer, who will automatically register you for the ACC levy when you start work. ACC contributions for employees are at 1.3 per cent of income up to $99,817 (i.e. a maximum contribution of $1,297.62). Your employer also makes a contribution to the scheme, known as the 'employer's levy', which is used to provide compensation for accidents in the workplace. The self-employed pay the same ACC levy as employees, although they're exempt if their net earnings are less than $19,760 per year ($15,808 for those aged under 20).

Visitors are also covered by the ACC scheme, without the need to make contributions. If you should suffer an accident and make a claim (the procedure is explained on the website of the Accident Compensation Corporate Office – see below), the ACC will cover your medical and associated expenses in New Zealand; but it won't cover repatriation, or medical expenses arising abroad in connection with an accident or loss of earnings abroad.

Compensation made under the ACC scheme used to be extremely generous lump sum payments, but this resulted in large amounts of money being paid to people with relatively minor injuries. The Injury Prevention and Rehabilitation Act of 2000 resulted in a general tightening of the ACC budget, and the emphasis now lies on injury prevention and rehabilitation, rather than the payment of compensation, as was previously the case. Compensation ranges from a minimum of $2,500 to a maximum of $100,000. The aim of the Act, which also established a 'code of claimants' rights', is to prevent fraud, and to ensure that the more seriously injured claimants receive greater compensation than the less seriously injured. The Act has come in for much criticism, particularly from employers, but the ACC scheme is much more generous than most other countries' public schemes, most of which don't pay out a penny to accident victims, certainly not without a long legal struggle. Expenses covered by the ACC are comprehensive, and include medical and hospital treatment, hospital surgery, loss of earnings, loss of future earnings, physiotherapy, home nursing care, expenses involved with rehabilitation or future disability, and an allowance if you're unable to work.

> Note that suing the party who 'caused' an accident isn't usually possible under New Zealand law – a situation that that would have grossly overpaid personal injury lawyers in the US gasping in horror!

You must simply accept the payment awarded by the ACC, which, although it means you're unlikely to receive a multi-million dollar payout (as you may in the US), ensures that a lot of money isn't wasted on drawn-out court cases. However, if you wish, you can take out personal injury insurance, which is likely to pay considerably higher compensation in the case of an accident, and may also compensate you for damage to property (which the ACC doesn't).

For further information about the scheme, contact the Accident Compensation Corporate Office (☎ 04-918 7700, 🖥 www.acc.org. nz). Further information about ACC contributions can be obtained from your local Inland Revenue Department (IRD) office or from the ACC.

HOLIDAY & TRAVEL INSURANCE

Holiday or travel insurance is recommended for anyone who doesn't wish to risk having a holiday or travel ruined by financial problems or to arrive home broke. As you know, anything can and plenty often does go wrong with a holiday, sometimes before you leave home (particularly if you **don't** have insurance). Travel insurance is available from many sources, including airlines, banks, insurance brokers, motoring organisations, tour operators and travel agents, but not all policies provide adequate cover.

Level of Cover

Before taking out travel insurance, carefully consider the level of cover required and compare policies. Most policies include cover for accidents (including evacuation home if necessary), delayed or lost baggage, departure delay at both the start **and** end of a holiday (a common occurrence), loss of deposit or holiday cancellation, legal expenses, medical expenses (up to $4m), missed flight, lost or stolen money (e.g. $500 to $1,000) and personal effects (e.g. $3,000), personal liability ($2m or $4m), and a tour operator going bust. You should also insure against missing your flight after an accident or transport breakdown, as almost half of travel insurance claims are for cancellation (you should also be covered for transport delays at the end of your holiday, e.g. the flight home). With some policies, the amount you can claim for belongings may be limited to around $400 per item. Some home contents policies include cover for belongings worldwide.

> ☑ **SURVIVAL TIP**
>
> Your insurance company won't pay out if you're negligent, e.g. you leave your camera in a taxi or on a beach.

Medical Expenses

Medical expenses are an important aspect of travel insurance and you shouldn't rely on reciprocal health agreements, cover provided by charge and credit card companies, house contents policies, or private medical insurance, none of which usually provide the necessary cover. When you pay for your travel costs with some credit cards, your family (possibly including children under the age of 25) are provided with free travel accident insurance up to a specified amount, e.g. $300,000. **Don't rely on this insurance, as it usually covers only death and serious injury.** Flight and travel insurance are available from insurance desks at most airports, covering in-transit baggage, personal accident, travel accident and worldwide medical expenses.

The minimum medical insurance recommended by experts is $500,000 for Europe and $2m for North America and the rest of the world. Personal liability should be at least $2m for Europe and $4m for the rest of the world. **Many travel and holiday insurance policies don't provide the level of cover that may be needed.**

Always check any exclusion clauses in contracts by obtaining a copy of the full policy document, as all relevant information won't be contained in insurance leaflets.

Exclusions

Health or accident insurance included in travel insurance policies usually contains exclusions, e.g. dangerous sports such as crocodile wrestling, hang-gliding, kangaroo boxing, mountaineering, scuba-diving, skiing, white-water rafting, and even riding a motorbike in some countries. Check the small print and find out exactly what terms such as 'hazardous pursuits' include or exclude. Skiing and other winter sports should be specifically **listed** in a policy if you expect to be covered for accidents. Winter sports policies are available, which are usually more expensive than normal holiday insurance but may cover you for all relevant eventualities.

Cost

The cost of travel insurance varies considerably according to your destination. Many companies have different rates for different areas, e.g. Australia, Europe, North America and worldwide excluding North America. Premiums for travel within New Zealand are around $30 to $45 per person for two weeks, European destinations are usually from $150 for two weeks, and North America (where

medical treatment costs an arm and a leg) and a few other destinations cost from $200 for three weeks. The cheapest policies offer reduced cover but may not be adequate. Premiums may be higher for those aged over 65 or 70. Generally, the longer the period covered, the cheaper the daily cost, although the maximum period may be limited, e.g. six months. With some policies, an excess (e.g. $50) must be paid for each claim.

Annual Policies

For people who travel overseas frequently, whether for business or pleasure, an annual travel policy is often an excellent idea, costing around $250 to $400 per year for worldwide cover for an unlimited number of trips. However, always carefully check exactly what is included and read the small print (some insist that travel is by air). Most annual policies don't cover you for travel within New Zealand and there's a limit on the length of a trip, e.g. one to three months. Some companies offer 'tailor-made' insurance for independent travellers (e.g. backpackers) for any period from a few days to a year.

Claims

Although travel insurance companies quickly and gladly take your money, they aren't so keen to pay claims, and you may need to persevere before they pay up. Fraudulent claims against

travel insurance are common, so unless you can produce evidence to support your claim, insurers may think that you're trying to cheat them. Always be persistent and make a claim irrespective of any small print, as this may be unreasonable and therefore invalid in law.

⚠ **Caution**

Insurance companies usually require you to report any loss (or any incident for which you intend to make a claim) to the local police within 24 hours and to obtain a report. Failure to do this usually means that a claim won't be considered.

Art gallery, Christchurch

9.

LETTING

I f you're planning to buy a holiday or future retirement home in New Zealand, it may be possible to let it to generate income to cover the running costs and help with mortgage payments (or to supplement a pension). Whatever type of property you have, you should check with your insurance company whether your policy covers tenants (and any damage they may cause to your home or its contents).

If you're planning to let a property, it's important not to overestimate the income, particularly if you're relying on letting income to pay the mortgage and running costs.

If you have a mortgage on a property in New Zealand, you're highly unlikely to meet your mortgage payments and running costs from rental income alone. Most experts recommend that you don't purchase a second home if you need to rely heavily on rental income to pay for it.

Buyers who over-stretch their financial resources often find themselves on the rental treadmill, constantly struggling to earn enough money to cover their running costs and mortgage payments. In many holiday areas there's a surfeit of short-term rental accommodation, and many property owners have discovered that rental returns are below their expectations.

LOCATION

If letting income is a priority, you should buy a property with this in mind, in which case location is paramount. In particular, you should consider the following factors.

Climate

Properties in an area with a pleasant year-round climate have the greatest letting potential, particularly outside the high season. Fortunately, this applies to most of the North Island, but much of the South Island doesn't have good weather all year. Avoiding these areas is also important if you wish to use the property yourself outside the high season; for example, you could let a property during the summer months, when rental rates are at their highest, and use it yourself in May or October and still enjoy fine weather.

Accessibility

A property should be within comfortable travelling distance of a major airport, as most holidaymakers won't consider travelling more than an hour to their destination after arriving at the airport. Make sure you choose an airport with frequent flights from your home country and (if applicable) the main New Zealand cities. It isn't wise to rely on an airport served only by budget airlines, as they may alter or cancel routes at short notice. It's also an advantage if a property is served by public transport (e.g. buses or trains)

or is situated in a town where a car is unnecessary.

If a property is located in a town or development with a maze of streets, you should provide a detailed map. On the other hand, if it's in the country where signposts are all but non-existent, you'll not only need to provide a detailed map (with plenty of landmarks), but you may also need to erect signs (for which permission may be necessary). Holidaymakers who spend hours driving around trying to find a holiday home are unlikely to return or recommend it! Maps are also helpful for taxi drivers, who may be unfamiliar with the area.

Attractions

The property should be as close as possible to a major attraction (or more than one), e.g. a beach, theme park, area of scenic beauty or tourist town, although this will depend on the sort of clientele you wish to attract. If you want to let to families, a property should be within easy distance of leisure activities such as theme parks, water parks, sports activities (e.g. tennis, watersports, fishing) and nightlife. If you're planning to let a property in a rural area, it should be somewhere with good hiking possibilities, preferably near one of New Zealand's many natural parks. Proximity to one or more golf courses is also an advantage to many holidaymakers and is an added attraction outside the high season, when there may otherwise be little to attract visitors.

SWIMMING POOL

A swimming pool is desirable, particularly in warmer regions, as properties with pools are much easier to let than those without (unless a property is situated near a beach, lake or river). It's usually necessary to have a private pool with a single-family home, but a shared pool is sufficient for an apartment or townhouse. You can also charge a higher rent for a property with a pool and you may be able to extend the season by installing a heated or indoor pool. Some private letting agencies won't handle properties without a pool. Note that there are safety regulations regarding pools used by the public, which include pools at private homes that are let for holidays (see **Swimming Pools** on page 123).

LETTING RATES

To get an idea of the rent you should charge, simply ring a few letting agencies and ask them what it would cost to rent a property such as yours at the time of year you plan to let. They're likely to quote the highest possible rent you can charge. You should also check the advertisements in newspapers and magazines. Set a realistic rent, as there's a lot of competition. Add a returnable deposit (e.g. $200) as security against loss (e.g. of keys) or

breakages, although this cannot be more than 25 per cent of the rental fee or be requested more than six months in advance. A deposit should be refundable only up to six weeks before a booking. It's normal to have a minimum two-week rental period in December and January.

COSTS

When letting your property, make sure you allow for the numerous costs that inevitably reduce the amount of profit you can expect to make. These may include cleaning between and during lets; laundry; garden and pool maintenance; maintenance of appliances; replacement of damaged or soiled items; insurance and utility bills (electricity bills can be high if your property has air-conditioning or electric heating).

 Caution

Costs can account for up to half the rental income.

FURNISHINGS

If you let a property, don't fill it with expensive furnishings or valuable belongings. While theft is rare, items will eventually be damaged or broken. When furnishing a property that you plan to let, you should choose durable furniture and furnishings and hard-wearing, dark-coloured carpets that won't show the stains. Properties should be well equipped with cooking utensils, crockery and cutlery, and you must also provide bed linen and towels. You may need a cot or high chair for young children. Two-bedroom properties usually have a sofa-bed in the living room. Depending on the price and quality of a property, your guests may also expect central heating, a washing machine, dishwasher, microwave, television, internet access (possibly wireless), covered parking, a barbecue (compulsory!) and garden furniture. Some owners provide bicycles and sports equipment (e.g. badminton and table tennis). It isn't usual to have a telephone in rental homes, although you could install a credit card telephone or a phone that will receive incoming calls only.

CONTRACTS

It's usual to have a written contract for all rentals. Most people who let a property for holiday accommodation draw up a simple agreement that includes the property description, the names of the clients, and the dates of arrival and departure. However, if you do regular letting, you may wish to check with a lawyer that your agreement is legal and contains all the necessary safeguards. For example, it should specify the types of damage for which the tenant is responsible. If you're letting through an agent, he will provide a standard contract. If you offer long-term lets outside the high season,

you must ensure that you or your agent uses an appropriate contract, as there are usually different regulations for short- and long-term lets.

You must decide whether you want to let to smokers or accept pets or young children (some people don't let to families with children under five because of the risk of bed-wetting and breakages). Some owners also prefer not to let to young, single groups. Note, however, that this reduces your letting prospects.

KEYS

You'll need several sets of spare keys, which will inevitably get lost at some

time. If you employ a management company, its address should be on the key fob and not the address of the house. If you let a home yourself, you can use a 'keyfinder' service, whereby lost keys can be returned to the company providing the service by anyone finding them. You should ensure that 'lost' keys are returned, or you may need to change the locks (in any case it's wise to change the external locks periodically if you let a home). You don't need to provide clients with keys to all the external doors, only the front door (the others can be left in your home). If you arrange your own lets, you can post keys to clients in your home country, or they can be collected from a caretaker in New Zealand. It's also possible to install a key-pad entry system, changing the code regularly, although this isn't as secure as a good lock.

USING AN AGENT

If you're letting a second home, the most important decision is whether to let it yourself or use a letting agent (or agents). If you don't have much spare time or don't live in New Zealand, you're better off using an agent, who will take care of everything and save you the time and expense of advertising and finding clients.

Take care when selecting a letting agent, as they sometimes go bust owing customers thousands of dollars. Make sure that your income is kept in an escrow account and paid regularly, or even better, choose an agent with a bonding scheme who pays you the rent before the arrival of guests (some do). It's absolutely essential to employ an efficient, reliable and honest company, preferably long-established. Ask a management company to substantiate rental income claims and occupancy rates by showing you examples of actual income received from other properties. Ask for the names of satisfied customers and check with them. It's also worthwhile inspecting properties managed by an agency to see whether they're well looked after.

☑ **SURVIVAL TIP**

Things to ask letting agents include the following:

- who they let to;
- where they advertise;
- what information they send to potential and actual clients;
- whether they have contracts with holiday and travel companies;
- whether you're expected to contribute towards marketing costs;
- whether you're free to let the property yourself and/or use it when you wish.

The larger companies market homes via newspapers, magazines, overseas agents, colour brochures and the internet, and have representatives in many countries.

Bear in mind that if you use a letting agent to let a property, your costs will be even higher, although this may be compensated by increased rental income.

You should also check whether you'll receive a detailed analysis of income and expenditure and what notice you're required to give if you decide to terminate the agreement. Agency contracts usually run for a year.

Some agencies act as management companies, whose services should include the following:

- arranging routine and emergency repairs;

- reading meters (if electricity is charged extra);

- routine maintenance of house and garden, including lawn cutting and pool cleaning;

- arranging cleaning and linen changes between lets;

- advising guests on the use of equipment;

- providing guest information and advice (possibly 24 hours a day in the case of emergencies).

Agents may also provide someone to meet and greet clients, hand over the keys and check that everything is in order. A letting agent's representative should also make periodic checks when a property is empty to ensure that it's secure and that everything is in order. The services provided may depend on whether a property is basic one- or two-bedroom apartment or a luxury four-bedroom detached house.

> You may wish (or need) to make periodic checks on an agency to ensure that all bookings are being declared and that your property is being well managed and maintained.

DOING YOUR OWN LETTING

Some owners prefer to let a property to family, friends and colleagues, which allows them more control (and with luck the property will be better looked after). In fact, the best way to get a high volume of lets is usually to do it yourself, although many owners use a letting agency in addition to doing their own marketing.

Rates & Deposits

Whereas if you use an agency your rates may be fixed, if you do your own letting you must decide what to charge. To get an idea of the rent you should charge, simply ring a few letting agencies and ask them what it would cost to rent a property such as yours at the time of year you plan to let. Note, however, that they're likely to quote the highest possible rent you can charge. You should also check the advertisements in newspapers and magazines. Set a realistic rent, as there's a lot of competition. Add a returnable deposit (e.g. $200) as security against loss (e.g. of keys) or breakages, although this cannot be more than 25 per cent of the rental fee or be requested more than six months in advance. A deposit should be refundable only up to six weeks before a booking. It's normal to have a minimum two-week rental period in December and January, and it's common to have a two-night minimum stay in rural areas. You'll need to have a simple agreement form that includes the dates of arrival and departure and approximate times (see **Contracts** on page 202).

Marketing

Good marketing (which doesn't just mean lots of expensive advertising) is the key to successful letting – provided, of course, you have an attractive property in a good location. The more marketing you do, the more income you're likely to earn. It also pays to work with other local people in the same business and send surplus guests to competitors (they will usually reciprocate). It isn't necessary to just market locally or stick to your home country; you can extend your marketing to other countries or internationally via the internet. Ideally you should have an email address and possibly also an answer-phone and fax machine.

Advertising

If you wish to let a property yourself, there's a wide variety of publications and internet sites where you can

place an advertisement. Most owners, however, find it prohibitively expensive to advertise a single property in a national newspaper or magazine. A cheaper and better method is to advertise in property directories or websites, both in your home country and in New Zealand. UK options include Holiday Rentals (☐ www.holiday-rentals.co.uk) and Holiday Lettings (☐ www.holidaylettings.co.uk), although most UK property directories have few properties in New Zealand. You can reach a wider market by advertising in an Antipodean property directory such as ☐ www.holidayrentals.com.au, ☐ www.ozstays.com and ☐ www.takeabreak.com.au. Property owners pay for the advertisement on the website and handle bookings themselves. Advertising fees vary from a one-off annual charge, e.g. $100 to a fixed fee (e.g. $10) for every booking made.

You can also 'advertise' among friends and colleagues, in company and club magazines (which may even be free), and on notice boards in companies, stores and public places.

Internet Site

As well as (or instead of) placing an advertisement on an agent's site or property directory (see above), you can set up your own site. Although more expensive initially (though less so in the long run), a personalised website can include photographs, brochures, booking forms and maps of the area, in addition to comprehensive information about your property. You can also provide information about flights, car hire, local attractions and sports facilities and links to other useful websites. A good website should be easy to navigate (don't include complicated page links or indexes) and must include contact details, preferably via email. The key is to make your site 'visible', i.e. appear on the first page or two of popular search-engine results; there are ways of achieving this (e.g. to make sure your site contains plenty of search engine-friendly phrases such as 'holiday accommodation') and it's worth spending the time to research them and implement them. You can also exchange links with other websites, which helps to improve visibility.

Brochures & Leaflets

If you don't have a website containing photographs and information, you should produce a coloured brochure or leaflet. This should contain external and internal pictures, comprehensive details, the exact location, information on local attractions and details of how to get there (with a map included). You should enclose a stamped addressed envelope when sending out details

and follow up within a week if you don't hear anything. It's necessary to make a home look as attractive as possible in a brochure or leaflet without distorting the facts – advertise honestly and don't over-sell the property.

Added Value

It's possible to increase rental income outside the high season by offering special interest or package holidays, which can be done in conjunction with other local businesses in order to broaden the appeal and cater for larger parties. These may include the following:

- activity holidays, such as golf, tennis, cycling, hiking, fishing or Kiwi wildlife spotting;

- cooking, gastronomy and wine tours/tasting;

- arts and crafts such as painting, sculpture, photography and writing courses.

You don't need to be an expert or conduct courses yourself, but can employ someone to do it for you.

Handling Enquiries

If you plan to let a home yourself, you need to decide how to handle enquiries about flights and car rentals. It's easier to let clients make their own bookings, but you should be able to offer advice and put them in touch with airlines, travel agents and car hire companies. Finally, keep detailed records and ensure that you never double book!

INFORMATION PACKS

You should also provide information packs for clients who have booked: one to be sent to them before they leave home and another for them to use after they arrive.

Pre-arrival

After accepting a booking, you should provide guests with a pre-arrival information pack containing the following:

- information about local attractions and the local area (available free from tourist offices);

- a map of the local area and instructions how to find the property;

- emergency contact numbers in your home country (e.g. the UK) and New Zealand in case guests have any problems or plan to arrive late;

- the keys (or instructions where to collect them on arrival).

☑ SURVIVAL TIP

It's ideal if someone can welcome your guests when they arrive, explain how things work, and deal with any special requests or problems.

Post-arrival

You should also provide an information pack in your home for guests explaining the following:

- how things work, e.g. kitchen appliances, TV/video/DVD player, heating and air-conditioning;

- security measures (see page 209);

- what not to do and possible dangers (for example, if you allow young children and pets, you should make a point of emphasising dangers such as falling into the pool – which may be required by your insurance company);

- local emergency numbers and the numbers for health services such as a doctor, dentist, clinic and a hospital with an emergency department;

- contact numbers for emergency assistance such as a general repairman, plumber, electrician and pool maintenance (you may prefer to leave the telephone number of a local caretaker – see below – who can handle any problems);

- a list of recommended shops, restaurants and attractions.

Many people provide a visitor's book, in which guests can write their comments and recommendations regarding local restaurants and attractions, etc. Some owners also send out questionnaires.

If you really want to impress your guests, you may wish to arrange for fresh flowers, fruit, a bottle of wine and a grocery pack to greet them on their arrival. It's personal touches like this that ensure repeat business and recommendations. If you go 'the extra mile', it will pay off and you may even find after the first year or two that you rarely need to advertise. Many people return to the same property each year and you should do an annual mail-shot to previous clients. Word-of-mouth advertising is the cheapest and always the best.

Maintenance

If you do your own letting, you'll need to arrange for cleaning and maintenance, including pool cleaning and a gardener if applicable. You should also allow for the consumption of electricity, gas, water, etc. by your tenants and the cost of additional equipment (e.g. cots and highchairs for children).

> ☑ **SURVIVAL TIP**
>
> When letting a property, you should take care not to underestimate maintenance and running costs, which can be considerable.

Caretaker

If you have a second home in New Zealand, you'll find it beneficial or even essential to employ a local caretaker, irrespective of whether you let it (unless you use an agency). You may also need to employ a gardener. You can have your caretaker prepare the house for your family and guests as well as looking after it when it isn't in use. If you have a holiday or future

retirement home in New Zealand, it's wise to have your caretaker check it periodically (e.g. fortnightly) and give him authority to authorise minor repairs. If you let a property yourself, your caretaker can arrange for (or do) cleaning, linen changes, maintenance and repairs, and possibly gardening as well as pay bills. Ideally you should have someone on call seven days a week who carry out or arrange any necessary maintenance or repairs.

SECURITY

Most people aren't security conscious when on holiday so you should provide detailed instructions for guests regarding security measures and emphasise the need to secure the property when they're out. It's also important for them to be security-conscious when in the property, particularly when having a party or in the garden, as it isn't unusual for valuables to be stolen while guests are outside.

When leaving a property unattended, it's important to employ all the security measures available, including the following:

- storing valuables in a safe (if applicable) – hiding them isn't a good idea, as thieves know **all** the hiding places;

- closing and locking all doors and windows;

- locking grilles on patio and other doors;

- closing shutters and securing any bolts or locks;

- setting the alarm (if applicable) and notifying the alarm company when you're absent for an extended period;

- making it appear as if a property is occupied through the use of timers for lights and a television or radio.

Bear in mind that prevention is always better than cure, as stolen property is rarely recovered. If you have a robbery, you should report it to your local police station, where you must make a statement. You'll receive a copy, which is required by your insurance company if you make a claim. See also **Home Security** on page 187.

Closing a Property for the Winter

Before closing a property for the winter, you should turn off the water at the mains and drain all pipes, remove the fuses (except the one for a dehumidifier if you leave it on while you're away), empty the food cupboards and the refrigerator/freezer, disconnect gas cylinders, bring in any outdoor furniture and empty dustbins. All exterior doors, large windows and shutters should, of course, be locked, but you should open interior doors and a few small windows (with grilles or secure shutters), as well as wardrobes, to provide ventilation.

Secure anything of value against theft or leave it with a neighbour. Check whether any essential work needs to be done before you leave and if necessary arrange for it to be done in your absence. Most importantly, leave a set of keys with a neighbour and have a caretaker check your home periodically (e.g. once a month). It's worth making yourself a checklist of things to be done each time you leave a property unattended.

☑ **SURVIVAL TIP**

Many people keep their central heating on a low setting during the winter when they're absent to prevent pipes from freezing, which can occur in parts of New Zealand.

In humid areas you may wish to leave the air-conditioning on in order to prevent mildew and have someone check your property periodically.

If your property is in an area liable to flooding, move valuable and easily damaged items to an upper floor, raise the fridge, washing machine and other apparatus off the floor (e.g. on pallets) and, if necessary, fit flood boards across external doors and lay sand bags against them.

rain forest

Maori handicrafts

10.

MISCELLANEOUS MATTERS

This chapter contains miscellaneous, but nevertheless important, information for homeowners in New Zealand, including facts about crime, heating and air-conditioning, home security, postal services, shopping for household goods, radio and television, telephone services, time difference and utilities.

CRIME

New Zealand has a reputation as a low-crime country and is safe by international standards, although both serious crime (such as murder) and petty crime (such as burglary) have risen considerably in the last few decades. The only real 'no-go' areas are certain parts of Auckland, where residents of the more affluent parts of the city dare not venture. (The North Shore area of Auckland has successfully experimented with New York-style 'zero tolerance' policing.) Nevertheless, although strangers wandering into high-crime areas are at some risk of being mugged, knifed or even murdered, that risk is much lower than, for example, in most American cities.

A worrying trend is that an increasing number of violent attacks and rapes in New Zealand are racially inspired, particularly against Asians and Pacific Islanders. However, it should be noted that, overall, race relations in New Zealand are excellent and the envy of many other countries.

There's a huge difference between crime levels in the major cities and in rural areas: in the latter it's still common to find communities where people never lock their homes or their cars when leaving them unoccupied, a practice which used to be common throughout New Zealand. In urban areas, however, good door and window locks and an alarm system are considered essential. Car theft is a problem in cities and it's wise to have an immobiliser and alarm system fitted to your car (although little notice may be taken of an alarm when it's triggered).

Crime statistics show that these measures have been at least partially successful: burglary and car theft rates have decreased by almost 15 per cent and the resolution of crime is the highest for a decade. Violent crime, however, is still on the increase, and convictions for domestic violence have risen significantly, although it's believed that this may be due to greater public awareness of the problem and the fact that more domestic violence is reported to the police. Further information and statistics on crime can be obtained from the Minister of Justice, PO Box 180, Wellington (☎ 04-918 8800, 💻 www.justice.govt.nz).

Despite the statistics, you can safely walk almost anywhere at any time of the day or night in most parts of the country. However, it's important to take the same precautions as you would in any country. Beware of pickpockets and bag-snatchers in cities and keep a close eye on your belongings in shops and when using public transport, particularly trains and the Interislander ferry. If your luggage is stolen on public transport, you should make a claim to the relevant authority, as they may make an ex-gratia payment for lost, stolen or damaged baggage.

Most New Zealanders are law abiding and their 'criminal' activities amount to little more than speeding, 'pulling a sickie' (i.e. taking a day off work to go to the beach), or exaggerating a road or workplace

A Crime and Safety Survey carried out among the New Zealand population revealed that 1 in 14 houses had been burgled in the previous year and one in five people had been the victim of some kind of assault. In the light of these worrying findings and the general rise in crime, the government has introduced a series of measures designed to reduce the rate of crime (such as the DNA testing of criminals, including burglars, and greater police funding) and provide increased support for victims of crime. Another recent initiative has been a task force on young offending, which is a particular problem in some cities.

accident in order to secure a more generous payout from the ACC. (Insurance companies recently reported that insurance claims were believed to be inflated by at least $50m annually by otherwise law-abiding citizens.) White-collar fraud and corruption have become a more serious problem in recent years, and a number of respected companies have been rocked by financial scandals, which were previously unknown in New Zealand.

Gangs

Gangs are a problem in some cities, particularly in the poor inner-city areas of Auckland and Wellington, although there's some gang activity in most large towns. As the gangs' main activity tends to be inter-gang warfare, most people rarely come into contact with them, except when a gang organises a 'convention' in a public place or at a major rock concert or sporting event. However, gang 'meets' are usually well publicised, and characterised by a much larger than usual police presence. The best advice is never to consider buying or renting a home in an area known for gang activity, and to stay well away from events or areas where gangs are likely to congregate.

Prisons

Tougher sentencing in recent years has created something of a prison crisis in New Zealand, where the prison population in May 2007 was 8,076 – a rate of almost 200 per 100,000 population, which is high by the standards of most developed countries (not the US, of course). The authorities are experimenting with more liberal punishments, such as home detention, electronic tagging and community work.

Drugs

New Zealand has been described as having the perfect climate for the cultivation of cannabis, and plantations are tucked away in most parts of the country, particularly in Northland, which is dubbed New Zealand's 'cannabis capital'. Police regularly trace and destroy plantations, but many more are believed to remain undiscovered, and this doesn't take into account plants that are grown literally on the window sills and balconies of homes throughout the country.

> ⚠ **Caution**
>
> **Recreational smoking of cannabis or marijuana ('electric puha' as it's known in some places) is commonplace, although illegal, and its possession is punishable by a $1,000 fine and/or 12 months' imprisonment.**

As in many other countries, there's pressure on the government to legalise cannabis, headed by the National

Organisation For The Reform of Marijuana Laws (NORML, 🖥 www.norml.org.nz) and, while most people feel that this is unlikely to happen, plans to punish possession by on-the-spot fines, similar to parking tickets, have been seriously proposed in recent years. Currently, possession of small amounts of cannabis can lead to a fine of up to $500 or sometimes to up to three months in prison, although the latter penalty is rarely used. Having over 28g classifies you as a dealer (with much heftier penalties), unless you can prove otherwise. The police tend to concentrate on tracing and prosecuting growers (using helicopter patrols in rural areas) and dealers, rather than users, and they rarely raid homes in search of small quantities. However, vehicles driven by 'likely looking' drug users (those with glazed eyes and flowers in their hair?) that are stopped for traffic offences may be searched for drugs.

Ecstasy is a popular alternative to cannabis, particularly among teenagers, and the use of hard drugs such as heroin and cocaine is increasing (the official 'Just Say No' anti-drugs campaign is often criticised for its lack of impact). However, drugs are much less of a problem than in the US or western Europe, as New Zealand conducts relatively effective border controls aimed at keeping 'nasties' (including illicit fruit and vegetables) out of the country.

HEATING & AIR-CONDITIONING

Although the weather in New Zealand is generally mild in summer, you shouldn't assume that you won't need heating at other times of the year; there are few areas of New Zealand where you won't need effective heating and good insulation (older properties aren't usually well insulated) if you want to be warm – the average New Zealand home is colder than the World Health Organisation's recommended 18C (64F), which explains why a lot of Kiwis spend the winters wrapped up in sweaters (indoors).

Only a few areas, such as Northland (the northernmost tip of the North Island), are warm enough

Ice cave, Fox glacier

o manage without central heating n winter, although you may want an air-conditioning system or individual heaters instead. Most newer homes (and many older homes) have central heating systems, consisting of heated water systems or ducted air. These are powered by electricity or mains/bottled gas and often double as air-conditioning in summer. Many homes also have a fireplace, as much for show as for effect. Older properties often have free-standing electric or gas heaters rather than a central heating system, and some may have a wood burner, which is essentially a stove that heats the room but also provides hot water. Note, however, that although it's attractive, a wood burner requires a good deal of care and attention, and wood is expensive.

HOME SECURITY

Security is obviously an important consideration for anyone buying a home in New Zealand (or anywhere else), particularly if it's a holiday home that will be unoccupied for long periods. While it's important not to underestimate security risks, even in rural areas, where crime rates are generally low (see **Crime** on page 213), you should avoid turning your home into a fortress, which will deter visitors as well as would-be thieves! Bear in mind that your home is generally more at risk from fire and storm damage than from burglary.

Generally, the minimum level of security required by insurance companies is fairly basic, e.g. security locks on external doors and shutters on windows (small windows generally have bars rather than shutters). Some owners fit additional locks on external doors, alarm systems (see below), grilles on doors and windows, window locks, security shutters and a safe for valuables, although such systems are rarely required by insurance companies. The advantage of grilles is that they allow you to leave windows open without inviting criminals in (unless they're **very** slim). You can also install UPVC (toughened clear plastic) security windows and doors, which can survive an attack with a sledge-hammer, and external steel security blinds (that can be electrically operated), although these are expensive. A policy may specify that all forms of protection on doors must be employed when a property is unoccupied, and that all other protection (e.g. shutters) must also be used after 10pm and when a property is left empty for two or more days.

> ☑ **SURVIVAL TIP**
>
> In New Zealand, your home is generally more at risk from fire and storm damage than from burglary.

When moving into a new home, it's often wise to replace the locks (or lock barrels) as soon as possible, as you have no idea how many keys are in circulation for the existing locks. This is true even for new homes, as builders may give keys to sub-contractors. In any case, it's wise to change the external locks or lock barrels periodically if you let a home. If they aren't already fitted, it's best to fit high security (double cylinder or dead bolt) locks. Modern properties are usually fitted with high-security locks that are individually numbered. Extra keys for these locks cannot be cut at a local hardware store and you need to obtain details from the previous owner or your landlord. Many modern developments and communities have gates and guards.

You may wish to have an alarm fitted, which is usually the best way to deter thieves and may also reduce your household insurance (see page 183). The system should include external doors and windows, internal infra-red security beams, and possibly an entry keypad (whose code can be frequently changed) and 24-hour monitoring. With a monitored system, when a sensor (e.g. smoke or forced entry) is activated or a panic button is pushed, a signal is sent to a 24-hour monitoring station. The duty monitor will telephone to check whether it's a genuine alarm (a code must be given); if he cannot contact you, someone will be sent to investigate. Note, however, that an insurer may require you to have a particular alarm fitted; check before buying one that may be unacceptable. More sophisticated security systems using internet technology are now available, including cameras and sound recorders that can be monitored via a computer or mobile phone.

You can deter thieves by ensuring that your house is well lit at night and not conspicuously unoccupied. External security 'motion detector' lights (that switch on automatically when someone approaches); random timed switches for internal lights, radios and televisions; dummy security cameras; and tapes that play barking dogs (etc.) triggered by a light or heat detector, may all help deter burglars. A dog can be useful to deter intruders, although it should be kept inside where it cannot be drugged or given poisoned food. Irrespective of whether you actually have a dog, a warning sign with a picture of a fierce dog may act as a deterrent. If not already present, you should have the front door of an apartment fitted with a spy-hole and chain so that you can check the identity of a visitor before opening the door. Remember, prevention is better than cure, as stolen property is rarely recovered.

> ⚠ **Caution**
>
> **Holiday homes are particularly vulnerable to thieves and in some areas they're regularly ransacked.**

No matter how secure your door and window locks, a thief can usually obtain entry if he's determined enough, often by simply smashing a window or even breaking in through the roof or knocking a hole in a wall. In isolated areas thieves can strip a house bare at their leisure and an unmonitored alarm won't be a deterrent if there's no one around to hear it. If you have a holiday home, it isn't wise to leave anything of great value (monetary or sentimental) there.

If you vacate your home for an extended period, it may be obligatory to notify a caretaker, landlord or insurance company, and to leave a key with someone in case of emergencies.

If you have a robbery, you should report it immediately to your local police station, where you must make a statement. You'll receive a copy, which is required by your insurance company if you make a claim.

Safety deposit boxes are provided at most bank branches, and are an effective (although expensive) way of keeping your valuables secure. The annual rental charge for a small box is usually $50 to $100, plus a key deposit (bond). Most banks conduct extensive security checks, including fingerprinting, when you use a deposit box.

When closing a property for an extended period, e.g. over the winter, you should ensure that everything is switched off and that it's secure (see **Closing a Property for the Winter** on page 210). Another important aspect of home security is ensuring that you have early warning of a fire, which is easily accomplished by installing smoke detectors. Battery-operated smoke detectors can be purchased for around $15 and should be tested weekly to ensure that the batteries aren't exhausted. You can also fit an electric-powered gas detector that activates an alarm when a gas leak is detected.

POSTAL SERVICES

The New Zealand Post Office (known as NZ Post) is a national institution and has a rich past, similar to the American

postmen deliver a variety of goods, including bread, milk, newspapers and even animals. They also offer a haulage service and, in some cases, carry passengers in their trucks or post buses to and from villages and isolated farms. A lot of sorting is still done by hand and postmen need to rely on their geographical and personal knowledge. Some 80 per cent of New Zealand's 1,000 post shops are operated in this way. Nevertheless, the system is efficient enough, and NZ Post, which operates the post offices in cities and major towns, manages to deliver even poorly addressed letters on time (most of the time).

Post shops offer a friendly, personal service as well as providing a range of other goods and services, such as bill payment (BillPay) and national lottery (Lotto) tickets, and acting as a focal point for the local community. Some post shops provide cheque cashing and deposit services (there's usually a sign indicating the services available).

Information about NZ Post services is available from post offices in a variety of leaflets, and via Customer Service (☎ freephone 0800-501 501) or NZ Post's website (🖥 www.nzpost.co.nz), which provides numerous *Step by Step* guides to using the postal service.

'Pony Express'; tales abound of how postmen in bygone days struggled through forests and mountains to ensure that the mail was delivered. Today the postal service remains a mainstay of New Zealand life, particularly for those living in remote regions. The spirit of private enterprise extends to rural post office (post shop) employees, who aren't NZ Post staff but self-employed individuals with a concession to deliver mail, and who offer various other delivery and collection services to supplement their income. In addition to delivering (and collecting) letters and parcels, rural

SHOPPING FOR FURNITURE & HOUSEHOLD GOODS

New Zealand isn't noted for offering a very interesting or exciting shopping experience. Traditionally, many New Zealanders were almost self-sufficient and shopped only for necessities that they couldn't grow or make themselves (they still have a strong preference for making or growing things themselves wherever possible, particularly in rural areas). However, the situation has improved considerably in recent years, with an influx of international chain stores and 'boutiques' in towns and cities. Naturally, you won't find the same choice of shops or merchandise on offer in New Zealand that you will in the US, the UK or even Australia, as the market is so much smaller. However, a shopping trip in New Zealand is now a much more rewarding experience than previously.

Furniture

The average New Zealand home is furnished much like those in Europe or North America. The staple items of furniture are the three-piece suite (usually called a lounge suite) and the dining table with four or six chairs. All kinds of furniture are available, from antique or reproduction to modern, and quality ranges from bargain-priced flat-packed or secondhand furniture to exclusive handmade and 'designer' items. Most properties in New Zealand have large fitted wardrobes in the American style, which are often walk-in rooms with shelves and rails, thus rendering bedroom furniture other than a bed and a dressing table unnecessary. Fitted kitchens are also standard in new properties and basic appliances (oven, hob and refrigerator, and possibly also a washing machine and dishwasher) are normally included in the price.

Household Goods

New Zealand used to be notorious for the high cost of domestic appliances, which was a result of swingeing import taxes designed to protect local industries. In the '80s, however, the government decided to allow imports on more favourable terms and as a result New Zealanders have been able to replace their ageing home appliances with modern equipment at more reasonable prices.

A huge choice of home appliances is available in New Zealand, and smaller appliances such as electric irons, grills, toasters and vacuum cleaners aren't expensive and are usually of good quality.

All electrical goods sold in New Zealand must conform to local safety standards. It pays to shop around, as quality, reliability and prices vary considerably (the more expensive imported brands are usually the most reliable). Before buying household appliances, whether large or small, it may pay you to check the test reports in consumer magazines.

It isn't usually worthwhile shipping bulky domestic appliances to New

Zealand, such as a dishwasher, refrigerator or washing machine, which, irrespective of the shipping expense, may not meet local safety regulations or fit into a New Zealand kitchen. On the other hand, if you own good quality small household appliances it's worth bringing them to New Zealand, as all that's usually required is a change of plug, provided you're coming from a country with a 220/240V electricity supply (see page 237).

☑ **SURVIVAL TIP**

Don't bring a TV to New Zealand (other than from Australia), as it won't work.

Second-hand Bargains

There's a lively second-hand market in New Zealand for almost everything, from antiques to motor cars, computers to photographic equipment. You name it and somebody is selling it second-hand. With such a large second-hand market there are often bargains to be found, particularly if you're quick off the mark. Many towns have a local second-hand or junk store and charity shops, selling new and second-hand articles for charity, where most of your money goes to help those in need. There are a number of national and regional weekly newspapers devoted to bargain hunters.

If you're looking for a particular item, such as a boat, camera or motorcycle, you may be better off browsing the small ads in specialist magazines rather than those in more general newspapers or magazines. Classified ads in local newspapers are also a good source of bargains, particularly for furniture and household appliances. Shopping centre (mall) and newsagent bulletin boards and company notice boards may also prove fruitful. Expatriate club newsletters are a good source of household items, which are often sold cheaply by those returning home. Another place to pick up a bargain is at an auction, although it helps to have specialist knowledge about what you're buying (you'll probably be competing with experts). Auctions are held in the major cities in New Zealand throughout the year for everything from antiques and paintings to motorcars and property.

There are antiques shops and centres in most towns, and street markets and fairs are common in the major cities (where you can pick up interesting local artefacts – but you must get there early to beat the dealers to the best buys). Ask at your tourist office or library for information about local markets. Car boot (trunk) sales are gaining popularity in New Zealand, and yard sales, where people sell their surplus belongings at bargain prices, are also popular. Sales may be advertised in local newspapers and signposted on local roads (they're usually held at weekends).

TELEPHONE SERVICES

New Zealand has a low number of telephone land lines per 100 people (43 – the 34th-highest ratio in the world) and mobile phone ownership is also low by international standards. However, New Zealanders have always been enthusiastic telephone users due to the long distances (or at least long travelling times) that separate many communities, and the fact that many New Zealanders are immigrants with family members and friends overseas. Many New Zealand households have two or more telephone lines, which enable them to connect a fax machine or modem or to remain contactable when teenage children spend hours (and hours) gossiping to their friends.

The telephone system in New Zealand has been extensively modernised in the last decade or so and all areas are now served by modern digital exchanges (the last exchange on which subscribers could make calls only via the operator was closed in 1991).

The New Zealand telecommunications industry has been extensively deregulated in recent years. The main telecommunications operator is Telecom New Zealand (TCNZ), known simply as Telecom (🖥 www.telecom.co.nz), which used to be state owned (and part of the Post Office) but became a separate company in 1987 and was privatised in 1990. The deregulated environment has allowed Telecom to offer a number of other telecommunications services, including cable and internet. After deregulation, other telecommunications companies, notably TelstraClear (🖥 www.telstraclear.co.nz) and WorldxChange (🖥 www.wxc.co.nz), entered the marketplace, although they remain small compared with Telecom.

Installation

In the more populated parts of New Zealand, there's a choice of companies for line installation and rental; in more remote parts, your only supplier is likely to be Telecom. The easiest way to find out whether there's a choice of telephone companies in your area is to ask your neighbours or look in the local telephone directory. If a line and telephone are already installed in your property, you can usually take over the connection, but you aren't obliged to if an alternative supplier is available. For example, In Auckland and Wellington, you can receive your telephone service via fibre optic cables (owned by First Media, yet another offshoot of Telecom), which also deliver TV signals.

Before connecting your line, a telephone company will need your name and address, date of birth, proof of your address (e.g. driving licence), details of your previous address (and proof) and employer, and the address of a relative or friend in New Zealand (if applicable) whom you can use as a reference (plus six pints of blood or your first-born as security!). If you've just arrived in New Zealand, your immigration documents should be acceptable as proof of identity; otherwise, ask your employer (if you have one) to confirm your identity.

Once your application has been approved, your telephone will be connected within 24 hours if your home has an existing line, or within 48 hours if it hasn't but there are lines nearby. The fee is $45 to reconnect an existing line. If you need a line installed or you live in a remote area, you'll be quoted a price for the labour and materials involved. You can call ☎ 123 for a quote.

You can no longer rent a telephone from Telecom. However, you can choose from a wide variety of telephones of all shapes and sizes (plus answering machines and other equipment) at telephone and electrical shops, with prices starting at around $20, which is a cheaper option than renting anyway.

☑ SURVIVAL TIP

The emergency number in New Zealand is 111, which can be dialled free from any telephone, including all types of public phone; you're connected to the emergency operator, who puts you through to the police or fire or ambulance service, as required. Be ready to tell the emergency operator which service you require and your name. You don't need to give your location, as the telephone from which you're calling automatically 'sends' its identity.

Using the Telephone

Using the telephone in New Zealand is simplicity itself. All standard telephone numbers now have nine digits, beginning with a two-digit area code, which corresponds to one of five regions, as shown in the table below, followed by a three-digit district code and a four-digit subscriber number.

Code	Region
03	South Island
04	Wellington
06	South of North Island
07	Waikato/Bay of Plenty
09	Auckland and Northland

When calling a number in another region, you must dial the whole nine-digit number; when calling within a region, you can simply dial the seven-digit number (which you must do even when dialling within the same district). The only drawback to the system is that many people don't quote the regional code in their numbers because they expect callers to know what it is.

Numbers prefixed 01 usually connect you to a telephone company service, such as the operator. Mobile telephone numbers are identified by the prefixes 021 or 025. Numbers beginning with 0800 are freephone numbers (although some businesses use 0508), which are common in New Zealand. 0900 numbers are premium-rate services, e.g. information lines, where the cost of the call is typically $3 per minute but can be over $10 per minute.

When you dial a major company (such as a bank or airline), you dial the same number from anywhere in the country, rather than a local number. The telephone system then 'reads' your telephone number to find your location and routes your call, through what's known as a 'value added network', to the office dealing with your location. So, for example, when you dial an 0800 number from Christchurch you could end up speaking to someone in Christchurch or, equally, to someone in Auckland.

If you're unable to get through to a number, dial the operator on 010. If you wish to make a reverse charge (collect) call, dial 010 for domestic calls and 0170 for international calls. For information about Telecom services dial 123.

Charges

New Zealand has a regulatory body which rules on whether telephone charges are 'fair and reasonable', but otherwise leaves the market to its own forces.

Line Rental

Line rental fees vary with the supplier (where you have a choice), the 'package' and sometimes the location. For example, Telecom's Homeline plan costs between around $36 (in the 04 calling region and in Christchurch city and its suburbs) and $45 per month, including unlimited local calls. Most packages include some or all local calls; the area which qualifies as 'local' is listed in your telephone directory and **doesn't** cover the whole of your regional code area.

Charge Plans

As in most other countries, calls aren't subject to fixed charges but are 'packaged' according to your use (e.g. whether you make mainly local or long-distance calls) so that you never know whether or not you've got the best deal. Telecom offers a range of such packages (known as 'plans'), with various rates for non-local calls (local calls are usually 'free' with your line rental – see above). The most popular are the Anytime and Anytime Plus plans, in which calls are priced as shown below

The above rates apply 24 hours a day, seven days a week, and represent a discount of between 30 and 60 per cent off Telecom's standard rates.

Alternative Networks

Although most people rent their telephone line from Telecom, there's no obligation to make all your calls via the Telecom network. Under deregulation, other companies can provide your telephone service, even when you have a Telecom line, and it's no longer necessary to enter a code before making calls with another service provider. The cost of calls is charged

| | Anytime | | Anytime Plus | |
	Per Minute	Cap*	Per Minute	Cap*
National Calls	18¢	$2.50	14¢	$2
Home to Mobile (025 and 027)	44¢	-	35¢	-
Home to Mobile (021 and 029)	51¢	-	41¢	-

*The capped rate is the maximum charge for any call of up to two hours.

to you by the alternative company (usually to a credit or debit card) and doesn't appear on your Telecom bill.

The main alternative network is TelstraClear (☎ 0508-888 800, 🖥 www.telstraclear.co.nz), which offers a number of calling plans, including the following:

1. **Talk 24/7** – includes both capped call charges and competitive per-minute rates, 24 hours a day, seven days a week. The national call rate is 25¢ per minute, with a $2.75 cap for calls not exceeding to two hours (excludes calls to mobiles). Calls to UK and US landlines cost 28¢ per minute, with a two-hour capped rate of $5.75.

2. **Ztalk** – Calls to NZ landlines costs 10¢ per minute, and calls to mobiles 45¢ per minute. Calls to a UK or US landline cost 10¢ per minute and calls to UK mobiles 40¢ per minute.

3. **Big Back Yard** – allows you to make free calls within your phone book area (i.e. Auckland, Bay of Plenty, Christchurch, Nelson and Bays, Otago, Waikato or Wellington). There's a minimum sign-up period of 12 months.

4. **Kiwi Anytime Yak Paks** – recommended if you make lots of (mostly short) calls to New Zealand landlines. Each month you receive a number of minutes you can use to make national calls, at any time of the day or night, for a fixed charge. You can choose from Kiwi 3 (three hours or 180 minutes, costing around $13), Kiwi 5 (five hours or 300 minutes, $19), or Kiwi 100 (100 hours or 6,000 minutes, $20). Conditions may apply.

WorldxChange Communications (🖥 www.wxc.co.nz) offers a SuperCap plan allowing you to call any or all of a number of countries (for example, Plan A includes Australia, Canada, China, Hong Kong, Ireland, New Zealand, Singapore, Taiwan, the UK and the US) for 1,000 minutes (over 16 hours) per month for a flat fee of around $20. For $30, you can also call mobile phones in these countries.

Bills

Telephone bills are issued monthly, and you have around a week to pay before a reminder is sent. You can pay bills by post, at post shops and other outlets that act as Telecom agencies, by direct debit from a bank account, or via the internet. Telephone bills are automatically itemised, unless you request a non-itemised bill. You can also decide the level at which itemisation begins, e.g. calls over 50¢, $1 or $5. This is handy if you just want to keep an eye on the more expensive calls and don't want to receive reams of paper listing all your calls (other telephone companies please take note!).

> Bill Online is a system whereby you can receive and pay your telephone bill via the internet, and includes the option to schedule when and how much you pay each month. To use this system you must register online (🖳 www.telecom.co.nz).

International Calls

You can direct dial international calls from private and public telephones in New Zealand through the ISD (International Subscriber Dialling) system. A full list of country codes is shown in the information pages of your telephone directory. To make an international call, dial the international access code of 00, followed by the country code (e.g. 1 for the US, 44 for the UK) and the number you want, usually omitting the initial 0. For international operator assistance dial 0170.

International calls via Telecom are charged according to the time of day and the part of the world (zone), Australia being in the cheapest zone and the UK in one of the most expensive. Other companies usually charge a different rate for each country. It's sometimes cheaper to use a company other than Telecom to make international calls.

If you're travelling overseas, you can use Telecom's Direct service to call New Zealand. By dialling the relevant local access number you can speak to an operator in New Zealand and charge the call to your Telecom account or a calling card or credit card, or place a reverse charge (collect) call. For information and access numbers contact Telecom.

It's possible to make Home Country Direct (HCD) calls in New Zealand by dialling 0009 followed by the country code of the country you wish to call. You'll then be connected directly to an operator in the country you're calling, who will place the call for you and charge it either to the number you're calling or your bill, assuming you have a telephone account in that country. Needless to say, this is much more expensive than paying for the call yourself.

Public Telephones

Public telephones (payphones) can be found in the streets of towns and villages and at various other locations, including airports, bus stations and post offices. All payphones allow ocal, national and international calls. nternational calls can also be made via the operator or the Home Direct Service (see **International Calls** above). Most payphones are in kiosks rather than 'boxes' and these are different colours to indicate that they accept coins (blue), PhoneCards (green) or credit cards (yellow); no boxes accept more than one method of payment. The majority of public telephones (around 4,500) accept only PhoneCards (see below). This is to save Telecom money by not having to empty coin boxes (or repair telephone kiosks that have been broken into for the cash) rather than for customer convenience. Credit card telephones are found mainly in cities.

Local calls aren't free from public telephones (as they usually are from a private telephone) and the minimum charge is around 50¢ per minute.

Coin Telephones

Telephones in blue kiosks usually accept 10¢, 20¢ and 50¢ coins. You must lift the receiver and insert at least 50¢ before dialling (the minimum cost of even the shortest local call). In older phone boxes you should insert only small coins (one at a time), because if you speak for less than the time you've paid for, you won't receive any change. In newer boxes (where the amount in reserve is shown on a digital display), you can insert as much money as you like, as completely unused coins

are automatically refunded at the end of the call. However, you still won't receive any change from a partly used coin, e.g. if you insert a $1 coin but make only a 50¢ call.

Making an international call from a coin telephone can be difficult, as you need to insert at least $3 in coins. Even if you plan to use the Home Direct Service, you must insert 20¢ (which isn't refunded) to access the service.

PhoneCard Telephones

Telecom PhoneCards are available from post offices, petrol stations, Telecom Centres and shops (such as dairies) displaying a Telecom PhoneCard symbol (a green, yellow and blue illustration of a card being inserted into a telephone receiver). Cards are sold in denominations of $5,

$10, $20 and $50 and have various designs, usually scenic views of New Zealand (many people collect them, and some issues are much sought-after and consequently worth far more than their face value!).

PhoneCards have an expiry date, so don't buy a high value card unless you're sure that you'll use it, as there are no refunds.

The procedure when using a PhoneCard in most public telephones is as follows:

1. Lift the receiver and listen for the dial tone.

2. Insert your PhoneCard into the slot.

3. Wait (while your card is checked).

4. When your card's remaining credit is displayed, dial the number.

5. Hang up when you're finished, and **don't forget to remove your card**.

Credit Card Telephones

In some places, mainly city centres and airports, there are public telephones which accept international credit cards (e.g. American Express, Bankcard, Diners Club, MasterCard and Visa), where the cost is automatically debited to your credit card account; there's a minimum call charge of $2. Credit cards cannot be used in PhoneCard payphones and vice versa.

Private Payphones

There are private payphones in bars, hotels, shops and other businesses. They're usually portable units, rather

than telephone kiosks, and operate like any other public telephone, except that they don't usually give change, so you should insert only the amount that you expect a call to cost. The main point to note is that the owner of the telephone can set whatever rates he wishes, which are usually much higher than Telecom's (and he has no obligation to display what the charges are). The same apples to calls from hotels.

Calling Cards

If you do a lot of travelling, you can obtain a Telecom calling card. Calls can be made with a calling card from any telephone, public (including credit card telephones) or private (including mobile telephones), and are charged to your home or business Telecom account or a credit card. You can also use the card to make calls to New ealand from overseas, using the NZ Direct service. A calling card can be mited to 20 pre-selected numbers or o numbers with a particular prefix, and personal identification number (PIN) rotects you against misuse of your ard. Additional cards can be allocated o family, friends or business associates. Jote, however, that although cards are ee and convenient to use, **call charges re high.**

Mobile Telephones

Given the remoteness of many parts f New Zealand, mobile (cellular) elephones are popular and there are ell over 2m mobiles in use (although, y international standards, this is quite ow when calculated as a percentage f population). Coverage is surprisingly ood despite the difficult terrain in many laces. Recently, however, there have een scare stories about the risks to ealth from mobile telephones and the ntennae towers (one garage owner who lanned to mount a tower on his land djacent to a primary school received eath threats!).

The cellular market is dominated y Telecom Mobile and Vodafone. Competition for business is fierce, prices re keen and it's no longer necessary o have a contract. Both firms offer (sometimes bewildering) range of ayment plans. Telecom's offerings clude Telecom FLEXI, Freetime, nytime Go, Go Onebill, Go Prepaid nd Multi-phone plans. Vodafone

has a similar range, including Talker, TXTer, You Choose, Motormouth and Supa Prepay. Calls to and from mobile telephones are generally expensive but vary according to the payment plan.

Pre-pay ('pay-as-you-talk') telephones are increasingly popular in New Zealand, as elsewhere, and you can buy cards for $20, $30 and $50 in many shops, including post shops.

You can buy a mobile telephone directly from Telecom or Vodafone or from a mobile telephone shop, where you can be connected to a network.

It's possible to rent mobiles by the day or week, starting at around $20 per day.

Internet

The internet is extremely popular in New Zealand, where most companies and all government bodies are online, and internet time is free if you have free local calls and your service provider has a local access number. There are numerous internet service providers (ISPs), mainly based in the large cities, including Telecom's Xtra (www.telecom.co.nz), TelstraClear (www.telstraclear.co.nz), ihug (www.ihug.co.nz), owned by Vodafone, Paradise (www.paradise.net.nz) and Xnet (www.xnet.co.nz). Most companies offer dial-up and broadband lines, although the latter aren't available in all areas; check the relevant websites.

Prices are competitive and limited free access (e.g. two hours per month) is available from a few dollars per month or unlimited access from around $30 per month. The monthly magazine *NZ PC World* publishes a comparison of rates and packages, which can also be viewed online (🖥 www.pcworld.co.nz), and the Consumers' Institute provides an online comparison of ISP rates (🖥 www.consumer.org.nz).

Internet Telephony

If you have a broadband internet connection, you can make long-distance and international phone 'calls' for free (or almost free) to anyone with a broadband connection. Voice over internet protocol (VOIP) is the latest technology which is reshaping the telecoms landscape and will eventually (some say within five years) make today's telephone technology (both land lines and mobile networks) obsolete. The leading company in this field is Skype (🖥 www.skype.com), recently purchased by eBay, which has over 50m users worldwide. There are numerous other companies in the market – a search on 'internet phone' will throw up many other internet phone providers. All you need is a broadband connection and a headset (costing as little as $10) or a special phone. Calls to other computers anywhere in the world are free, while calls to landlines are charged at a few cents a minute.

TIME DIFFERENCE

New Zealand lies within a single time zone, 12 hours ahead of Greenwich Mean Time (GMT). However, summer daylight saving time – an advance of one hour – is observed between the last Sunday in September and the first Sunday in April, whereas in the UK summer time operates between the last Sunday in March and the last Sunday in October. This means that there's only a brief period when the two countries are 12 hours apart; for most of the UK's summer (NZ winter), New Zealand is 11 hours ahead of the UK, and for most of the rest of the year 13

TIME DIFFERENCES					
Sydney	**London**	**Cape Town**	**Tokyo**	**Los Angeles**	**New York**
10am	1am	2am	9am	4pm (previous day)	7pm (previous day)

hours ahead. Therefore, unless the person you're calling is on night shifts or an insomniac, you need to phone the UK either first thing in the morning or last thing at night. There's also a considerable time difference between New Zealand and the US. You should check the local time abroad before making international telephone calls. The time in some major foreign cities when it's noon in Wellington in January is shown above.

New Zealand hasn't taken to the 24-hour clock, and times in most timetables are shown according to the 12-hour clock system, i.e. 'am' or 'pm', or are printed in light type to indicate before noon and heavy type to indicate after noon. If in doubt, it's better to ask than to arrive 12 hours late (or early) for your flight or bus!

TELEVISION & RADIO

Broadcasting in New Zealand and the ownership of TV and radio stations used to be strictly regulated by the government. There has been deregulation since 1991, however, and a number of companies (particularly foreign media corporations) have entered the market, making the broadcasting industry somewhat volatile. New radio and TV companies are constantly starting up or buying existing stations and, just as frequently, closing down. (It doesn't pay to become too attached to a particular programme, as you may find that the next time you sit down in front of 'the box' your favourite station has disappeared!) The situation has stabilised in recent years, however.

Despite the influx of foreign companies, television programming is still highly regulated by the Broadcasting Standards Authority; evening programmes receive a classification according to their suitability for younger viewers, e.g. PG (parent guidance).

New Zealand is converting to digital television and radio, and the analogue 'switch-off' is planned for some time between 2013 and 2017. There's no TV or radio licence in New Zealand.

Television

Television is popular in New Zealand, where most households have at least one TV, and it's estimated that the vast majority of people watch some television every day. There are six terrestrial, national free-to-air TV stations in New Zealand. The three main stations are imaginatively named: TV One, TV2, TV3. The other three terrestrial channels are C4, a youth, music-based channel, Prime and Triangle (see below). TV One and TV2 are operated by the state-owned company TVNZ (🖥 www.tvnz.co.nz), while TV3 and C4 are privately owned by Ironbridge Capital. (The government has long-term plans to sell off TVNZ, although this has been delayed for years.) There are also state and privately owned regional TV stations in some areas (e.g. Triangle Stratos in Auckland and Wellington, Canterbury TV in Christchurch, and Channel 9 in Dunedin). All stations, even those that are state owned, carry advertising, although the amount of revenue that state-funded channels can raise from advertising is limited.

TV One is TVNZ's most popular channel, with an audience share of around 40 per cent in 2007, and provides a staple diet of news broadcasts, home-produced and imported dramas, and the inevitable 'lifestyle' programmes. TV2 broadcasts children's programmes, drama series and films, and had a share of some 20 per cent in 2007. TV3 claims to target the 18-to-49 age range (50-year-olds should switch over) and offers mainly home-produced and international series. It had around 20 per cent of the audience share in 2007, while

C4, Prime and Triangle each had less than 2 per cent. The balance of the TV audience is made up by cable and satellite viewers (see below).

Prime Television New Zealand (🖥 www.primetv.co.nz) is a small national free-to-air TV station, now owned by Sky Television. It airs a mixture of programming largely imported from Australia, the UK and the US, as well as rugby (league and union) and cricket matches. Prime's terrestrial signals cover over 90 per cent of the population, although it has 100 per cent national cover via Sky Television's satellite service, with a paid subscription.

Triangle Television (run by Triangle Stratos, 🖥 www.stratostv.co.nz), which is available in Auckland and (since

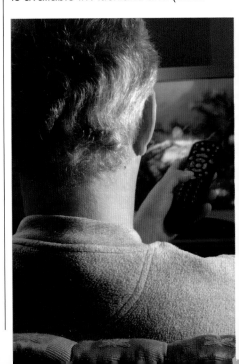

25th August 2006) Wellington, is a non-profit trust that runs a public service. It broadcasts programmes in many languages and is a popular channel among ethnic communities in the city, who cannot see programmes in their own languages anywhere else on New Zealand television. Triangle TV has also broadcast on Freeview (a digital service now usually built in to new televisions) since 2007.

Terrestrial TV is short on the Kiwis' passion, sport, because the major sporting events have been sold to the highest bidder, namely satellite or cable TV, although this has changed to some extent following the agreement between Sky TV and TV3. Otherwise, if you like watching sport, you need to invest in a satellite dish or cable connection to watch the big matches (although you can watch them free at pubs that show live sport on large-screen TVs, but the drinks aren't free!).

Cable TV

Despite initial optimistic predictions, cable television has made slow progress in New Zealand and is available only in certain areas, including Wellington and the Kapiti Coast, Greymouth, Gisborne and several suburbs of Auckland. Cable TV offers exclusive channels as well as terrestrial TV broadcasts and satellite channels such as CNN.

One way to find out whether cable TV is available in your area is to ask your neighbours; the presence of cable 'pillars' (junction boxes) and unsightly, subsiding trenches in the roads of Auckland and Wellington's smartest suburbs are also a good indication!

> The main cable operator is TelstraClear (🖳 www.telstraclear.co.nz) – available in Christchurch, Kapiti and Wellington – which offers a 'menu' pricing system. A basic package costs around $73 per month, but you can pay considerably more if you add film and sports channels.

Satellite TV

Owing to New Zealand's rugged topography and sparse population outside the cities, where terrestrial TV signals can be poor and cable TV isn't cost-effective, satellite TV is sometimes the only option for those who cannot live without the 'electric goldfish bowl'. It's operated by Sky (🖳 www.skytv.co.nz), which offers a wide range of films, music, sport and general content across 70 channels.

A start-up package to receive Sky TV, including a dish, decoder and installation, costs around $300, although occasional special offers reduce this to around $100. Sky viewers pay a monthly subscription fee of around $48 for a basic package of channels, but an increasing number of channels are on a pay-per-view basis, in addition to the basic cost, e.g. up to $25 per month for the 'premium' sports channels.

Radio

As with television, there are state-operated and commercially run radio stations. Radio New Zealand (RNZ, 🖥 www.radionz.co.nz) operates three national stations: Concert FM and National Radio, which are similar to the BBC's Radio 3 and 4 respectively, and the AM Network, which relays parliamentary proceedings. RNZ has a good reputation for the quality of its broadcasting, although programmes are rather staid and have a mainly older (and declining) audience. The stations are entirely state-funded and don't carry advertising. RNZ also operates local radio stations throughout the country, which are partly state-funded and partly funded from advertising. They broadcast mainly rock, pop and easy listening music, local and regional news, and sport.

Ironbridge Capital (the owner of TV3 and C4) operates RadioWorks, the second-largest national radio network, which broadcasts mainly pop music. There's a wealth of other national commercial radio stations, mainly broadcasting pop music, and several special interest stations, such as Radio Sport (whose commentaries have been widely acclaimed) and a number of religious stations. A student station, b.NET, broadcasts from universities and polytechnics around the country. There's also an abundance of local commercial radio stations, with around 100 FM stations alone, plus others broadcasting on the AM frequency. These play pop or easy listening music and broadcast local news and sports results, being closely involved with their local communities.

Most radio stations broadcast in English, but there are a number of state and private stations broadcasting in Maori, particularly in regions with large Maori communities, such as Auckland and the north-west tip of the North Island.

BBC World Service

The BBC World Service (the insomniac's station) broadcasts worldwide, in English and around 35 other languages, with a total output of over 750 hours per week (a **very** long week). The World service can be received on 810AM in the Auckland area, 107FM in Coromandel/Pacific Coast and 107.3FM in Matakohe/Kaipara. A programme guide can be found on the BBC's website (💻 www.bbc.co.uk/worldservice/index.shtml).

UTILITIES

Utilities is the collective name given to electricity, gas and water supplies, which are discussed separately below.

Electricity

The electricity supply in New Zealand is 240/250 volts AC, with a frequency of 50 Hertz (cycles). It's generated mostly by hydroelectric power plants, so conservationists can consume energy to their hearts' content. The energy market in New Zealand is completely privatised and most major areas have at least two electricity suppliers, so you can shop around. The main companies are Bay of Plenty/King County Energy (💻 www.bopelec.co.nz), Empower (part of Contact Energy, 💻 www.contactenergy.co.nz), Energy Online (Genesis Power, 💻 www.energyonline.co.nz), Genesis Energy (💻 www.genesisenergy.co.nz), Meridian Energy (💻 www.meridianenergy.co.nz), Mighty River Power (💻 www.mightyriverpower.co.nz), Mercury Energy (💻 www.mercury.co.nz) and Trustpower (💻 www.trustpower.co.nz).

If you move into a new home, the electricity supply may have been disconnected. In this case, you must contact a local electricity company and complete a registration form; you should allow at least two days to have the electricity reconnected and the meter read. There's usually a charge for connection and a security deposit may be payable.

> The electricity supply is usually reliable, despite the catastrophic and well publicised cable failures in Auckland in 1998, which left the centre of the city without full power for several weeks.

Power Supply

The electricity supply in New Zealand is 240/250 volts AC, with a frequency of 50 Hertz (cycles). Power cuts are rare in most parts of the country, although fairly frequent in some areas or during bad weather. In remote areas where there's no mains electricity, you must usually install a generator, although some people make do with gas and oil lamps.

A problem with some electrical equipment is the frequency rating, which in some countries, e.g. the US, is designed to run at 60 Hertz (Hz) and not New Zealand's 50Hz. Electrical equipment **without** a motor is generally unaffected by the drop in frequency to 50Hz (except TVs). Equipment with a motor may run with a 20 per cent drop in speed, but clocks, cookers, record players, tape recorders and washing machines are unusable if they aren't designed for 50Hz operation. To find out, look at the label on the back of the equipment: if it says 50/60Hz, it should be safe; if it says 60Hz, you can try it anyway, **but first ensure that the voltage is correct (see below)**. If the equipment runs too slowly, seek advice from the manufacturer or the retailer.

> Bear in mind that the transformers and motors of electrical devices designed to run at 60Hz run hotter at 50Hz, so make sure that equipment has sufficient space around it for cooling.

Converters & Transformers

Electrical equipment rated at 110 volts (e.g. from the US) requires a converter or a step-down transformer, although some electrical appliances (e.g. electric razors and hair dryers) are fitted with a 110/240 volt switch. Check for the switch, which may be located inside the casing, and make sure it's switched to 240 volts **before** connecting it to the power supply. Converters can be used for heating appliances but transformers, which are available from most electrical retailers, are required for motorised appliances (they can also be bought secondhand). Add the wattage of the devices you intend to connect to a transformer and make sure that its power rating **exceeds** this sum.

Generally, all small, high-wattage, electrical appliances such as heaters, irons, kettles and toasters need large transformers. Motors in large appliances such as cookers, dishwashers, dryers, refrigerators and washing machines need replacing or fitting with a large transformer. In most cases it's simpler to buy new appliances in New Zealand, which are of good quality and reasonably priced.

Plugs, Fuses & Bulbs

Unless you've come to New Zealand from Australia, all your plugs will require changing, or you'll need a lot of adapters. Plug adapters can be difficult to find locally, so you should bring a number of adapters with you, although using these isn't recommended it's better to use extension leads fitted with local plugs. Australian and New Zealand plugs have three pins: two diagonally slanting flat pins above one straight (earth) pin. Plugs aren't fused. Some electrical appliances are earthed and have a three-core flex – you must **never** use a two-pin plug with a three-core flex. **Always make sure that a plug is correctly and securely wired, as bad wiring can prove fatal**.

Most apartments and all houses have fuse boxes, which are usually of the circuit breaker type in modern homes. When a circuit is overloaded, the circuit breaker trips to the OFF position. When replacing or repairing fuses of any kind, if the same fuse continues to blow, contact an electrician and **never fit a fuse of a higher rating than specified, even as a temporary measure**. When replacing fuses, don't rely on the blown fuse as a guide, as it may have been wrong. If you use an electric lawnmower or power tools outside your home or in your garage, you should have a Residual Current Device (RCD) installed. This can detect current changes of as little as a thousandth of an amp and in the event of a fault (or the cable being cut) it switches off the power in around 0.04 seconds.

Electric light bulbs (called globes) in New Zealand are of the Edison type with a bayonet, not a screw fitting. Low-energy light bulbs are also available and, although more expensive than ordinary bulbs, save money due to their longer life and reduced energy consumption. Bulbs for non-standard electrical appliances (i.e. appliances not made for the local market) such as lamps, refrigerators and sewing machines may be unavailable locally, so you should bring spares with you.

Connection & Payment

To have the electricity supply connected (or the bill transferred to your name when moving into a new home), simply call a local electricity company. Connection charges are around $40, although if the electricity hasn't been disconnected you won't be charged. You may need to pay a bond if you don't own your home, which can be around $250 if you don't meet the company's credit criteria or $100 if you rent a property. You're billed every two months – most people pay by direct debit from a bank account. The typical bill for an average house is around $200 (for two months).

Gas

Gas is popular for cooking (it costs less than electricity), although it's less commonly used to provide heating and hot water (gas heaters are, however, becoming more popular).

Mains gas (natural gas) is available in all of the North Island with the exception of a few remote corners, but not in the South Island. Liquefied petroleum gas (LPG) is distributed nationally in bottled form. Mains gas is used by around 200,000 commercial, industrial and residential customers and, despite not being available in the South Island, is one of New Zealand's most important energy sources. It's produced in local fields and supplies a third of the country's energy needs.

Like electricity, gas is supplied by local companies, listed in telephone directories. Contact Energy (🖥 www. contactenergy.co.nz) and the Natural Gas Corporation (🖥 www.ngc.co.nx) are two of the largest mains gas suppliers. There may be no gas supply in older homes or modern properties. If you're looking to rent a property and want to cook by gas, make sure it already has a gas supply (some houses have an unused gas service pipe).

In areas without mains gas, you can buy appliances that operate on bottled gas. On payment of a deposit, a local supplier will provide you with gas bottles and replace them when they're empty. Large users can have a storage tank installed and have gas delivered by tanker. If you need to purchase gas appliances, such as a cooker or fire, you should shop around, as prices vary considerably.

If you buy a home without a gas supply, you can usually arrange with a local gas company to install a line between your home and a nearby

gas main, provided there's one within a reasonable distance; otherwise the cost will be prohibitive. If a home already has a gas supply, simply contact a local gas company to have it reconnected or transferred to your name (there's a connection fee of around $50). A security deposit (e.g. $100) is usually payable if you're renting. You must contact your gas company to obtain a final reading when vacating a property. In areas where mains gas is unavailable, some properties are plumbed for bottled gas.

Bottle rental for two 45kg bottles costs between $100 to $150 per year (it may vary between the North and South islands) and you pay around $90 for each refill. The price may vary according to where you live (prices are higher in rural areas due to delivery costs). Alternatively, you can buy 9kg gas bottles (around $50) and refill them at most petrol stations for $20 to $23.

Gas central heating boilers, water heaters and fires should be checked annually. Ask for a quotation for any work in advance, and check the identity of anyone claiming to be a gas company employee (or any kind of 'serviceman') by asking to see an identity card and checking with his office.

⚠ Caution

Bear in mind that gas installations and appliances can leak, and cause explosions or kill you while you sleep. If you suspect a gas leak, first check to see if a gas tap has been left on or a pilot light has gone out. If not, there's probably a leak, either in your home or in a nearby gas pipeline. Ring your local gas company immediately, and vacate your home as quickly as possible.

Gas leaks are extremely rare, and explosions caused by leaks even rarer, although they're often spectacular and therefore widely reported. Nevertheless, it pays to be careful. You can buy an electric-powered gas detector which activates an alarm when a gas leak is detected.

Water

Although much of New Zealand usually has an abundant supply of water (see **Climate** on page 20), the country suffers from recurring droughts. The first half of 2005 saw some very dry months; for example, April had less than 25 per cent of the normal rainfall. Mains water is available everywhere in New Zealand except in the most remote areas (where it sometimes shoots up in boiling form directly out of the ground!). All tap water is drinkable, although it's heavily chlorinated in towns (as in many other countries).

Water is supplied and billed by a local water company, which may be a division of your local council. Usually, you pay an annual water 'rate', which is set according to the size and value of your property. In most areas, the water rate is included in the local property tax (see page 174), but in some areas water is billed separately, e.g. in Auckland some households pay several hundred dollars per year. In some areas, properties (generally newer homes) have a water meter and you're charged according to use. If you're on water rates, it's usually possible to ask for a metered supply. It's generally cheaper to pay for your water on the rated system, although modest users living in large properties find it cheaper to have a meter fitted.

Mains drainage is found throughout New Zealand except in remote areas, where properties usually have a septic tank.

WILLS

It's an unfortunate fact of life, but you're unable to take your worldly goods with you when you take your final bow (even if you have plans to return in a later life). Once you've accepted that you're mortal (the one statistic you can confidently rely on is that 100 per cent of all human beings eventually die), it's wise to make a will leaving your estate to someone or something you love, rather than leaving it to the government, or leaving a mess which everyone will fight over (unless that's your intention). Many people in New Zealand die intestate, i.e. without making a will, in which case their property is subject to New Zealand's intestacy laws. In general, these divide your estate equally between your spouse and children. If you die in New Zealand without making a will, and aren't domiciled there, the intestacy laws of your home country apply to the disposal of your estate.

As a general rule, New Zealand law entitles you to make a will according to the law of any country and in any language. If you're a foreign national and don't want your estate to be subject to New Zealand law, you should be eligible to state in your will that it's to be interpreted under the law of another country. However, to avoid being subject to New Zealand inheritance laws, you must establish your domicile in another country. If you don't specify in your will that the law of another country applies to your estate, then New Zealand law will apply. A legal foreign will made in an overseas country dealing with overseas assets is valid in New Zealand and will be accepted for probate there. However, you should have a New Zealand will to deal with your New Zealand assets.

> It isn't a legal requirement in New Zealand to use a lawyer to prepare your will, although the relatively small fee (e.g. $200) may save problems later. If you want to make your own will, you can simply write your instructions and sign them, which is known as a holographic will and doesn't need to be witnessed.

If your circumstances change dramatically, e.g. you get married, you must make a new will, as under New Zealand law marriage automatically annuls an existing will. A husband and wife should make separate 'mirror' wills.

Similarly, if you separate or are divorced, you should consider making a new will, although divorce doesn't automatically annul a will. A new bequest or a change can be made to an existing will through a document called a codicil. You should check your will every few years to make sure it still fulfils your wishes and circumstances (your assets may have increased significantly in value). A will can be revoked simply by tearing it up.

You also need someone to act as the executor of your estate, which can be costly even for modest estates. Your bank, building society, solicitor or other professional will usually act as the executor, although this should be avoided if possible, as fees can be **very** high. If you appoint a professional as the executor of your estate, check the fees in advance (and whether they could increase in future). **It's best to make your beneficiaries the executors, as they can instruct a solicitor after your death if they need legal assistance.** The good news about dying in New Zealand (at least for your beneficiaries) is that there's no inheritance tax or death duties.

Keep a copy of your will in a safe place (e.g. a bank), and another copy with your solicitor or the executor of your estate. It's useful to leave an updated list of your assets with your will to assist the executor in distributing your estate. You should keep information regarding bank accounts and insurance policies with your will(s), but don't forget to tell someone where they are!

All Blacks performing the haka

punting on the river Avon, Christchurch

APPENDICES

APPENDIX A: USEFUL ADDRESSES

Embassies & Consulates

Most foreign embassies in New Zealand are located in the capital Wellington, although some countries have their missions in Auckland. A selection of embassies in Wellington is shown below; a full list is available from the New Zealand Ministry of Foreign Affairs and Trade (💻 www.mfat. govt.nz/Embassies/2-Foreign-Embassies/index.php). Note that business hours vary considerably and embassies close on their national holidays as well as on New Zealand's public holidays. Always telephone to check the business hours before visiting.

Argentina: Level 14, 142 Lambton Quay, Wellington (☎ 04-472 8330).

Australia: 72-76 Hobson Street, Thorndon, PO Box 4036, Wellington (☎ 04-473 6411).

Austria: 57 Willis Street, Wellington (☎ 04-499 6393).

Belgium: 12th Floor, 1-3 Willeston Street, PO Box 3841, Wellington (☎ 04-472 9558).

Brazil: 10 Brandon Street, Wellington (☎ 04-473 3516).

Canada: 3rd Floor, 61 Molesworth Street, PO Box 12-049, Wellington (☎ 04-473 9577).

Chile: 19 Bolton Street, PO Box 3861. Wellington (☎ 04-471 6270).

China: 2-6 Glenmore Street, Kelburn, Wellington (☎ 04-472 1382).

Finland: Simpson Grierson Building, 195 Lambton Quay, PO Box 2402, Wellington (☎ 04-499 4599).

France: 34-42 Manners Street, Wellington (☎ 04-384 2555).

Germany: 90-92 Hobson Street, Thorndon, PO Box 1687, Wellington (☎ 04-473 6063).

Greece: 5-7 Willeston Street, PO Box 24–066, Wellington (☎ 04-473 7775).

India: 180 Molesworth Street, PO Box 4045, Wellington (☎ 04-473 6390).

Indonesia: 70 Glen Road, Kelburn, PO Box 3543, Wellington (☎ 04-475 8699).

Iran: 151 Te Anau Road, Roseneath, Wellington (☎ 04-386 2976).

Ireland: 6th Floor, 18 Shortland Street, PO Box 279, Auckland (☎ 09-977 2252).

Israel: 13th Floor, Equinox House, 111 The Terrace, PO Box 2171, Wellington (☎ 04-472 2368).

Italy: 34-38 Grant Road, Thorndon, PO Box 463, Wellington (☎ 04-473 5339).

Japan: Level 18-19, Majestic Centre, 100 Willis Street, Wellington (☎ 04-473 1540).

Korea: Level 11, ASB Bank Tower, 2 Hunter Street, PO Box 11–143, Wellington (☎ 04-473 9073).

Malaysia: 10 Washington Avenue, Brooklyn, PO Box 9422, Wellington (☎ 04-385 2439).

Mexico: Level 8, 111 Customhouse Quay, PO Box 11-510, Wellington (☎ 04-472 0555).

Netherlands: Investment House, Corner Ballance & Featherstone Streets, PO Box 840, Wellington (☎ 04-471 6390).

Papua New Guinea: 279 Willis Street, PO Box 197, Wellington (☎ 04-385 2474).

Peru: Level 8, Cigna House, 40 Mercer Street, Wellington (☎ 04-499 8087).

Philippines: 50 Hobson Street, Thorndon, PO Box 12-042. Wellington (☎ 04-472 9848).

Poland: 51 Granger Road, Howick, Auckland (☎ 09-534 4670).

Russia: 57 Messines Road, Karori, Wellington (☎ 04-476 6113).

Singapore: 17 Kabul Street, Khandallah, PO Box 13-140, Wellington (☎ 04-470 0850).

Sweden: 13th Floor, Vogel Building, Aitken Street, Thorndon, Wellington (☎ 04-499 9895).

Switzerland: Panama House, 22 Panama Street, Wellington (☎ 04-472 1593).

Thailand: 2 Cook Street, Karori, PO Box 17-226, Wellington (☎ 04-476 8616).

Turkey: 15-17 Murphy Street, Thorndon, Wellington (☎ 04-472 1292).

United Kingdom: 44 Hill Street, Wellington (☎ 04-924 2888).

USA: 29 Fitzherbert Terrace, PO Box 1190, Wellington (☎ 04-462 6000).

Selected Government Departments

Citizenship Office, PO Box 10-680, Wellington (☎ 0800-225 151, 💻 www.dia.govt.nz).

Department of Building & Housing, PO Box 10-729, Wellington (☎ 04-494 0260, 💻 www.dbh.govt.nz).

Department of Child, Youth and Family Services, PO Box 2620,

Wellington (☎ 04-918 9100, 🖥 www.cyf.govt.nz).

Department of Internal Affairs, PO Box 805, Wellington (☎ 04-495 7200, 🖥 www.dia.govt.nz).

Department of Labour, PO Box 3705, Wellington (☎ 04-915 4400, 🖥 www.dol.govt.nz).

Department of the Prime Minister & Cabinet, Parliament Building, Wellington (☎ 04-471 9743, 🖥 www.dpmc.govt.nz).

Land Information New Zealand (LINZ), Private Bag 5501, Wellington (☎ 04-460 0110, 🖥 www.linz.govt.nz).

Ministry for the Environment, PO Box 10-362, Wellington (☎ 04-917 7400, 🖥 www.mfe.govt.nz).

Ministry of Agriculture & Forestry, PO Box 2526, Wellington (☎ 04-474 4100, 🖥 www.maf.govt.nz).

Ministry of Foreign Affairs & Trade, Private Bag 18-901, Wellington (☎ 04-439 8000, 🖥 www.mft.govt.nz).

Ministry of Health, PO Box 5013, Wellington (☎ 04-496 2000, 🖥 www.moh.govt.nz).

Ministry of Transport, PO Box 3175, Wellington (☎ 04-472 1253, 🖥 www.transport.govt.nz).

New Zealand Customs, PO Box 2218, Wellington (☎ 0800-428 786, 🖥 www.customs.govt.nz).

New Zealand Immigration Service, PO Box 3705, Wellington (☎ 0508-558 855, 🖥 www.immigration.govt.nz).

Customs Offices

Auckland: Customhouse, 50 Anzac Avenue, PO Box 29 (☎ 09-359 6655).

Auckland International Airport: PO Box 73-003, Mangere (☎ 09-275 9059).

Christchurch: 6 Orchard Road, PO Box 14-086, (☎ 03-358 0600).

Dunedin: 32 Portsmouth Drive, Private Bag 1928 (☎ 03-477 9251).

Invercargill: Business Centre, Ground Floor, Menzies Building, 1 Esk Street, PO Box 840 (☎ 03-328 7259).

Napier: 215 Hastings Street, PO Box 440 (☎ 06-835 5799).

Nelson: 10 Low Street, PO Box 66 (☎ 03-548 1484).

New Plymouth: 54-56 Currie Street, PO Box 136 (☎ 06-758 5721).

Opua: PO Box 42 (☎ 029-602 1669).

Tauranga: 27-33 Nikau Crescent, PO Box 5014 (☎ 07-575 9699).

Wellington: Head Office, The Customhouse, 17-21 Whitmore Street, PO Box 2218 (☎ 04-473 6099).

Whangarei: PO Box 4155 (☎ 029-250 9305).

Miscellaneous

Archives New Zealand, PO Box 12-050, Wellington (☎ 04-499 5595, 🖳 www.archives.govt.nz).

National Library of New Zealand, PO Box 1467, Wellington (☎ 04-474 3000, 🖳 www.natlib.govt.nz).

Statistics New Zealand, PO Box 2922, Wellington (☎ 04-931 4600, 🖳 www.stats.govt.nz).

TeachNZ, PO Box 1666, Wellington (☎ 0800-832 246, 🖳 www.teachnz. govt.nz).

APPENDIX B: FURTHER READING

Magazines & Newspapers

A directory of New Zealand's national and local newspapers, with links to their websites, is available from 🖥 www.onlinenewspapers.com/nz. Some leading publications are listed below:

The Dominion Post – Wellington (🖥 www.stuff.co.nz/dominionpost). The capital's leading newspaper.

Migrant News (🖥 www.migrantnews.co.nz). New Zealand's primary resource for migrants.

The National Business Review (🖥 www.nbr.co.nz). New Zealand's premier business publication.

The New Zealand Herald – Auckland (🖥 www.nzherald.co.nz). New Zealand's largest newspaper online.

New Zealand News UK, South Bank House, Black Prince Road, London SE1 7S6 (☎ 020-7476 9704, 🖥 www.nznewsuk.co.uk). Subscription newspaper for prospective migrants.

New Zealand Outlook, Consyl Publishing, 13 London Road, Bexhill-on-Sea, East Sussex TN39 3JR, UK (☎ 01424-223111, 🖥 www.consylpublishing.co.uk). Subscription newspaper for prospective migrants.

The Opinion (🖥 www.theopinion.co.nz). National monthly newspaper that examines and analyses in depth, the performance of government, its bureaucracy and political system

The Otago Daily Times – Dunedin (🖥 www.odt.co.nz). Their website contains a good summary of regional, national and international news and sport.

TNT Magazine New Zealand, 14-15 Child's Place, London SW5 9RX, UK (☎ 020-7373 3377, 🖥 www.tntmagazine.com). Free weekly magazine for expatriate New Zealanders in the UK, but of interest to anyone planning to live in New Zealand.

The Waikato Times – Hamilton (🖥 www.stuff.co.nz/waikatotimes). Hamilton's leading newspaper.

Books

A selection of books about New Zealand is listed below (the title is followed by the name of the author and the publisher's name in brackets). Some of the books listed may be out of print, but you may still be able to find a copy in a book shop or library.

Culture

Cultural Atlas of Australia, New Zealand and the South Pacific, Gordon Johnson (Facts on File)

Cultural Questions: New Zealand Identity in a Transitional Age, Ruth Brown (Kapako)

Culture Wise New Zealand, Graeme Chesters & John Irvine (Survival Books)

A Destiny Apart: New Zealand's Search for a National Identity, Kenneth Sinclair (Allen & Unwin)

Food & Wine

Celebrating New Zealand Wine, Joelle Thomson & Andrew Charles Coffey (New Holland)

Edmonds Illustrated Cookbook, Edmonds (Hachette Livre NZ)

Harvest: Naturally Good New Zealand Food, Penny Oliver & Ian Batchelor (New Holland)

New Taste New Zealand, Lauraine Jacobs & Stephen Robinson (Ten Speed Press)

Pocket Guide to the Wines of New Zealand, Michael Cooper (Mitchell Beazley)

Rough Guide to Auckland Restaurants, Mark Graham (Rough Guides)

Simply New Zealand: A Culinary Journey, Ian Baker (New Holland)

Wine Atlas of New Zealand, Michael Cooper (Hodder Moa)

History

The New Zealand Wars, James Belich (Penguin)

History of New Zealand, George William Rusden (Elibron Classics)

A History of New Zealand, Keith Sinclair (Pelican)

New Zealand and the Second World War: The People, the Battles and the Legacy, Ian McGibbon (Hodder Moa Beckett)

New Zealand's Top 100 History-makers, Joseph Romanos (Trio Books)

Oxford Illustrated History of New Zealand, Keith Sinclair (Oxford University Press)

The Penguin History of New Zealand, Michael King (Penguin)

Language

A Concise Dictionary of New Zealand Sign Language, Graeme Kennedy (Bridget Williams)

A Dictionary of Maori Words in New Zealand English, John Macalister (Oxford University Press)

Dictionary of New Zealand English, H. W. Oarsman (Oxford University Press)

The Godzone Dictionary, Max Cryer (Exisle)

Languages of New Zealand, Alan Bell & others (Victoria University Press)

New Zealand English: Its Origins and Evolution (Cambridge University Press)

New Zealand Ways of Speaking English, Allan Bell & Janet Holmes (Multilingual Matters)

A Personal Kiwi-Yankee Dictionary, Louis S. Leland Jr

The Reed Dictionary of New Zealand Slang, D. McGill (Reed NZ)

Sign Language Interpreting: Theory and Practice in Australia and New Zealand, Jemina Napier (Federation Press)

Living & Working

Living and Working in New Zealand, edited by David Hampshire (Survival Books)

Maori New Zealand

The Rough Guide to Maori New Zealand (Rough Guides)

Exploring Maori Values, John Patterson (Dunmore Press)

Maori Art and Culture ed. D. C. Starzecka (British Museum Press)

Maori Legends, Alistair Campbell (Viking Sevenseas)

Maori Myths and Tribal legends, Antony Alpers (Longman)

Te Marae: a Guide to Customs and Protocol, Hiwi Tauroa (Reed Books)

People

Being Pakeha: An Encounter with New Zealand and the Maori Renaissance, Michael King (Hodder & Stoughton)

The Governors: New Zealand's Governors and Governors-General, Gavin Mclean (Otago University Press)

A Land of Two Halves: An Accidental Tour of New Zealand, Joe Bennett (Scribner)

A Man's Country? The Image of the Pakeha Male, Jock Phillips (Penguin)

My Home Now: Migrants and Refugees to New Zealand Tell Their Stories, Gail Thomas et al (Cape Catley)

Visitor Guides

25 Ultimate Experiences New Zealand, Mark Ellingham (Rough Guides)

Australia and New Zealand on a Shoestring (Lonely Planet)

Blue Guide New Zealand (A & C Black)

Eyewitness Travel Guide New Zealand (Dorling Kindersley)

Frommer's New Zealand from $50 a Day, Elizabeth Hanson & Richard Adams (Macmillan)

Insight Guide New Zealand, Craig Dowling (APA Publications)

Kiwi Tracks: New Zealand Journey, Andrew Stevenson (Lonely Planet)

Let's Go New Zealand (Macmillan)

Lonely Planet New Zealand, Carolyn Bain & others (Lonely Planet)

Maverick Guide to New Zealand, Robert W. Bone (Pelican)

Rough Guide to New Zealand, Laura Harper & others (The Rough Guides)

Fiction

All the Nice Girls, Barbara Anderson (Vintage)

The Bone People, Keri Hulme (Picador)

The Collected Stories of Katherine Mansfield, Katherine Mansfield (Penguin)

Dogside Story, Patricia Grace (Talanoa)

Fifty Ways of Saying Fabulous, Graeme Aitken (Headline)

The God Boy, Ian Cross (Penguin)

The Miserables, Damien Wilkins (Faber)

Once Were Warriors, Alan Duff (Virago/Random House)

Potiki, Patricia Grace (Penguin)

The Stories of Frank Sargeson, Frank Sargeson (Penguin)

Strangers and Journeys, Maurice Shadbolt (Hodder/Atheneum)

Miscellaneous

AA Road Atlas New Zealand (Automobile Association)

Back Country New Zealand (Hodder)

Beach Houses of Australia and New Zealand 2, Stephen Crafti (Images Publishing)

Facts New Zealand, Nicky Chapman (David Bateman)

Landscapes of New Zealand, Warren Jacobs & Jill Worrall (New Holland

New Zealand: A Natural History, Tui De Roy & Mark Jones (Firefly)

The Penguin Natural World of New Zealand, Gerald Hutching (Penguin)

Politics in New Zealand, Richard Mulgan (Auckland UP)

Sanctuary: New Zealand's Spectacular Nature Reserves, Eric Dorfman (Penguin Putnam)

Tramping in New Zealand, Jim DuFresne (Lonely Planet)

Truth About New Zealand, A. N. Field (Veritas)

Whale Watching in Australian and New Zealand Waters, Peter Gill & Cecilia Burke (New Holland)

APPENDIX C: USEFUL WEBSITES

A selection of websites is listed below by subject (in alphabetical order) – it isn't intended to be exhaustive. Websites relevant to specific aspects of buying a home in New Zealand are listed in the appropriate section.

Government

Arts Council of New Zealand (🖥 www.creativenz.govt.nz). Provides information about the world of the arts, arts funding and the work of the Arts Council.

Immigration New Zealand (🖥 www.immigration.govt.nz). Information about New Zealand's culture, history and lifestyle, plus extensive information about entry requirements and the skills sought.

Inland Revenue (🖥 www.ird.govt.nz). Everything you need to know about taxation in New Zealand, whether you're a resident, non-resident or visitor.

Ministry for Culture & Heritage (🖥 www.mch.govt.nz).

Ministry of Education (🖥 www.minedu.govt.nz).

Ministry of Health (🖥 www.moh.govt.nz). Extensive information about everything health-related, including an informative a–z of health topics.

Ministry of Women's Affairs (🖥 www.mwa.govt.nz). Information and statistics about the lot of women in equal-opportunity New Zealand, and about the Ministry's work, including its Action Plan for New Zealand Women.

New Zealand Elections (🖥 www.elections.org.nz). New Zealand electoral system explained in detail.

New Zealand Government (🖥 www.govt.nz). In addition to extensive information about government organisations and services, this website also contains useful information and news about various aspects of visiting and living in New Zealand.

New Zealand Trade and Enterprise (🖥 www.nzte.govt.nz). Advice and information for those contemplating doing business in or with New Zealand.

Statistics New Zealand (🖳 www.stats.govt.nz). Facts and figures about many aspects of life in New Zealand.

Te Ara (🖳 www.teara.govt.nz) The encyclopaedia of New Zealand (*te ara* is 'the pathway' in Maori).

Maori

Maori (🖳 www.maori.org.nz). Dubs itself the 'main Maori site on the net', with information and features about Maori customs, genealogy, language, performing arts and more.

Maori News (🖳 http://maorinews.com). Maori news, views, commentary and writings.

Maori Television (🖳 www.maoritelevision.com). The website of the television channel devoted to Maori culture and life.

Maori UK (🖳 www.maori.org.uk). Providers of Maori language & culture courses in London, UK.

Media

The New Zealand Herald (🖳 www.nzherald.co.nz). New Zealand's largest newspaper online. As well as coverage of business, news and sport, there are articles about culture, employment, entertainment, lifestyle, motoring, property, technology and travel.

NZ On Air (🖳 www.nzonair.govt.nz). Promotes and fosters the development of New Zealand's culture on the airwaves by funding locally-made television programmes, public radio networks and access radio.

Online Newspapers (🖳 www.onlinenewspapers.com/nz.htm). Links to the websites of all New Zealand's major newspapers.

Otago Daily Times (🖳 www.odt.co.nz). A good summary of regional, national and international news and sport.

Television New Zealand (🖳 http://tvnz.co.nz). The public TV service that operates TV One and TV2.

Migrants

Auckland Regional Migrant Services (🖥 www.arms-mrc.org.nz). A non-profit organisation which helps migrants and refugees to settle in the Auckland region.

Citizens Advice Bureau (🖥 www.cab.org.nz)

Emigrate NZ (🖥 www.emigratenz.org). New Zealand immigration guide.

The Emigration Group (🖥 www.jobfastrack.co.nz/tegindex.php). The leading consultants regarding New Zealand emigration.

Human Resource Institute of New Zealand (🖥 www.hrinz.org.nz). Information about all aspects of human resources and employment in New Zealand.

Job Fast Track (🖥 www.jobfastrack.co.nz/jobindex.php). Find a job in New Zealand.

Kiwi Ora (🖥 www.kiwi-ora.com). Information to help new immigrants settle in New Zealand.

Real Estate Institute (🖥 www.realestate.co.nz). Peruse a wealth of properties and check prices online.

Miscellaneous

Enzed (🖥 www.enzed.com). Information from websites in New Zealand and the rest of the world.

Film New Zealand (🖥 www.filmnz.com). A website that covers all aspects of New Zealand's burgeoning film industry, including plenty of information for those considering making a film there, including data about film crews, locations, permits, tax and transport. There's also a feature about the making of the *Lord of the Rings* trilogy.

Geography New Zealand (🖥 www.nzgeography.com). New Zealand's online geographical resource.

Met Service (🖥 www.metservice.co.nz/default/index.php). New Zealand's National Meteorological Service.

NZ English to US English Dictionary (🖥 http://nz.com/NZ/Culture/NZDic.html). A useful resource for Americans bewildered by Kiwis's sometimes unusual way with the English language.

New Zealand in History (🖳 http://history-nz.org). This website describes itself as 'a brief overview of prehistoric, colonial and modern periods.'

New Zealand Museums Online (🖳 www.nzmuseums.co.nz). This website allows you to take a tour of New Zealand's museums, by area, collection or name.

New Zealand Post (🖳 www.nzpost.co.nz). Everything you need to know about the country's postal services.

New Zealand Rugby World (🖳 www.nzrugbyworld.com). Everything you could want to know about the latest happenings in the world of New Zealand rugby, the central plank of many a Kiwi life.

New Zealand Wine and Grape Industry (🖳 www.nzwine.com). Information about the country's wine exports, events, production statistics, regions and styles.

NZ History (🖳 www.nzhistory.net.nz). New Zealand's history online.

Sport and Recreation New Zealand (🖳 www.sparc.org.nz). Information about all aspects of sport in New Zealand and becoming active and healthy.

Trade me (🖳 www.trademe.co.nz). Online auction site – New Zealand's answer to Ebay.

Wikipedia New Zealand (🖳 http://en.wikipedia.org/wiki/New_Zealand). Comprehensive information about all aspects of New Zealand.

Travel & Tourism

Air New Zealand (🖳 www.airnewzealand.co.nz). Book a flight online.

Backpacker Board (🖳 www.backpackerboad.co.nz). Travel guide for backpackers in New Zealand.

Destination New Zealand (🖳 www.destination-nz.com). Information about accommodation, activities, facts and figures, tours and transport, plus commercial information, maps and a newsletter.

The New Zealand Guide Book (🖳 www.nz.com). Information about places in New Zealand, facts and figures, food, history, language and natural history.

The New Zealand Site (🖳 http://thenewzealandsite.com). Site for travellers.

New Zealand Tourism (🖥 www.tourism.net.nz). A wealth of information about accommodation, attractions, culture, history, key facts, travel, weather and more.

Tourism New Zealand (🖥 www.newzealand.com). The official New Zealand tourist website; as well as the usual tourist information there are some informative feature articles about various aspects of New Zealand's culture, history and lifestyle.

Want (🖥 www.want.co.nz). Information about things to do and places to go in New Zealand.

APPENDIX D: WEIGHTS & MEASURES

New Zealand uses the metric system of measurement. Those who are more familiar with the imperial system of measurement will find the tables on the following pages useful. Some comparissons shown are only approximate, but are close enough for most everyday uses. In addition to the variety of measurement systems used, clothes sizes often vary considerably with the manufacturer. The following websites allow you to make instant conversions between different measurement systems: 💻 www.omnis.demon.co.uk and 💻 www.unit-conversion.info.

Women's Clothes

Continental	34	36	38	40	42	44	46	48	50	52
NZ/UK	8	10	12	14	16	18	20	22	24	26
US	6	8	10	12	14	16	18	20	22	24

Pullovers

	Women's						Men's					
Continental	40	42	44	46	48	50	44	46	48	50	52	54
NZ/UK	34	36	38	40	42	44	34	36	38	40	42	44
US	34	36	38	40	42	44	sm	med	lar	xl		

Men's Shirts

Continental	36	37	38	39	40	41	42	43	44	46
NZ/UK/US	14	14	15	15	16	16	17	17	18	-

Men's Underwear

Continental	5	6	7	8	9	10
NZ/UK	34	36	38	40	42	44
US	sm	med		lar	xl	

Note: sm = small, med = medium, lar = large, xl = extra large

Children's Clothes

Continental	92	104	116	128	140	152
NZ/UK	16/18	20/22	24/26	28/30	32/34	36/38
US	2	4	6	8	10	12

Children's Shoes

Continental	18	19	20	21	22	23	24	25	26	27	28	29	30	31	32
NZ/UK/US	2	3	4	4	5	6	7	7	8	9	10	11	11	12	13
Continental	33	34	35	36	37	38									
UK/US	1	2	2	3	4	5									

Shoes (Women's and Men's)

Continental	35	36	37	37	38	39	40	41	42	42	43	44
NZ/UK	2	3	3	4	4	5	6	7	7	8	9	9
US	4	5	5	6	6	7	8	9	9	10	10	11

Weight

Imperial	Metric	Metric	Imperial
1oz	28.35g	1g	0.035oz
1lb*	454g	100g	3.5oz
1cwt	50.8kg	250g	9oz
1 ton	1,016kg	500g	18oz
2,205lb	1 tonne	1kg	2.2lb

Length

British/US	Metric	Metric	British/US
1in	2.54cm	1cm	0.39in
1ft	30.48cm	1m	3ft 3.25in
1yd	91.44cm	1km	0.62mi
1mi	1.6km	8km	5mi

Capacity

Imperial	Metric	Metric	Imperial
1 UK pint	0.57 litre	1 litre	1.75 UK pints
1 US pint	0.47 litre	1 litre	2.13 US pints
1 UK gallon	4.54 litres	1 litre	0.22 UK gallon
1 US gallon	3.78 litres	1 litre	0.26 US gallon

Note: An American 'cup' = around 250ml or 0.25 litre.

Area

British/US	Metric	Metric	British/US
1 sq. in	0.45 sq. cm	1 sq. cm	0.15 sq. in
1 sq. ft	0.09 sq. m	1 sq. m	10.76 sq. ft
1 sq. yd	0.84 sq. m	1 sq. m	1.2 sq. yds
1 acre	0.4 hectares	1 hectare	2.47 acres
1 sq. mile	2.56 sq. km	1 sq. km	0.39 sq. mile

Temperature

°Celsius	°Fahrenheit	
0	32	(freezing point of water)
5	41	
10	50	
15	59	
20	68	
25	77	
30	86	
35	95	
40	104	
50	122	

Notes: The boiling point of water is 100°C / 212°F.

Normal body temperature (if you're alive and well) is 37°C / 98.6°F.

Temperature Conversion

Celsius to Fahrenheit: multiply by 9, divide by 5 and add 32. (For a quick and approximate conversion, double the Celsius temperature and add 30.)

Fahrenheit to Celsius: subtract 32, multiply by 5 and divide by 9. (For a quick and approximate conversion, subtract 30 from the Fahrenheit temperature and divide by 2.)

Oven Temperatures

Gas	Electric	
	°F	°C
-	225–250	110–120
1	275	140
2	300	150
3	325	160
4	350	180
5	375	190
6	400	200
7	425	220
8	450	230
9	475	240

Air Pressure

PSI	Bar
10	0.5
20	1.4
30	2
40	2.8

Power

Kilowatts	Horsepower	Horsepower	Kilowatts
1	1.34	1	0.75

APPENDIX E: COMMUNICATIONS MAP

The map below shows the main airports, road and railways in New Zealand.

APPENDIX F: GLOSSARY

Agreement: A written contract for the sale of a property, agreed by the buyer and seller.

Amortise: To pay off a debt gradually, usually referring to regular payments to clear a mortgage (the principal and interest).

Appraisal: An informal, non-binding verbal assessment of a property by an estate agent.

Appreciation: The increase in a property's value over time.

Asking price: The sum for which a property owner will sell a property (usually negotiable).

Assignment: The transfer of a lease or mortgage from one party to another.

Auction: A public sale of land or property, which is sold to the highest bidder (provided that the vendor's reserve price is equalled or exceeded).

Balloon payment: A lump sum paid to clear a debt.

Beneficiary: The recipient of a deed of trust, estate or trust.

Body corporate: An administrative body consisting of the owners of the apartments or units in a strata building. The owners usually elect a committee to handle the administration and upkeep of the building.

Bond: A sum of money paid by a tenant when he signs a tenancy agreement, which is a guarantee against damage or loss to the property or missed rental payments.

Boundary: A property's perimeter.

Bridging loan: A short term (often expensive) loan taken out to cover the cost of buying a new property before your present home has been sold.

Building Consent: A local authority permit issued to an owner or occupier undertaking building work, to ensure that all work complies with relevant codes.

Buyers' market: A property market with more sellers than buyers.

Capital gain: The profit made when an asset increases in value over the price paid for it.

Capital valuation: A local authority's valuation of a property, used to set its rateable value.

Capped interest rate: When the interest rate on a loan can fluctuate (up or down), but cannot exceed a certain rate.

Caveat: A caveat is a legal document which, when lodged in the Land Registry Office, gives the caveator the opportunity to protect an existing right or establish an existing claim in property.

Certificate of title: A certificate detailing the name of a property's registered owner and any mortgages. It must be presented by the seller before the sale of a property.

Chattels: Moveable (and removable) items in a property, e.g. carpets, curtains and light fittings. In order to count as part of the property, chattels must be specified in the sales and purchase agreement.

Clear title: A title free of any ambiguities or doubts as to the ownership of a property.

Code Compliance Certificate (CCC): A certificate issued when building work is completed, confirming that the building complies with the New Zealand Building Code.

Collateral: An asset or assets that guarantee the repayment of a loan.

Commission: The amount paid to an estate agent by the owner of a property as a fee for negotiating the sale of the property (usually a percentage of the sale price).

Common property: An area or areas jointly owned by all the owners within a strata property, e.g. a drive or garden.

Conditional agreement: A sales and purchase agreement that's subject to certain conditions being met by a certain date, e.g. a satisfactory survey or the arrangement of a mortgage.

Contract of sale: The terms and conditions of a sale at auction.

Conveyance: An instrument or document which transfers property or a right in property from one person to another.

Covenant: An agreement or promise by deed by which one party pledges to another that something will be done or has been done.

Credit history: The record of a person's debt repayment history, used by lenders to assess the creditworthiness of potential borrowers.

Cross Lease: A form of multi-unit tenure in which each owner has a share of the freehold as tenants in common, as well as a long-term (usually 999 years) registered leasehold of a particular unit, e.g. an apartment.

Cul-de-sac: A street with only one entrance/exit, meaning that there's no through-traffic, making the street quieter and safer.

Deed: A legal document which conveys title to a property.

Default: A failure to comply with a mortgage's terms and conditions.

Deposit: A percentage of the purchase price paid by the buyer when the price has been agreed, but before completion of a sale.

Depreciation: A reduction in the value of a property.

Due Diligence: The process by which careful consideration of every aspect of a proposed asset purchase or lease is reviewed, including an in-depth financial, legal and physical investigation.

Duplex: A property which shares a common wall or walls with other properties, e.g. a semi-detached or terraced property.

Easement: Somebody's right to access or use somebody else's land or property, e.g. utility companies sometimes have easement to certain properties for maintenance purposes, etc.

Effective Interest Rate: An annualised interest rate that incorporates the effects of compounding at less than annual intervals.

Encroachment: Part of a property which illegally overhangs a neighbouring property or the street.

Equity: The difference between the value of a property and the amount outstanding on the mortgage, i.e. the amount actually owned.

Exclusive listing/sole listing: When a property is listed with only one estate agency for sale (usually for a specified time).

Fiduciary: A fiduciary is deemed by law to have a duty to act mainly for the benefit of the person employing them (estate agents are deemed to be fiduciaries towards their clients).

Fixtures & fittings: Fixtures are fixed items that cannot be removed without damaging them or a property, while fittings are items that can be removed without damaging a property.

Floating/variable interest rate: A loan where the interest rate rises and falls in line with market forces.

Foreclosure: A legal procedure by which a borrower who has defaulted under a mortgage has his interest in the property terminated, usually by the property being auctioned and the proceeds paid to the lender.

Freehold: The most common type of property ownership in New Zealand, by which the owner owns the land and the property with very few restrictions.

Gearing: Commonly refers to the effect of debt. Expressed as the ratio of debt to equity. Also referred to as leveraging. An investment is said to be negatively geared when the cost of debt exceeds the return from the investment.

General listing: A listing that is shared among a number of agents. Different commission rates may apply between agents.

Gross Lease: A lease whereby the tenant pays a gross rent and the lessor pays the operating expenses.

Guarantor: The individual who guarantees a loan if the holder of the loan defaults on it.

Interest-only loan: A loan on which only the interest is paid by the borrower, with the original amount being repaid at the end of the loan period.

Joint Agency: Generally a joint sole agency where two or three agents are employed to sell a property on an exclusive basis. Both agents may advertise, other agents may or may not be invited to participate at the joint agent's discretion.

Joint tenancy: A form of ownership that gives tenants equal shares in the property.

Leasehold: Ownership in which the owner owns the property and leases the land on which it stands for a certain period.

Lessee: One who possesses the right to use or occupy a property under a lease agreement. Commonly termed a tenant.

Lessor: One who holds title to, and conveys the rights to use and occupy a property, under a lease agreement. Commonly termed a landlord.

Liabilities: Outstanding debts and financial responsibilities.

Lien: A legal claim against a property that has to be paid when the property is sold.

Life estate: A freehold interest in a property that expires when the owner dies.

LIM report: A Land Information Memorandum report, which is prepared by the local council and details information about a property.

Listing: A written contract between a property owner and estate agent, which authorises the agent to sell the property.

Lump sum payment: An additional sum paid towards clearing a mortgage.

Mortgage discharge fee: The fee charged by some lenders when a borrower pays off a mortgage in full.

Mortgagee: The lender of funds who takes mortgage security over the assets of the borrower.

Mortgagee sale: An auction to sell a property when a borrower defaults on the loan, with the proceeds going to pay off the mortgage. Any money raised in excess of the mortgage amount goes to the borrower.

Mortgagor: The party borrowing funds whose property assets are mortgaged as security in favour of the lender.

MRIENZ: Member of the Real Estate Institute of New Zealand.

MWP: Marketing without a price.

Negative gearing: When the income generated by an investment is insufficient to cover the costs.

Nominal Interest Rate: The generally quoted annual percentage rate (APR) of interest, ignoring the effects of compounding at less than annual intervals.

Notice of default: The written notice to a borrower that he has defaulted on a loan and that legal action may be taken to recover the debt.

Notice to quit: The written notice to a tenant to vacate a property.

Notification: Notification of a resource consent application, which involves the placement of a public notice in a local newspaper and notification of people most likely to be affected, including adjoining owners, and a sign displayed at or near the property to indicate what is proposed, e.g. building alterations.

Off plan/off the plan: Buying a property before it's completed, i.e. after only having seen the plan.

Passed in: The highest bid in an auction which fails to reach the seller's reserve price.

PIM: Project Information Memorandum, i.e. a report detailing potentially dangerous contaminants, erosion, subsidence, water, etc.

POA: Price on application, i.e. only revealing the asking price of a property when potential buyers specifically request it.

Pre-approval: Ascertaining how much somebody can borrow before he formally applies for a loan.

Principal: The amount still to be repaid on a mortgage.

Private sale: Where an owner sells a property himself without using an estate agent.

QV: Quotable value; a government document detailing the prices of properties in an area you're interested in.

Ratchet: A clause in a lease whereby the rent payable by the tenant can increase or remain static at review, but not fall.

Refinancing: Paying off one loan with another, using the same property as security.

REINZ: The Real Estate Institute of New Zealand.

Requisitions on title: A buyer asking a seller for additional information about the title of a property.

Reserve: The minimum price a seller at auction will accept.

Right of first refusal: Giving somebody the first opportunity to buy or rent a property, before it's offered for general sale or rental.

Right of Renewal: A clause within a lease giving a lessee the right to renew an existing lease for a specified term on specified conditions.

Right of way: A right of access to or across a property.

Riparian Rights: Rights of access to (and the use of) natural waterways, rivers, streams and coastline, etc.

Second mortgage: A second loan taken on a property, which can only be paid off after the first mortgage has been paid when the property is sold.

Sellers' market: A property market with more buyers than sellers.

Semi-detached: Two properties that share a common wall.

Sinking Fund: The allocation of regular payments which provide a reserve fund for future expected or emergency capital or maintenance costs.

Sole agency: When an estate agent has the exclusive right to sell a property, usually for a limited time.

Strata title/unit tile: A term used about apartments, townhouses and units, meaning that a property's owner owns his own property, but the common property belongs to the whole body.

Tenants in common: A joint tenancy whereby two or more buyers own a property in unequal shares. Shares can be sold without consulting the other owner(s).

Term of a loan: The length of time over which a loan extends.

Terraced house: A house that shares a wall or walls with other houses.

Title: A legal document detailing an individual's ownership of or right to a property.

Townhouse: A house with one or more attached houses of a similar type.

Unconditional: The point at which all conditional clauses within a sale and purchase or lease agreement have been satisfied or dispensed and the transaction is contractually binding on both parties.

Unit: An apartment or townhouse.

Unit Title: A unit title, under the Unit Titles Act 1972, provides individual ownership or freehold title in multi-unit developments.

Unsecured loan: A loan that isn't backed by an asset or guarantee.

Utilities: Services, e.g. electricity, gas, sewerage, telephone and water.

Vendor: Seller.

Warrant of Fitness: An annual certificate which confirms that the requirements of a compliance schedule have been met.

Yield: The income or interest earned on an investment.

Zoning: Council rules on the permitted use of land.

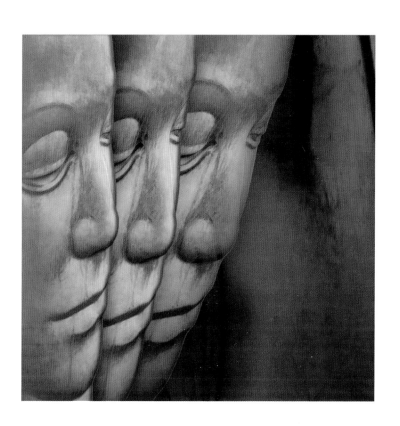

sunset, New Plymouth, North Island

INDEX

Survival Books

Essential reading for anyone planning to live, work, retire or buy a home abroad

Survival Books was established in 1987 and by the mid-'90s was the leading publisher of books for people planning to live, work, buy property or retire abroad.

From the outset, our philosophy has been to provide the most comprehensive and up-to-date information available. Our titles routinely contain up to twice as much information as other books and are updated frequently. All our books contain colour photographs and some are printed in two colours or full colour throughout. They also contain original cartoons, illustrations and maps.

Survival Books are written by people with first-hand experience of the countries and the people they describe, and therefore provide invaluable insights that cannot be obtained from official publications or websites, and information that is more reliable and objective than that provided by the majority of unofficial sites.

Survival Books are designed to be easy – and interesting – to read. They contain a comprehensive list of contents and index and extensive appendices, including useful addresses, further reading, useful websites and glossaries to help you obtain additional information as well as metric conversion tables and other useful reference material.

Our primary goal is to provide you with the essential information necessary for a trouble-free life or property purchase and to save you time, trouble and money.

We believe our books are the best – they are certainly the best-selling. But don't take our word for it – read what reviewers and readers have said about Survival Books at the front of this book.

Order your copies today by phone, fax, post or email from:
Survival Books, PO Box 3780, Yeovil, BA21 5WX, United Kingdom.
Tel: +44 (0)1935-700060, email: sales@survivalbooks.net,
Website: www.survivalbooks.net

Buying a Home Series

Buying a home abroad is not only a major financial transaction but also a potentially life-changing experience; it's therefore essential to get it right. Our Buying a Home guides are required reading for anyone planning to purchase property abroad and are packed with vital information to guide you through the property jungle and help you avoid disasters that can turn a dream home into a nightmare.

The purpose of our Buying a Home guides is to enable you to choose the most favourable location and the most appropriate property for your requirements, and to reduce your risk of making an expensive mistake by making informed decisions and calculated judgements rather than uneducated and hopeful guesses. Most importantly, they will help you save money and will repay your investment many times over.

Buying a Home guides are the most comprehensive and up-to-date source of information available about buying property abroad – whether you're seeking a detached house or an apartment, a holiday or a permanent home (or an investment property), these books will prove invaluable.

For a full list of our current titles, visit our website at www.survivalbooks.net

Living and Working Series

Our Living and Working guides are essential reading for anyone planning to spend a period abroad – whether it's an extended holiday or permanent migration – and are packed with priceless information designed to help you avoid costly mistakes and save both time and money.

Living and Working guides are the most comprehensive and up-to-date source of practical information available about everyday life abroad. They aren't, however, simply a catalogue of dry facts and figures, but are written in a highly readable style – entertaining, practical and occasionally humorous.

Our aim is to provide you with the comprehensive practical information necessary for a trouble-free life. You may have visited a country as a tourist, but living and working there is a different matter altogether; adjusting to a
new environment and culture and making a home in any foreign country can be a traumatic and stressful experience. You need to adapt to new customs and traditions, discover the local way of doing things (such as finding a home, paying bills and obtaining insurance) and learn all over again how to overcome the everyday obstacles of life.

All these subjects and many, many more are covered in depth in our Living and Working guides – don't leave home without them.

The Expat's Best Friend!

Culture Wise Series

Our **Culture Wise** series of guides is essential reading for anyone who wants to understand how a country really 'works'. Whether you're planning to stay for a few days or a lifetime, these guides will help you quickly find your feet and settle into your new surroundings.

Culture Wise guides:

- Reduce the anxiety factor in adapting to a foreign culture
- Explain how to behave in everyday situations in order to avoid cultural and social gaffes
- Help you get along with your neighbours
- Make friends and establish lasting business relationships
- Enhance your understanding of a country and its people.

People often underestimate the extent of cultural isolation they can face abroad, particularly in a country with a different language. At first glance many countries seem an 'easy' option, often with millions of visitors from all corners of the globe and well-established expatriate communities. But, sooner or later, newcomers find that most countries are indeed 'foreign' and many come unstuck as a result.

Culture Wise guides will enable you to quickly adapt to the local way of life and feel at home, and – just as importantly – avoid the worst effects of culture shock.

Culture Wise – The Wise Way to Travel

The essential guides to Culture, Customs & Business Etiquette

Other Survival Books

Investing in Property Abroad: Essential reading for anyone planning to buy property abroad, containing surveys of over 30 countries.

The Best Places to Buy a Home in France/Spain: Unique guides to where to buy property in Spain and France, containing detailed regional profiles and market reports.

Buying, Selling and Letting Property: The best source of information about buying, selling and letting property in the UK.

Earning Money From Your Home: Income from property in France and Spain, including short- and long-term letting.

Foreigners in France/Spain: Triumphs & Disasters: Real-life experiences of people who have emigrated to France and Spain, recounted in their own words.

Making a Living: Comprehensive guides to self-employment and starting a business in France and Spain.

Renovating & Maintaining Your French Home: The ultimate guide to renovating and maintaining your dream home in France.

Retiring in France/Spain: Everything a prospective retiree needs to know about the two most popular international retirement destinations.

Running Gîtes and B&Bs in France: An essential book for anyone planning to invest in a gîte or bed & breakfast business.

Rural Living in France: An invaluable book for anyone seeking the 'good life', containing a wealth of practical information about all aspects of French country life.

Shooting Caterpillars in Spain: The hilarious and compelling story of two innocents abroad in the depths of Andalusia in the late '80s.

Wild Thyme in Ibiza: A fragrant account of how a three-month visit to the enchanted island of Ibiza in the mid-'60s turned into a 20-year sojourn.

For a full list of our current titles, visit our website at www.survivalbooks.net

 Photo Credits